The
Economics of
The Noösphere

The Economics of The Noösphere

Why Lyndon LaRouche Is The World's Most Successful Economic Forecaster Of the Past Four Decades

by Lyndon H. LaRouche, Jr.

EIR News Service, Inc.
Washington, D.C., 2001

LaRouche, Lyndon H., Jr. The Economics of the Noösphere: Why
Lyndon LaRouche Is The World's Most Successful Economic
Forecaster of the Past Four Decades

First printing: August 2001.

Library of Congress Catalog Number: 2001 131740
ISBN 0-943235-20-0

Please direct all inquiries to the publisher:
EIR News Service, Inc.
P.O. Box 17390
Washington, D.C. 20041-0390

Cover design: Alan Yue, World Composition Services, Inc.
Front cover photos: Painting of Vladimir Ivanovich Vernadsky from
Kiev, Ukraine (photo EIRNS); Virginia landscape with power lines
(photo EIRNS/Stuart Lewis). Back cover photo: Lyndon LaRouche
at the Lebedev Institute, Moscow (phone EIRNS).

Printed in the United States of America

EIRBK 2001-2

Contents

*Lyndon H.
LaRouche, Jr.,
seen here during
his Year 2000
Presidential
campaign.*

*There is a crucial link between Lyndon
LaRouche's epistemology, and his work on
physical economy. A successful approach to
economics depends, at bottom, upon a
commitment to a Classical humanist method of
investigation and thought, which LaRouche
preeminently represents today; and a mastery
of that method is critical for ensuring
mankind's future.*

Why Lyndon LaRouche Is The World's Most Successful Economic Forecaster Of the Past Four Decades

AS THE BUSH Administration goes into ever-deeper modes of self-destruction, the most pressing question on the minds of rational governments and U.S. citizens should be: Where can I find the alternative to this disaster? Those with good brains and memories, will turn to the personality, and writings, of economist Lyndon H. LaRouche, Jr.*

The most striking fact which recommends LaRouche, is the record of his economic forecasts, which have been correct in every essential aspect since he began making such projections in the late 1950s. In contrast to today's establishment economists, like, for example, Gene Rothberg, a former vice president and treasurer of the World Bank.

On April 24, 2001, Rothberg told a Capitol Hill audience that no one could have predicted the current world economic disaster and the downturn in the United States. Published forecasts issued personally by LaRouche had repeatedly forecast the then-current long-term direction of the world economy over a period of 40 years. During the most recent 30 years, since the August 1971 collapse of the original Bretton Woods system,

---

* LaRouche is also a candidate for the 2004 Presidential nomination of the Democratic Party.

vii

LaRouche and his forecasts have been the center of an international controversy in these matters. In each case of these forecasts, he had identified the specific policy errors which have determined the pathway leading toward the present worldwide financial collapse.

When confronted by an *EIR* reporter on LaRouche's accuracy, Rothberg lied. He asserted that he had deliberately avoided mentioning LaRouche's forecasts. In the effort to defend his suppression of that fact, he claimed, LaRouche had been "predicting" a depression every quarter for the last 35 years, and should therefore be dismissed. That description by Rothberg was simply an outright lie.

In one respect, Rothberg's response can be considered a back-handed admission that LaRouche has been right. In reality, LaRouche has presented very few short-term forecasts. Those few include a November 1979 projection of a sudden and protracted downturn which would result, probably by February 1980, if Federal Reserve chairman Paul Volcker's interest-rate policy were not reversed. Similarly, during May and June 1987, he repeatedly warned of a probable stockmarket crash by mid-October 1987. In each of the rare cases LaRouche has made short-term forecasts, those forecasts have been borne out dramatically. Otherwise, LaRouche has avoided short-term forecasts; he has concentrated, instead, on identifying the *long-range* results in physical economy which can be forecast from crucial economic and financial policy decisions.

Beginning with his first long-range forecast, first made in 1959, and in later long-range forecasts issued at various points, through 1994, economist LaRouche has produced stunningly accurate projections of the succession of results caused by successive policy shifts in the direction of a post-industrial, free-trade, globalized economy. His first long-range forecast, issued during 1959-60, foresaw the threat of the kind of downturn which was actually set into motion with a vengeance, after President Kennedy's death.

Let us review four of LaRouche's major economic forecasts, to refresh the reader's memory.

The Post-Industrial Shift

LaRouche's first long-range forecast was made in 1959, following the success of an earlier short-term forecast of 1956, which he had made in the course of his duties as a management consultant. The way in which that earlier, short-term forecast of late 1956 was crafted, is key for understanding how his subsequent, long-term forecasts were developed.

During 1954-56, he had applied his earlier work in the branch of science known as physical economy, to analyze a developing crisis in automobile marketing. Looking at mid-1956 developments in that and related sectors, he pointed to a paradoxical development in a growing gap between wholesale prices of used cars at auctions, and the much higher inventory valuation of used-car inventories in new-car dealerships' accounting. By extending the study of the same general pattern in other sectors, it was clear to him that the accumulated shifts in Federal Reserve and related policies, under, first, Truman and then Eisenhower, had created a credit-expansion bubble similar to the "John Law" model, a bubble to pop. Typically, by mid-1956, an increasing number of those who had purchased consumer "hard goods" on "low monthly payments plus concluding 'balloon-note,' " owed substantially more unpaid balance on the loan than the cost of purchasing a more or less exactly equivalent item on the market for used goods. This line of investigation led LaRouche to foresee the impending eruption of the "biggest recession of the postwar U.S. to date," beginning no later than spring 1957.

He pointed out, that since 1955, output per hour had risen, but that the number of production-operative workers was declining, and that the number of administrative and sales jobs had increased; thus, as he put it, "It has cost more administrative and sales effort to account for, supervise, and distribute each man-hour of production output." The U.S. economy had begun to decay, he wrote, and he pointed out that "each production worker now has to carry on his back a constantly growing cost for administration, selling, and idle plant capacity." The gap so generated, was being filled, at that time, by an escalating reliance on dubious and reckless modes of consumer-credit financing.

As the data confirming such an ongoing recession poured in, beginning February 1957, the results of that "experiment" in short-term forecasting led him to extend his study to the longer-term trends embedded in the accumulated, post-FDR economic-policy shifts of Truman and Eisenhower Administrations.

In constructing the long-term forecast first outlined in 1959-60, LaRouche focussed upon those trends toward shifts in composition of employment and capital investment which had erupted in the 1957-1958 recession. Looking at the shift which was then underway in patterns of U.S. employment, consumption, and productivity, and the axioms behind the shaping of such policies, LaRouche concluded that the 1957 recession was "the turning point in America's postwar prosperity," and he warned of "another great depression that seemed to loom up for the middle or late '60s." He warned, specifically, and repeatedly, that, unless radical changes back to a pre-Truman policy were to occur, the second half of the 1960s, would see a series of increasingly menacingly international monetary crises, which would be followed by a collapse of the existing world monetary agreements in their present form.

The crucial question, of course, was how the financial and political establishment would deal with this decay. LaRouche's forecast was based upon two assumptions: that existing monetary policies would be continued, and that the response of the government and banking system to the series of crises, would be an increasingly savage austerity, modelled on the methods introduced by Hjalmar Schacht in Weimar and Nazi Germany.

In fact, President Kennedy introduced a significantly different policy, a return toward Franklin Roosevelt's thinking. This change delayed the onset of the monetary crises, through aid of such programs as the application of the investment tax credit, and the launching of the space program. These gave the economy a boost of productivity which briefly delayed the overall collapse. The assassination of President Kennedy halted further steps in that direction. The long-term trend foreseen by LaRouche continued.

The monetary crises against which LaRouche had warned, began with the British government's autumn 1967 devaluation of the pound sterling, a collapse which spread, chain-reaction style, into the U.S. dollar crises and dollar devaluation of January-March 1968. The dollar-mark crisis of 1969-1971, generated the Chrysler-Penn Central crisis of 1970, and led into the forecast collapse of the Bretton Woods monetary agreements in August 1971.

With that fateful August 1971 decision of the Nixon Administration, the policies of Schachtian austerity, which LaRouche had projected in his long-range forecasts of the 1959-65 interval, were instituted with a vengeance. This unleashed the *international* looting process which has defined the world economy for the last 30 years. The cruellest impact of this new, downward economic trend, was first felt most severely in the developing sector, and has now finally come home, with savagery, even to the United States itself.

When the 1971 crisis struck, recognition, and fear, of LaRouche spread among the majority of economists in the U.S.A. and Europe. LaRouche called them "quackademics," whose forecasts had been shattered by a reality which they had each and all denied possible. Those whom LaRouche called publicly "quackademics" at that time chose as their champion to debate LaRouche publicly, Queens College Professor Abba Lerner, considered the leading exponent of the work of Keynes. When Lerner confessed that his policies were copies of the model which Nazi Economics Minister Hjalmar Schacht had introduced in Germany, Lerner defended Schacht's policies. LaRouche had won the debate, but had also marked himself as a figure the establishment considered dangerous, a figure to be destroyed. Rothberg's lie is to be seen as a present-day echo of those developments around the LaRouche-Lerner debate of 1971.

It is of interest to look at what leading establishment figures were saying at the time that LaRouche was putting forward his first long-range forecast, and, we should not omit to mention, his alternative proposals for a new monetary system based on great projects, a new scientific revolution, and major infrastructure development. LaRouche never issued a forecast of disaster, without providing a policy alternative to improve mankind's situation.

On the one hand, it was the established "wisdom" that there could never be another depression. "Built-in stabilizers" ensconced in the financial system were supposed to prevent the kind of collapse in employment and living standards which were legendary from the 1930s.

On the other hand, the "avant-garde" of the financial establishment had made its own forecast of a major shift in the world economy based upon the move toward a post-industrial society. As recorded in *The Triple Revolution* document, published in 1964 and promoted by the Ford Foundation and other establishment liberal thinktanks, the establishment was counting upon the "cybernation revolution" creating such an "economy of abundance," that the major problem in the years to come would be to find enough socially valuable things for the "excess" manpower to do. In fact, this was a projection of the coming "Third Wave" economy, in which seemingly endless gains in productivity would totally transform the world. There's more to what the Triple Revolution promoters were up to, of course, in terms of social control and other projects, but this is the economic gist.

Now, ask yourself the question: Who was right? LaRouche, who said that post-industrial consumerism would lead to looting of the physical economy, including persons, in a Nazi-like fashion, or the Ford Foundation, which said that post-industrial consumerism and cybernation would bring us an "economy of abundance"?

The long range showed definitively that LaRouche was right.

The Ecological Disaster

The second major long-term forecast which LaRouche made, was issued in 1974, in the course of a study which took up the danger of the emergence of a biological holocaust worldwide. LaRouche's Ecological Holocaust Taskforce was commissioned to determine what would be the result of the pursuit of the policies of the zero-growth movement, and its financial enforcer-arm in the International Monetary Fund and the World Bank. LaRouche's researchers directly took on the assumptions of the zero-growthers at the start:

"What we are faced with is not a return to an earlier mode of functioning, not a return to the way things were a hundred years ago. . . . In this zero-growth view, we have an equilibrium that we can lower the level of society to . . . and stabilize the situation at that level. That is the zero-growth view. . . . That is completely and fundamentally wrong in an epistemological sense because there is no such equilibrium. There is no such development of the ecology except in the existence of such evolutionary or degenerative processes. There is no balance point between the two. The actual realization and practice, therefore, of zero-growth ideas is the ecological holocaust, which is now beginning, and which it is our task to halt."

The study which the researchers produced then projected the likely results of a continuation of austerity and deprivation of advanced technology and infrastructure, in the spread of disease: "To the extent that disease organisms have an increasing chance to mutate, as the resistance of the human population is lowered, given mutations are less likely to die out because of an unfavorable situation for the development of pathogens, because the population has become so ill-resistant, that practically any mutation will survive, then you have an increase in the mutation rate of pathogens. An increase in the total disease population leads to the possibility of an increase in evolution of any given disease, and the cycle continues."

The forecast next took up the question of "weak links": "To understand this entire process of ecological collapse, it is critical to understand it as a process of the ecology, not of individuals. The history of epidemics demonstrates that epidemic disease occurs only when a 'weak link' exists in the human species as a whole. Disease attacks the weakest, least-resistant area, when that area is surrounded by relatively low levels of resistance, even though the resistance is higher in surrounding areas than in the 'weak-link' area. Therefore, new diseases are produced in the areas of lowest standard of living, and then begin to spread. For example, at the beginning of the 19th century, cholera was unknown throughout the world. As the British Raj lowered the standard of living in India in approximately 1816, a pandemic started to spread outward from India, throughout the entire world.

"If we look at the situation today, if we do not reverse this process in the next two years, devolution will accelerate because of the vastly more integrated global attacks on the human race which the Rockefellers are carrying out. When you have, as you do in India and Bangladesh today, the spread of total breakdown of nutrition, absolute starvation, then a second phase of disease occurs. Diseases like influenza, pneumonia, etc., are replaced by diseases characteristic of the total collapse of resistance, of which the milder [form] is epidemic measles, and the most characteristic is the Black Death. The Black Plague, bubonic plague, and pneumonic plague recur precisely at those times in human history when resistance is the lowest, and in precisely the 'weak links' in human society . . . bubonic plague, the familiar type during the collapse of feudalism, spread by rats and mice, has approximately a 30% rate of death in an untreated, healthy population, and up to 80% in an untreated, unhealthy population. At the height of such a plague, rats are no longer necessary to spread the disease: Plague begins to spread directly man-to-man through pneumonic plague through coughing. Pneumonic plague in untreated forms or in forms resistant to antibiotics is invariably fatal.

"Taking the process of ecological holocaust as a whole, we see a series of interrelated cycles: the fall of soil fertility leading to a fall in food supply; leading to a fall in nutrition of both human beings and animals; leading to lower efficiency of human metabolism and further drops in nutrition; leading to increase in the disease population, further fall in human nutrition and further susceptibility to disease. The cycle as a whole leads to a general collapse of the cognitive abilities of the population, to mass psychosis, collapse of industry, destruction of wealth, and therefore, an increase in the driving force behind Rockefeller's holocaust, the rate of primitive accumulation.

"Knowing these cycles, we can outline what the inevitable

consequences of this process would be overall in the next few years." That process was the equivalent of a New Black Death.

Today there is no question but that LaRouche's biological holocaust forecast is hideously vindicated. In the January 2001 study by the CIA's National Intelligence Estimates section, it was reported that not only does AIDS, which developed over the post-1974 period, threaten the existence of humanity in Africa and other impoverished areas, but that at least 40 other previously unknown pathogens, and many epidemic diseases, have emerged, or re-emerged, to attack mankind. All attempts to deal with these diseases, and the devastation they have caused, have failed utterly—precisely because these attempts do not challenge the axioms of austerity and low technology, both imposed by the leading international financial institutions, which LaRouche condemned as responsible for the long-range trend of devolution.

Deregulation: The Carter Disease

Now, let's again look at what the "authorities" were saying about economic policy in the 1970s. Their stated view was that the path to "prosperity" (actually, only for the very few) was to free the economy of government controls. That direction began with the deregulation of the financial system, starting with the delinking of the dollar from gold in 1971, and then into the floating-exchange-rate regime for national currencies in 1974. In the immediately following period, especially under President Carter, the deregulation drive became a juggernaut, proceeding into areas of transportation like trucking and airlines, and then proceeding into other areas of communications and banking, toward basic social and economic services.

The idea was basically that of British imperial economist Adam Smith: Take government away, and submit every area of the economy to competition, and everyone will make more money. Everyone with their hands on crucial resources, that is.

In reality, as LaRouche had consistently stated, the elimination of government regulation on behalf of the public good, or general welfare, was just another pathway to looting by the banking establishment. Rather than creating any improvements, deregulation opened up government-created resources to looting by private industry, which then reduced the services. We've seen that process occur in health care, in transport, in communications, and now, with a vengeance, in energy. Deregulation has proven itself to be a pathway to the destruction of vital infrastructure, and to the collapse of a productive economy.

Do Americans have to freeze, or swelter, in the dark, before they admit that LaRouche was right?

Two More Forecasts

There are two more major, medium-term forecasts by LaRouche which should be brought to mind. The first is LaRouche's 1983 projection that, unless the Soviet Union adopted the policy represented by LaRouche's science driver/Strategic Defense Initiative policy, the Soviets were headed for the collapse of their economy over the period of the next five years. The fact that it took six years, not five, for this forecast to be fulfilled, hardly takes away from its incisiveness.

How did LaRouche know that the Soviet system was headed for collapse? He understood how the Soviet government was thinking about squeezing the last drops of production, especially military production, out of the Soviet bloc economy, and knew precisely where that would lead them. There was no romanticism in LaRouche's forecast, either, about the great strength of the Western "free market" in vanquishing the Soviet economy. LaRouche knew that the Western economies were also headed into the trash can during the 1980s, without a fundamental shift in economic policy. But the proposals which he had put forward, were adopted by neither, leading to the present conjuncture.

The final forecast worth noting here is what has been broadly circulated as the *Ninth Forecast,* written in the spring of 1994, shortly after LaRouche was released from the prison to which the *Washington Post's* Katharine Graham and her cronies had dispatched him. In the Ninth Forecast document, LaRouche put forward his conclusion that "the presently existing global financial and monetary system will disintegrate during the near term," and that "that collapse into disintegration is inevitable, because it could not be stopped now by anything but the politcally improbable decision by leading governments to put the relevant financial and monetary institutions into bankruptcy reorganization."

The vindication of this forecast is obvious to a vast number of statesmen, government leaders, and economists worldwide. They know that the series of crises which have hit the world monetary system since 1994, have been kept from leading to a global monetary breakdown by huge government bailouts, virtual "walls of money," in the words of hedge-fund megathief George Soros, and by the accelerated looting process against real living standards and production. The debt created by these bailouts is unpayable. And the process of hyperinflationary blow-out which has resulted in areas such as the energy sector in the United States, is even more rapidly creating gaping holes in the physical economy.

As lately as a few months ago, financial "experts" like Fed chairman Alan Greenspan were still waxing eloquent about the permanent revolution in "productivity" and "lack of inflation" in the U.S. economy. With the collapse of the financial bubble in the U.S. "New Economy" over the last year, the reality is irrefutable. Only the most fantasy-ridden deny the current collapse into depression, and the inevitable bankruptcy of financial institutions. The question simply remains: At what point will responsible citizens, and leaders, turn to the guidance of LaRouche?

The Deeper Questions

We can assure you that, in the face of the disastrous incompetence of Bush and a policy vacuum otherwise, many leaders from many nations are turning to LaRouche. In Russia, Poland, Italy, China, Mexico, Brazil, India, and many other places, LaRouche's proposals are under intensive review, with the prospect for immediate action.

But leading economists and political thinkers who want to remain relevant to currently unfolding world realities, will want to get deeper into the thinking behind LaRouche's proposals. It is largely for their benefit—as well as for the intellectually curious and politically astute among ordinary citizens—that we publish this collection of LaRouche's recent articles from *Executive Intelligence Review*.

Each of these three articles addresses the question of the scientific method behind the strictly economic and the social policy (cultural) aspects of LaRouche's proposals. The first article deals with this question from the prism of an examination of the roots of racism. The next two more directly address the question of man's voluntaristic role in changing and improving the universe. Each deals substantially with the necessity of Classical humanist educational policies in the rebuilding of world economy. In each, LaRouche has decided to use, for pedagogical reasons, the scientific contributions of Vladimir Vernadsky, the Russian biogeochemist, whose productive work dealt with crucial questions of the relationship of man's cognitive power (the noösphere) and the biosphere.

Thus, we have added in an appendix, for the readers' convenience, a brief review of Vernadsky's work, as well as an excerpt from an exemplary part of his work.

What should become clear in the course of reading these challenging works, is the crucial link between LaRouche's epistemology, and his work on physical economy. A successful approach to economics depends, at bottom, upon a commitment to a Classical humanist method of investigation and thought, which LaRouche preeminently represents today. A mastery of that method, especially by our youth, is critical for ensuring mankind's future today, just as it was 600 years ago. In the traditional words of Lyndon LaRouche, "have fun."

—The editors of *EIR*
May 30, 2001

The
Economics of
The Noösphere

The great American thinker and leader Frederick Douglass, shown here with his young grandson.

"With Plato's dialogues, we encounter a typification of the transition from Classical tragedy, to the higher principle of the sublime. In reviewing the works of the world's greatest modern dramatists, Shakespeare and Schiller, ... we may trace an upward development in their work, from the level of tragedy, to the sublime. ...

"See a certain likeness in the slave represented by the Negro Spiritual. Out of that condition, he affirms his humanity and his trust in God, and thus touches the sublime. It is always a song of humanity, of the humanity being crushed by servitude, but a cry of humanity which will not be stilled."

THE TRAGEDY OF U.S. EDUCATION

Shrunken Heads In America Today[1]

March 25, 2001

IT IS A FAIR rule-of-thumb, that until he thinks of himself as just another victim of the situation which the legacy of Richard Nixon's "Southern Strategy," has re-imposed upon those fellow-Americans considered to be of African descent, no citizen of the U.S. is capable of seeing the reality, that his own rights as a human being are impaired by the systemic defects in our nation's present culture.

The truth of this matter, does not lie in the situation seen as the usual individual victim views it, as if with eyes in shrunken heads, from inside-out, and bottom-up. Instead of the usually expressed, "TV talk-show" view of the issues, the individual must develop a scientifically efficient grasp of the centuries-long, even millennia-long historical process which has placed the victim, whoever you are, in that position.

We must view the situation of the victim, from outside himself, from the standpoint of considering his society as a whole, in which the individual exists only briefly as a mortal individual. What will be your continuing interest in the outcome

---

1. This was written for the included purpose of setting the stage for a coming Bad Schwalbach, Germany conference of May 4-8, which had as an included feature some deliberations on urgent contemporary issues of Africa itself.

of your mortal life, later? Thus, the meaning, and self-interest of that individual mortal life, could be competently conceptualized only as the principal authors of the 1776 Declaration of Independence and general welfare clause of the 1789 Preamble to the Federal Constitution situated the individual, only in two respects. Narrowly, by the individual's acting from the vantage-point of a top-down comprehension of that long-term historical process in which he is situated; but, broadly, by the individual's contribution to improving the culture within which his individual actions and their consequences are situated.

In the course of this report, I shall clarify that matter, of inside-out versus top-down, as a central matter of the scientific principle to be brought to bear; but, meanwhile, expect my proof, in a later part of this report, that the problem of racism in America today, could not be efficiently explored for durable solutions, without bringing in the issue of the top-down outlook.

As I shall show, the racism radiating from former President Nixon's 1966-68 launching of his "Southern Strategy," and permeating U.S. society, top-down, today, is not a only a matter of society oppressing those considered as of African descent. It is an included symptom and product of the systemically oppressive, all-pervasive, degenerative, present condition of the society in which that specially oppressed stratum is nothing different than an integral part.

The problem immediately before us, is a matter of Nixon's abruptly reversing the trend toward civil rights, his reenergizing of a long-existing, axiomatic legacy of racist intention, as expressed in U.S. society at the moment of the assassination of Rev. Martin Luther King. This is an oppression which continues to be directed not only against so-called African-Americans, but against each and all of the members of our society, whether they are conscious of this state of their affairs, or not. The effects, already actual and worse threatened, produced by the presently accelerating, new general collapse of the world's present financial system and economies, are an expression of these connections.

As I shall show in this present report, the truth of the matter at issue is exposed, most efficiently, from the standpoint of studying those defective policies which are usually practiced in the often-misused name of education, the policies experienced by nearly all students, in virtually all schools and universities, still today. It is in the footprints left by the trends of change in U.S. public and higher education, and the relationship of education to citizens' voting rights, rather than such matters as employment and housing as such, that the principled issues are most immediately and clearly expressed. Patterns of employment and housing can be changed; but it is only proper education, armed with their struggle to acquire and maintain voting rights, which can enable the victims of unfair practices in employment and housing, to change their situation in the only way possible, *politically*.

As a first step toward that knowledge, look over my shoulder, to see that problem, so defined, as my experience has shown it to be.

My first actual knowledge of the institution of racism in the U.S.A., came, more than seventy years ago, from the dinner-table discussions at the Ohio parsonage of my maternal grandfather, the late Reverend George Weir. For me, as a child, this repeated experience was like sitting, rapt, at the performance of a great Shakespeare drama; it was living history of a recent past century, brought to life, reenacting itself before me. The dominant figure on stage in those dinner-table conversations, taken as a whole, was the family's vivid anecdotal memory of my great-great grandfather, the Rev. Daniel Wood, a Quaker abolitionist in the following of John Woolman, and a contemporary of Abraham Lincoln's generation, who had resettled in the area north of Columbus, Ohio, in what is known as Woodbury. Rev. Wood had run one of the "underground railroad stations" in Ohio, and was known by handed-down family reputation as a "Henry Clay Whig" in his leanings.[2]

---

2. George Weir was the teetotalling son of a professional Scottish dragoon, the latter equally adept with whisky and saber, who immigrated into the Fall River, Massachusetts area, circa 1861, to join the First Rhode Island cavalry. George Weir's uncle, Captain William Weir, was a Scottish sea-captain, who took the assignment of commanding a U.S.-made steam-

During my early years, first, in a Rochester, New Hampshire childhood, and, later, adolescence in the area of Boston, Massachusetts, my understanding of institutionalized racism in the U.S.A., was limited to what was supplied to me from a combination of certain Quaker traditions and my adopted, adolescent, self-identification as a follower of President Abraham Lincoln and his Clay-Carey tradition generally.

It was during my war-time experience, in military and related settings, that I had any first-hand encounter with the institutionalized contemporary practice of anti-"African-American" racism, in a more concrete, personalized way. My concerns on this matter were strengthened by experience with the disgusting racism exhibited by the British, military and others, in India and Burma, during and following World War II. However, it was memories of my conflict with the hegemonic variety of oligarchical culture of the Greater Boston area, already during my childhood and adolescence, which I mined, in my adult reflections, for the depth of background needed to understand the top-down, anglophile cultural influences, by aid of which racism and its associated effects are spread in the U.S.A. more generally.

The shortfall in most academic and other specialist attempts at comprehension of the issue of racism in America, is exhibited by most of what is written in the U.S. today on the subject of education and its required content in general, including the subject of the education of so-called "African-Americans." For example, I have on my desk a copy of James D. Anderson's *The Education of Blacks in the South, 1860-1935*.[3]

The latter is, on balance, an amiable and valuable book, and a timely one for today's study, that chiefly because Anderson documents, anecdotally, and clearly, the statistical fact of a crucial difference, that expressed as *intention,* between education

---

ship from Rhode Island, down the Atlantic to Argentina. My paternal grandfather was a clever and energetic fellow of Quebec origin, but unfortunately a bit too soft on Clemenceau for my taste. A pedigree well suited to the requirements of an American Whig of the Clay-Carey-Lincoln tradition.

3. James D. Anderson, *The Education of Blacks in the South, 1860-1935* (Chapel Hill: University of North Carolina Press, 1988).

for freedom, as the figure of Frederick Douglass typifies the latter approach to U.S. chattel slavery historically,[4] and the contrary tendency of direction in education, notably that of Douglass' opponents. That of Douglass' opponents was intended to adapt most among its victims to acceptance of a more or less stereotyped future style of life, a life typified by the relatively lowest categories of employment, rather than the development of the individual as a citizen of a republic, in the fullest sense of the term.

However, the crucial problem, which, regrettably, prevented Anderson's effort from approaching the quality of "definitive," reflects his attempt to situate that important phenomenon within the wrong historical geometry, that of today's broadly accepted list of academic, so-called political-science categories, and, therefore, to ignore the essential, top-down features of the history of the relevant development of the policies and issues of education in the preceding approximately 2,600 years of European civilization. The overall result of those errors, is an example of the dangers of today's customary academic errors, of fallacy of composition in selection and treatment of the evidence considered.

I need not review Anderson's book itself here. I address the context in which I wish he had situated his approach to defining the deeper implications of the matter, and let the reader then read his book, this time in the context of the deeper issue which I set forth as follows.

1. Racism in Modern Society

Racism in the American colonies, and the U.S.A. itself, can not be competently understood, except as a product of the circumstances under which the imperial maritime power of Sixteenth- and Seventeenth-Centuries Venice, the leading European

---

4. The bellwether of that book's shortfalls, is the lack of emphasis on the case of Frederick Douglass, which should have been a central feature of Anderson's treatment of the very subject on which he focusses.

opposition to the networks and legacy of Cardinal Nicholas of Cusa, organized the modern African slave-trade.[5]

That slave-trade began in earnest at the outset of the Sixteenth Century, following the death of Spain's follower of Alfonso Sabio, Isabella I, through Venice's political control over the Iberian maritime powers and their monarchies. This same Venetian influence, was also exerted during that period by such figures as Henry VIII's marriage counsellor, Zorzi, who were associated, like the Plantagenet Cardinal Pole and the Newt Gingrich-like, Sir Thomas More-hater Thomas Cromwell, with the circles of the Paduan mortalist Pietro Pomponazzi.[6] Later, during the Seventeenth-Century hey-day of the relevant founder of empiricism, Venice's Paolo Sarpi,[7] the slave-trade became a typical practice among the customs of the Dutch and English India companies.

At the close of the Eighteenth Century, Britain began to dump the African slave-trade from vessels sailing under the "Union Jack," in favor of using the British merchant marine's bottoms for the East India Company's more lucrative opium traffic; but, Britain continued its participation in the slave-trade, deep into the Nineteenth Century, but then chiefly through its clients of the Portuguese and Spanish monarchies. In fact, the British monarchy has maintained the pro-genocidal legacy of that nation's slave-trade tradition, as Field Marshall Montgomery did, to the present day of British specialists Lynda Chalker's

---

5. Nicholas of Cusa, 1401-1464, was a key figure of his century, who played a crucial role in establishing the modern sovereign nation-state and also in launching modern experimental physical science.

6. Francesco Zorzi (1466-1540); Henry VIII (1491-1547, reigned 1509-1547); Pietro Pomponazzi (1462-1525). The significance of the emphasis on "mortalist" here, is of crucial significance for grasping the origins of modern European racism. Although Pomponazzi's fear of the reprisals by religious authorities, and warnings to this effect by his student Gasparo Contarini, prompted him to appear to recant on this matter, his argument for mortalism is implicit in his elaboration of the Aristotelean method. In social practice, all of the leading Venetian currents were practicing mortalists. Slavery was one expression of this.

7. Paolo Sarpi (1552-1623).

and Caroline Cox's currently continuing roles in shaping British and U.S. Africa policies.[8]

The characteristic feature of that modern slave-trade, is that it was premised on Venice's success in establishing a widely accepted convention as a "rule of law," *a presumed rule of international positive law, that any person of sub-Saharan African descent shall be defined as fair prey, to be made into a customary, and hereditary commodity and "shareholder value" of the modern slave-trade.* I refer to characteristics, distinct from the millennia-long, earlier practices of slavery, which first appeared in modern European civilization during the Sixteenth Century. This "rule of law" persists, in fact, as an active, and recently accelerated feature of the British monarchy's "Rhodes Plan" tradition of pro-genocidal policy of practice toward Zimbabwe and other regions of sub-Saharan Africa today.

The doctrine of "Life, Liberty, and Property," of English empiricist John Locke, typifies the doctrine under which the institutions of slavery and "shareholder value" have been hegemonic among what President Franklin Roosevelt recognized as our nation's treasonous "American Tory" faction, the faction represented by the combined forces of the anglophile current centered within Wall Street, and those, such as the self-styled "Nashville Agrarians,"[9] filled with nostalgic yearning for the quaintness of the Confederacy.

The mere details of the historical record on the documentation of slavery and Jim Crow, are so extensively documented,

---

8. Chalker and Cox have been key figures in the fomenting of genocidal conflict within sub-Saharan regions. Montgomery's Cecil Rhodes-echoing, homicidal statements on Africa policy are a matter of record, in his "Memorandum—Tour of Africa Nov/Dec 1947." See Linda de Hoyos, "African Unity: Community of Principle, or New Colonialism," *EIR*, July 30, 1999.

9. See Stanley Ezrol, "William Yandell Elliott: Confederate High Priest," *EIR*, Dec. 5, 1997; "Vanderbilt University and the Night Writers of the Ku Klux Klan," *New Federalist*, Oct. 7, 1996, p. 7; "Elliott and the Nashville Agrarians: The Warlocks of the Southern Strategy," *EIR*, Jan. 1, 2001.

that it would be superfluous to reprint that vast record as part of the present report. Useful as that documentation is for the purpose which it serves, such mere statistical and anecdotal documentation has so far failed, inevitably, to get to the crucial point of national policy at issue.

So much putatively scholarly and other attention, has been given to the interpretation of the emotionally charged phenomena of slavery and racism in America, that the most important side of the issue, *the causes for the interpreters' doubtful interpretation of that racism,* has been buried.[10] My point here, is to treat those interpretations of the facts as what they are, in net effect, often inflammatory distractions of attention from the underlying, determining, principled, functional features of the solution for the continuing injustice to be cured.

Therefore, I ask you to focus your attention on the axiomatic features underlying modern history as a whole. To this end, I focus upon that aspect of the practice of slavery, which has continued to be expressed as a continuing political alliance between the "American Tory" tradition of the Southern slaveholders and New York-centered Anglo-American financier interest, down to its fresh upsurge as the Nixon-led "Southern Strategy," which has dominated U.S. policy-trends increasingly since 1966-1968.

I say again, for emphasis, that the tradition of slaveholder interest, as defined by John Locke and his followers, has a vigorous reincarnation as the Locke doctrine of "shareholder interest" today. On today's global scale, that Locke doctrine, deployed under the name of "shareholder interest," has become as murderous and savage a pro-racist killer, as the old Locke doctrine of "slaveholder value" took pride in being. I shall not, and need not repeat here what is documented sufficiently elsewhere, on the relevant subject of the legacies of Jeremy Bentham's Aaron

---

10. Typical of such dubious interpretations, are the assumption that either sexual-cultural issues are determining, or that "white racism" is a reflection of so-called "Caucasians," and "black racism" a biologically determined cultural distinction of Africans.

Burr and Burr's Martin van Buren, as by Anton Chaitkin's *Treason in America*.[11]

The Central Issue of Law

The precondition for any competent discussion of the practice and legacy of chattel slavery, and of the education of populations of former slaves and their descendants, must begin by locating the central principle of intention of law at issue in all these cases.

That issue of law is, that, prior to the revolutionary introduction of the principle of a modern sovereign form of nation-state, itself based on the principle of the general welfare, all known forms of society degraded most of their subjects to the status of either wild creatures to be hunted, or, as the Roman imperial Code of the Emperor Diocletian did, and as the feudalism of Venice and its Norman and Plantagenet allies did, that of virtual human cattle. Like cannibalism, head-hunting, and Phoenician infanticide, slavery was but one of the typical expressions of the bestiality of man to man, which pervaded known or inferrable history and prehistory, prior to the great moral improvement introduced during the Fifteenth-Century birth-pangs of modern European civilization.

For recorded portions of ancient, medieval, and modern Mediterranean and European history, the prototype of ancient societies, was the continuity of the model of ancient Mesopotamia (e.g., Babylon), the Delphi cult of the Pythian Apollo, and pagan Rome. These societies were sometimes identified as expressions of an "oligarchical model," and, whether described so or not, fit that standard description. It is the continued legacy of that oligarchical model, commonly expressed in modern times as *Romanticism,* which is the ancient systemic root of the evil of racism, and of related phenomena, in all of modern European civilization, including the U.S.A. today.

---

11. Anton Chaitkin, *Treason in America: From Aaron Burr to Averell Harriman* (Washington: Executive Intelligence Review, 1999).

The modern African slave-trade, as launched, under Venetian influence, near the beginning of the Sixteenth Century, was first practiced by Portugal and Spain, and later by the ruling oligarchies of the Netherlands and England, that according to the precedent of pagan Roman law (i.e., Romanticism). As noted, these modern slave-traders treated so-called "black Africans" as, originally, wild prey to be hunted, and the captives held, bred, and culled as, quite literally, human cattle.

Three features of this Venetian innovation in the practices of slavery, as by the Portuguese and Spanish monarchies, are most notable.

First, that the introduction of the trans-Atlantic slave-trade into the Americas by the Sixteenth-Century Portuguese and Spanish monarchies, and under the Seventeenth-Century Dutch and English monarchies, was aimed, from the beginning, to prevent the successful development, in either the Americas or Europe, of the new form of independent nation-states modelled on the reforms of France's Louis XI and England's Henry VII.

The included aim was to plant and develop in the Americas a powerful oligarchical class, of the *compradore* type, as typified by the English-speaking North American slaveholders and their confederates, which would both loot the Americas for the profit of their European backers, and also serve to suppress the tendency toward emergence, in those Americas, of independent nation-state republics, the latter according to the Fifteenth-Century nation-state principle, the constitutional principle of the general welfare.[12]

---

12. Although the first attempts to establish nation-states in Europe are typified by the efforts of Staufer Emperor Frederick II, in peninsular Italy and Sicily, Alfonso Sabio in Spain, and the work and influence of Dante Alighieri, the first successes came directly out of work of Cardinal Nicholas of Cusa and his friends, in the context and aftermath of the great ecumenical Council of Florence. It was the Fall of Constantinople, in 1453, which impelled the circles of Cusa, such as his friends Fernão Martins and the astronomer Paolo Toscanelli, to launch what became known as the rediscovery and colonization of the continents and islands of the Americas. The included purpose of this project, and its included evangelization, was

The second feature, was the change in the way in which the virtually global marketing of African slaves and their produced product was practiced, relative to earlier periods in European history. The genocidal scale of loss of life among the victims, in their capture, culling, and transportation to the Americas, reflected the commercial programs used by Venice and its Portuguese, Spanish, Dutch, and English and French partners (chiefly). The appetite for the profit of such forms of looting, and the demands of those financier interests who funded these operations, resulted in a vast expansion of the scale of slavery; and the ratio of deaths caused, both directly and indirectly, by the combined capture and transport of slaves taken in Africa, zoomed to monstrous proportions.

The flooding of European markets with goods looted from the Americas and its growing slave populations, was, as has been generally recognized, a new, global, commercial scale and quality introduced to the practice of slavery.

This is a point addressed by the leading American economist, Henry C. Carey, in his work on the slave trade and the practice of slavery in the United States. Essentially, Carey's facts show that the pre-1861 U.S. economy as a whole did not profit from slavery, but, rather, lost money on slavery. The net economic benefit of that slavery was enjoyed, not by the internal economy of the U.S.A., but by the British monarchy, looting the U.S. physical economy, its people, and its natural resources, for

---

to outflank the combination of enemy forces, represented by Venice and the Ottoman Empire, by building up allies for modern European civilization in lands beyond the oceans. Thus, from the voyages of Columbus, the development of colonies in the Americas became a battleground between the pro-slavery Venetian faction, which took control of Spain's monarchy after the death of Isabella I, and the Christian forces of the Council of Florence. The battle between pro-slavery and anti-slavery forces in North America can not be understood competently as an historical phenomenon, except from this standpoint. The development of proto-republics in North America, beginning with the Massachusetts Bay Colony of the Winthrops and Mathers, and the continuation of that legacy under Benjamin Franklin and his circle, must be understood in light of that conflict.

Teachers arrive at school.   Claudio Celani

the enrichment of the parasitical British system.[13] The slave-owning U.S. planter class, was simply a local pack of predatory parasites, compradores acting as the de facto agents of the British monarchy in this business arrangement.

The third feature, was the use of the power of the initially

_____

13. Henry C. Carey, "The Slave Trade Foreign and Domestic," in W. Allen Salisbury, *The Civil War and the American System: America's Battle with Britain, 1860-1876* (Washington, D.C.: Executive Intelligence Review, 1992). Note, on the map of the Americas, the areas in which the practice of slavery was carried out in great concentration: Brazil, the Caribbean islands, and the Southeastern U.S.A. Then compare the vastly

Habsburg-centered European assets of Venice, to attempt to crush the accomplishments of the Fifteenth-Century Renaissance out of existence in Europe itself.

Their intent was to destroy and outlaw that institution of the sovereign nation-state based on the principle of the general welfare, such as Louis XI's France and Henry VII's England, which had been introduced by the Fifteenth-Century European Renaissance. The roles of the Habsburgs, as tools of Venice, in both the fostering of the trans-Atlantic slave-trade and the religious warfare of the 1511-1648 interval, were continued through the participation of the Nineteenth-Century Habsburg and Spanish monarchies in support of the cause of the slaveholders in North America against the United States, through the point of that assassination of Lincoln, conducted with political support from Habsburg circles in Rome and elsewhere, through the 1863-1865 interval. The British monarchy, although a rival of the Habsburg-centered pro-feudalist interests of continental Europe, played the same role in its own interest, often in concert with its imperial rival, the Habsburg interest.[14]

Thus, the three pro-slavery factors so indicated, are fully congruent with the adopted legacy of the so-called "conservative revolution" of the modern fascist tradition traced from Romantics such as Friedrich Nietzsche and like-minded existentialists, through Mussolini, Hitler, and the neo-Confederacy tradition of Presidents Theodore Roosevelt, Woodrow Wilson, and the

---

higher per-capita net product of agriculture in the Northern U.S. states. Islands were ideal locations for controlling large slave populations; areas of relatively warmed climates and relatively dense rainfall were indispensable for operations in which wealth extracted meant chiefly a looting of land and human bodies alike. Hence, the irony of Nixon's "Southern Strategy," which, in thirty-five years, has transformed the formerly richest, most productive region of the U.S. into a "rust belt."

14. This Habsburg anti-American tradition was defended by the Henry A. Kissinger (e.g., *The World Restored: Metternich, Castlereagh and the Problems of Peace 1812-1822* [Boston: Houghton-Mifflin, 1957]), who was trained at Harvard University under the neo-Confederate ideologue Professor William Yandell Elliott of *Nashville Agrarian* notoriety, as, implicitly, in his shameless London Chatham House address of May 10, 1982.

Nixon "Southern Strategy" campaign of 1966-1968.[15] As I have documented that point in an earlier published location, the Confederacy qualifies as a fascist state in the strictest sense, that of the 1789-1794 Jacobin Terror, the tyrannies of Napoleon Bonaparte and Napoleon III, and Twentieth-Century cases such as Benito Mussolini and Adolf Hitler, and their co-thinkers of the 1920-1945 interval. The "Southern Strategy" is, as Newt Gingrich described his "Contract With America" movement, in 1995, a strictly fascist movement, a "conservative revolution," as Armin Mohler defined it as an historical phenomenon, in the footsteps of Robespierre, the imperial Bonapartes, Mussolini, and Hitler.[16]

That defines, summarily, the context, within which the history of the modern slave-trade and its aftermath must be situated, for any competent understanding of the roots of racism in America today. It is only against that historical background, that the issues of law and related policy may be competently addressed.

The fundamental issue of law posed by the legacy of that modern slave-trade, is nothing different than the following. *Is there some absolute difference, corresponding to a physical-scientific notion of a universal physical principle, between the*

---

15. Theodore Roosevelt was raised as the nephew of the notorious Confederate spy and filibuster Captain James Bulloch. Woodrow Wilson was not only an unregenerate enthusiast for the original Ku Klux Klan, but played a leading role in reviving the Klan, publicly, from the White House, while President. President Grover Cleveland, a Democrat of the same political faction as Republican Theodore Roosevelt, orchestrated the changes in policy which led directly into the establishment of "Jim Crow." President Calvin Coolidge represented that faction in the Republican Party. Presidents Nixon and George Bush, Sr., have been an integral part of the "Southern Strategy" of racism, and the financier interests immediately associated with President George Bush, Jr., are fairly described as pro-racist, Southern-based carpetbaggers who have been looting the former agro-industrial power of the U.S. into a "rust belt" condition since Nixon's 1968 election. On the links to Nietzsche, et al., see Armin Mohler, *The Conservative Revolution in Germany* (Darmstadt, 1972).

16. Lyndon H. LaRouche, "What Is Fascism, Really?," *Executive Intelligence Review,* April 13, 2001.

nature of the individual human being and the nature of each and all lower forms of animal life? It is from the standpoint of this question, and in no other way, that the issues of slavery and of education policy in general, are competently posed. As experience to date should have shown anyone alert to the facts, any different standpoint has turned out to be a dead end, and an awful waste of time, sweat, and much blood.

The fundamental issue, as I have just identified it, is best brought into focus by concentration on the way that issue is expressed in terms of policies for universal education.

The basis in law and custom for the institution of both the modern slave-trade and its continuing offshoots, is what I have already referenced here as that legacy of pagan Roman law and custom which is strictly definable as *Romanticism*. Empiricism, as associated with the legacy of Thomas Hobbes, John Locke, and Adam Smith, is the most widespread and important expression of Romanticism in the past and present history of the United States, and has provided the geographical basis, in choice of climate, for the legalization of the custom of slavery and the slave-trade within some among the original thirteen English colonies of North America, most notably the Carolinas, Georgia, and Virginia.[17]

Since prior to Plato, the fundamental issue of law within

---

17. In the Northern states of the Union, the superior productivity of labor, per capita and per square kilometer, in agriculture and otherwise, was a reflection of a massive investment in development of the basic economic infrastructure of the locality and region. This included both the infrastructure of production as such, and that, such as schools, essential for promoting the productive potential of the population. In the practice of chattel slavery, the source of the wealth taken by both the planter class and the foreign (British) interest which that class served as compradore, was the looting, by what is called "primitive accumulation," of natural conditions, both the land and the living bodies of the slaves. Thus, the slave-system kept moving on, from looted areas, into new areas for production by slaves. Only where the climate allowed such looting to proceed, at least for a time, was this feasible. Hence, the relative brutishness of intellect and morals typical of the regions of the U.S. in which the tradition of slavery lurks on, to the present day.

globally extended European civilization, has continued to be
the conflict between two axiomatically irreconcilable notions
of law and government, between the Classical standpoint of
natural law, as typified by Plato and the Christianity of the
New Testament,[18] and that opposing, pagan tradition known
today as the Romantic school of law, whose precedents included
the customs of ancient Babylon and the Delphi cult of the
Pythian Apollo.

It is only from that standpoint respecting law, that the
phenomenon of racism in modern society can be competently di-
agnosed.

The effect of the influence of various forms of Romanticism,
in crippling the mental and emotional life of Americans, for
example, generally today, is pervasive, and is expressed in varieties of ways. Empiricism, as typified by the teachings of Locke,
as aggravated in the form of imported positivism and its offshoot,
the pragmatism of William James and John Dewey, or the behav-
iorism of Watson, et al., is to be recognized as the corrupting,
hegemonic current in present-day education, law, and scholarly
practices, in the U.S. It is also, specifically, the prevalent basis
in intellectual corruption for what has been taught as "political
science" and "sociology," during the past century. My concern
here is to show, how all of that is combined with a specific degree
and form of force, in the phenomenon rightly distinguished as
racism.

In the history of European civilization, this issue is best
typified by the irreconcilable opposition, both in principle and
in fact of practice, between, as I have said above, that Classical
Greek tradition typified by the dialogues of Plato and by Christian humanism, on the one side, and what is called Romanticism,

---

18. To simplify the point, I emphasize both the Gospel of John and the
Epistles of Paul, and the role of those portions of the New Testament employed by J.S. Bach for his *St. John Passion* and *St. Matthew Passion*. These
aspects of the New Testament typify Christianity's integration of the Platonic Classical Greek cultural tradition into Christianity; Bach's referenced
works, strictly reproduced in performance, express, most powerfully, the role
of what Friedrich Schiller defines as *the sublime* in Christianity's notions of
the Crucifixion.

on the other. The key to understanding all of the leading features of approximately 2,500 years of European civilization to date, is the conflict between the Classical Greek tradition of Solon, Plato, et al., on the one side, and the oligarchical model of ancient Babylon and the Delphi cult of the Pythian Apollo, and also, the legacy of pagan Rome.

That conflict between Classicism and Romanticism, is key to any competent understanding of the roots and effects of the modern slave-trade and its legacy as racism in the U.S. today. This locates the point of reference from which to understand educational policies of practice as the *political* battlefield on which the most essential fight against racism must be conducted.

Those who enjoy the right to a Classical humanist form of education, or its functional equivalent in self-education, are implicitly free; those who lack that education, are assuredly inviting, if not already suffering the conditions imposed upon virtual human cattle, even the conditions of slavery.

Plato's Meno Dialogue

In addressing the issue of slavery and its legacy in the U.S. today, the typification of this difference, as expressed in education, is Plato's *Meno* dialogue, as the lives of Classicist Frederick Douglass and of his family typify that distinction with a special practical excellence. Whereas, as I shall emphasize here, those who tolerate such swinishness as the policy of not compelling students to expose themselves to the ideas of "dead, white European males" (DWEMs) are, in fact, acting to defend and propagate the mentality of men and women who embrace the most essential features of slavery. The act of the fool who rejects study of the ideas of DWEMs, must therefore reject the lesson of Plato's *Meno,* and thus define himself as the fool whose part he is playing. The life of Frederick Douglass expresses the same connection emphasized by Plato.

The essence of the issue posed by racism, is to be located only in respect to that conflict between those two views on education. Either one takes the side of Frederick Douglass in that debate, or one is, in fact, dedicated to promoting what is recognized as the practice of racism, whether one believes that he, or she intends that result, or not.

The so-called African-American, for example, who defends the notion of an education free of the requirement of mastering the ideas of "dead white European males," is being a racist to himself; he is the slave who does not need to be enslaved, because he zealously puts his shackles on himself, and displays them proudly, even militantly. He is like that slave who insists, "Don't give me freedom; just give me reparations—money."

As Plato illustrates the proof of this, in his *Meno,* all human individuals have the developable cognitive potential to generate validated discoveries of universal physical principle. From that vantage-point, all human beings are equal in respect to their inborn nature, and all groups of human beings, from every society, share, as a group, that developable potential in virtually equal degree. The essential function of education, and of the conditions of family and community life in which education occurs, is to develop precisely that cognitive potential to the highest possible degree, in every possible young individual.

No lower form of life has this potential; that is the essential difference between man and beast. Beasts can learn, but only human beings can know; education which teaches children to learn to pass tests, to acquire habits needed for a specific form of employment, is education designed for beasts. Such forms of education, or of family relations, will tend to bestialize the students, and produce corresponding rations of bestialized adults. Unless your children are enjoying a Classical humanist form of education, they are being cheated; they are being bestialized, at least relatively so, that in the name of education.

It is important to emphasize, once more, that the result of accepting mere learning as a substitute for knowing, is not far from the condition of being a slave. At the very best, mere learning is a kind of obedience-training, as at a school for dogs, which produces an individual prone to many of the characteristics of behavior of a slave, the characteristics of a class of virtual human cattle.

Those who enjoy a Classical quality of education, and who are permitted to express that development in their practice as functioning members of society, are relatively "free," at least within and among themselves; those who lack such educational development, are not yet free within themselves.[19] Those who are not free within themselves, will find themselves, if not actually slaves, self-degraded to a condition fairly described as "human cattle," as today's U.S. popular opinion and mass entertainment, condition most Americans today to behave as did the Roman mob of spectators in the Colosseum, as human cattle, most of the time.

Now, turn again to Plato's *Meno* dialogue. Do not merely read it; relive it. Relive it as if you were, alternately, playing the part of the boy, and of Socrates: not acting out the recitation of the words, but reliving that experience of the paradox and discovery for which those words are, like sense-perceptions, mere shadows cast on the irregular wall of a dimly lit cave.

2. Education and Humanity

All of my own original discoveries of principle, during the approximately sixty years of my adult life, have been the harvest from a single germ, a germ whose existence I can date consciously, as a matter of knowledge, to no later than my child-

---

19. Public and higher education in the U.S.A. provided the more fortunate pupil a map of some of the crucial topics which should be known. Unfortunately, that map concentrated on the student's learning to recite the map, more often than actually knowing the discoveries to which the points on the map corresponded. If the pupil's entire education provided encounter with a few teachers who provoked the pupil into the kind of experience of knowing typified by the *Meno* dialogue, the student was thus prompted to apply that lesson to the effect of developing his, or her own self-education. Read the map, but discover the actual territory to which the map pretends to correspond! Then, go on to build a corrected map. The difference is typified, as I stress in my "Gravity of Economic Intentions" (see below, p. 179), by the difference between the student who has *merely learned* to recite the Newtonian version of gravitation, and he who has relived Kepler's step-by-step process of actually making the original discovery of universal gravitation. Knowing, like food, nourishes the body; that which is not food, such as mere learning, will, in its best performance, merely pass the course.

hood's family and community life, during my first three years of public school, in Rochester, New Hampshire. Some of the resulting, original discoveries, which first occurred early during my adult years, are shown to have been of outstanding, worldwide importance today, most emphatically so by the implications of the eruption of the presently ongoing, global, combined, existential financial, monetary, and economic crisis.[20]

As I have repeated that observation many times, it was during those childhood years in Rochester, that I recall today, reaching the conclusion that my parents, and most of the adults and peers I knew, lied habitually most of the time, as most of your friends and neighbors, and elected officials, still today.[21] It was also clear to me, that teachers, even then, were not necessarily a source of truthfulness. In my parental household, lying was filed, euphemistically, under such categories as "company manners," or falsehoods which, when caught out, were explained to the children as "I am only telling you this, for your own good." In school, the same type of practice prevailed, and tended, in my experience, to grow worse, not better, as the grade-levels succeeded one another.

In political life generally, lying is often called today, "Going along to get along." Dale Carnegie's *How To Win Friends and Influence People*, is an example of a ritual devotion to lying, as seen through the eyes of my own generation.[22] "Sensitivity," is

---

20. Among increasing numbers of leading circles around much of the world, the relative uniqueness of my successes as an economic forecaster, and in related matters, is no longer honestly debated among competent observers. Since that fact, and its implications are fairly established, it is not necessary to plead a case which has been, thus, already proven. There is a point, beyond which, the assertion of denial becomes either factitious lying, or conduct beyond the bounds of reasonable ignorance.

21. The most important forms of lying in the three Constitutional branches of the U.S. Federal government today, are lies made on the same pretext invoked by the spectactors of the pagan Roman Colosseum: "Go along, to get along."

22. Dale Carnegie, *How To Win Friends and Influence People* (New York: Simon and Schuster, 1936).

the code-word for widespread practices of lying popular among the so-called "Baby Boomer" generation. Those horrid, existentialist fanatics, who insist upon threatening school pupils with the Orwellian dogma, that there is no truth, only opinion, are perhaps the worst of the liars to be considered for the purposes of this report.

I recognized that what I was instructed to learn, was morally worthless to me, even if it might happen to be true factually, *unless I knew it to be true by my own intellectual resources.* I became, therefore, with but extremely rare exceptions, typically, the most knowledgeable person in any class I attended, among those most stubbornly resistant to merely learning what was prescribed. Some learned much more than I knew, but what I knew, I, unlike those peers, actually knew. I developed, more and more, the habit, that to say what one had merely learned to say, as to assert, as a matter of claims to *knowledge,* "What I read," or, "What I have been taught to believe," or "What I have been told by authorities I respect," is, itself, intrinsically, a form of lying, a form of habitual lying typical of the society and peer groups I knew.

Take, as an example, my rejection of the first year of high school geometry, from about the first day of class.

Earlier, I had observed carefully the structures seen during one among my not-infrequent family visits to the Charlestown (Boston), Massachusetts Navy Yard, and recognized that the holes made in the steel beams made the structures stronger, by eliminating the burden of weight not essential to the function of supporting the structure itself. Why should people concerned with the strength of the structures they had constructed, make those holes in the relevant beams? I decided that knowing the kind of geometry required for this use of materials, represented some principle to be discovered and mastered.

So, when the teacher challenged the members of the assembled geometry class to identify the useful purpose for studying geometry, I referred to the effect of making those holes in the beams seen at the Navy Yard: one cuts out the holes to make the structure stronger; there must be some reason why circular, or approximately circular holes had been chosen for those cases.

Those who ridiculed my response, which included some teachers at that high school, and most of the classmates, were not only clearly wrong on this and other issues expressing the same matter of method. This intellectual, and moral flaw expressed by my critics in that matter, is but all too typical of much of the adult population, even university science graduates with what are called, sometimes ironically, "terminal degrees," of the present day, and pathetically so.

In all my own teaching of university students, and in my leading role in the philosophical association which I have led, since more than three decades ago, I have recognized, and emphasized the importance of the individual's developing an epistemologically competent, critical insight into the characteristic panoply of ideology of his or her own culture, and of comparing the pathological quality inhering in that and all other ideologies of all cultures. Without that kind of self-conscious awareness of the invariably, ideologically polluted character of the prevalent assortment of leading ideologies within one's own cultural background, one is like a blinded beast struggling to survive in a swamp whose quicksands and other perils one is conditioned not to recognize.

Look at my immediate, and continuing disgust, in reaction to that classroom situation, from the standpoint of my frequent use, over recent decades of teaching and related activities, of the example of Johannes Kepler's original discovery of the principle of universal gravitation. The issue, that geometry must be studied from the standpoint of physics, rather than Euclidean ivory-tower geometry, was the same, in my relatively primitive, but accurate, adolescent's recognition of a pervasive, axiomatic fallacy in the classroom teaching of geometry and mathematics, and in Kepler's much more profound grasp of the same distinction, he echoing thus the insights of such among his named, relatively immediate predecessors as Nicholas of Cusa and Leonardo da Vinci.

Riemann's fundamental contribution to all modern physical science, was to free geometry from all such ivory-tower assumptions, and to base mathematics exclusively upon experimentally validated discoveries of universal physical principles. In my own principal original discoveries, I established the basis which enabled me, shortly thereafter, to view Riemann's work in the more general way required for a competent science of physical economy. It is mankind's relationship to the universe, as measured by increases in society's increased power to exist, per capita and per square kilometer of surface area of Earth, which is the foundation for all that truly sane people will regard as empirical knowledge, nominally physical-scientific or other.

That is the continuing tradition of Plato, Cusa, Kepler, Leibniz, et al., within which lie all of my principled contributions to society. So, the germ of all that began for me, in my rebellion against the kind of knee-jerk-reflex lying I witnessed, as a child, among my parents' household and their society. Herein lies also the germ of what must become our nation's general policy, respecting education for freedom.

As Kepler emphasized this fact, the astronomers Claudius Ptolemy, Copernicus, and Tycho Brahe, had each made the same specific mistake against which I rebelled in the secondary geometry class, as I rebelled, later in my student years, against swallowing a version of a differential calculus premised fatally upon the fraudulent, radically reductionist Cauchy "fraction," and as I, still later, in early 1948, rejected the fraud of Norbert Wiener's "information theory": in each case, on the same epistemological premises.

There is no exaggeration, or other incongruity, in my comparison of my adolescent reaction against the underlying error of secondary geometry instruction, to the reaction of Kepler to the fundamental errors of method by Ptolemy, Copernicus, and Brahe. *What I expressed in that act of rebellion, was like Kepler's recognizing the fallacies of Ptolemy et al., a defense of that same principle which is innate to all human beings, and which expresses the fundamental distinction between man and the apes. This, as I shall emphasize, is, as Frederick Douglass's life reflects this, a distinction inhering in every child of those liberated from slavery, or of newborn children of today.* This was expressed for me, as an adolescent, and also earlier, by a feeling of moral wrongness in the demand that one suppress in oneself the impulse to know, a demand that I do so for sake of the rewards proffered for obedience to the demand that one submit to learn as one is told.

More and more, especially as they grew older, most among those who had been my youthful peers capitulated, sooner or later, to the pressures for doing as one is told one must learn to do, especially as they acquired more and more of the burden of what are sometimes described as household life's hostages to fortune. The difference was, essentially, that I, like others of my kind, did not capitulate; being human was too important for us, to betray our birthright.

I shall return to that point as the pivotal feature of the argument developed in this report.

These three, Ptolemy, Copernicus, and Brahe, had constructed their astronomy on the basis of completely arbitrary, wrong-headed blind faith in the assumption, that events in space and time were organized according to a so-called Euclidean, infinitely linear, unscientific,[23] ivory-tower notion of space and time. Kepler, showing that any such construction as theirs, could not account for the variations in position and speed of the planet in its orbit, discovered an underlying, universal physical principle, universal gravitation, a discovery through which we are able, today, to *know* much about why the orbit behaves as it does.[24]

By "know," I mean, first of all, discovering paradoxical evidence, the kind of evidence which shows that reality contradicts absolutely what ivory-tower assumptions, such as those of Ptolemy, Copernicus, and Brahe, assume, still today, to be universally true. I mean also, solving the paradox posed by that

---

23. My use of "unscientific," here and elsewhere in this report, signifies arguments upon included arbitrary assumptions, including those of Euclidean geometry, rather than methods appropriate for defining universal physical principles.

24. LaRouche, op. cit. The thread of development of this principle of method, as applied to this problem by Kepler, is traced explicitly from Plato, through his follower Eratosthenes, and from Nicholas of Cusa, through Leonardo da Vinci, Kepler, Gottfried Leibniz, Abraham Kästner, Carl Gauss, and Bernhard Riemann.

contradiction; I mean, discovering, or rediscovering, through the perfectly sovereign cognitive powers of one's own individual mind, a Socratic form of *hypothesis,* which can be shown, physically, to be universally true, and is, therefore, an experimentally validated, universal physical principle. What you know in that way, and only in that way, is as much as you actually *know* about anything.[25]

This quality of *knowing,* as distinct from the beast-like ability *to learn,* is, once again, the essential, absolute distinction which sets the human species apart from all lower forms of life. In theological terms, this is the specific quality of the human individual, which is reflected in Genesis 1: man and woman as made equally in the image of the Creator of the universe, and, thus commanded to assume dominion within that universe, that in accord with the human individual's kinship to the nature of the Creator. This is no mere hand-me-down tradition; it is a scientific fact, as readily demonstrated as if that chapter of Genesis had never been written; sometimes, as the Apostle Luke writes, we must "let the stones cry out!"

Unless our natural human potential has been crippled by habituation to mere learning, when we, as such human beings, are faced with a paradox, in which something we had been taught to accept as universally true, such as a Euclidean geometry, is demonstrably false to physical reality, we reject the presumed authority of that mere learning. If we are then honest with ourselves, we cease to look for answers in "the back of the textbook," and cease attempting to pass the course by reciting what we have been taught to say.

Unless we are crippled by conditioning to accept conditioned learning, if we have not, like the Biblical Esau, sold our birthright for the mess of pottage called learning, we cease play-

---

25. Ibid., on *Analysis Situs.* This issue of method, was the thematic subject of the founding work of modern experimental physical science, Nicholas of Cusa's *De Docta Ignorantia.* It is the method of Plato, as richly developed, after Cusa, by Luca Pacioli, Leonardo da Vinci, William Gilbert, Kepler, Leibniz, Kästner, Gauss, Riemann, et al.

ing the game according to what we were told were "the accepted rules." We must strike out on our own, and discover a truthful solution.

However, this is no license for existentialism, or of kindred, inherently destructive, and evil forms of intellectual anarchy. In such matters, we must always act on behalf of discoverable truth, according to principles lacking in all beasts. We must act according to that specifically anti-reductionist quality of mind, which is indicated by a literate use of the term *reason,* reason, sometimes called *natural law,* as pointing toward some imperfectly known, but coherent set of principles underlying the ordering of the universe.

How shall we know that the crucial solution for a rigorously defined paradox, called a Socratic hypothesis, which we believe we have uncovered, is truthful? Plato's *Meno* dialogue confronts the reader with precisely such a problem, and that in the form a slave boy might be capable of not only solving the problem, but of knowing that he had solved it. There, in that example from Plato's work, lies the open door to a real education, a Classical mode of primary, secondary, and higher education.

I had the good fortune to meet a few teachers, in the course of my childhood and adolescence, who sometimes walked me through vivid experiences of discovery of the relatively simplest quality of universal physical principles, those of the type which the *Meno* and *Theaetetus* dialogues typify. In later life, Professor Robert Moon was notable among those whose impact upon me was of that quality.[26] With a bit of such help, here and there, what did most of the rest for me, were a similar approach to

---

26. Robert James Moon (1911-1989) expressed his intention early in life to master thermonuclear fusion. Arriving at the University of Chicago in 1928, he was directed to William Draper Harkins at the Department of Physical Chemistry, with whom he studied and worked, later also obtaining an advanced degree in physics. He taught both subjects at the university. Professor Moon built the first cyclotron at the University of Chicago; solved the problem of the contamination of the carbon moderator, which made the Chicago pile possible under the wartime Manhattan Project; and, conducted pioneering research on the action potential of the nerve after the war,

EIRNS/Philip Ulanowsky

Physicist Robert Moon teaching children at a summer camp. He walked them through vivid experiences of discovery of the relatively simplest quality of universal physical priniciples—giving children the kind of Socratic experience they will never forget.

study of books and my own critical, experimental view of what became an increasingly rich experience of, and appetite for the world at large

Once one has that kind of Socratic experience, as a child, perhaps one never really forgets it. In the first moments one is aware that one has confronted an actual paradox, produced the fruitful hypothesis, and proven the hypothesis by appropriate experimental standards, one must never forget that mental-emotional experience. It is something of a different quality than one experiences in any other way. That way of looking at the world, in terms of that special kind of cognitive experience, must become the core of our sense of "Who I am!"

In search of that truth of reason, about the age of twelve,

---

using the world's first scanning x-ray microscope, which he had designed and built.

I found myself lured into stumbling, as if purblind, but not accidentally, into a habit of reading philosophy, and, increasingly, debating, within my mind, with the authors of those writings.

During the ages of twelve through eighteen, I worked my way through the standard books authored by each of those certified to me as the leading English and French philosophers of the Seventeenth and Eighteenth Centuries. At the same time, I became more and more engaged by the writings of Gottfried Leibniz, and faced the challenge of Immanuel Kant's attack on Leibniz. About my fourteenth year, I had become a convert to Leibniz's approach, with special attention to the *Theodicy* and *Monadology,* and by sixteen had begun filling notebooks with composed arguments in defense of Leibniz against Immanuel Kant of the Kemp Smith presentation of the first and second editions of Kant's *Critique of Pure Reason.*

The issue was the same which arose, during that same adolescence, as my quarrel with the ivory-tower version of Euclidean geometry, at the beginning of the high school geometry course. What are ideas, and what is the provable relationship between ideas and the physical reality of the universe upon which we are acting willfully?

In fact, I knew virtually nothing, first hand, of Plato's work at that time, or for some time later, but I had become, through my objections to the empiricists (among whom I included Kant), an implicit Platonist, through the mediation of English translations of Leibniz, and through wrestling, as if in living controversy on the stage of my imagination, against the principal philosophers of the so-called English and French Enlightenment.

The point to emphasize is that with which I began the present section of this report: How does one find one's way, in a world in which parents, teachers, peers, and public officials, lie about almost anything, most of the time? For an "ugly duckling" like me, that was the most important, the most impassioned, of all questions. It is the crucial issue, for any student, of securing an education for the cause of freedom.

It is necessary that I continue a bit longer here in this direction, but I shall interrupt the part of the development of my argument for a moment, now, to make some needed remarks on the direction in which this report is now leading us.

Classical Education

What I have just illustrated by these autobiographical references, illustrates, both technically and morally, what is meant by *a Classical humanist mode of education,* as Classical humanist education differs from those sundry Romantic varieties and their offshoots, which predominate in the schools, universities, and popular culture of the Americas and Europe today. I emphasize Classical humanist education, against the satanic influences exerted in U.S. and other educational policy today, by truth-hating existentialists such as the Nazi philosopher Martin Heidegger and his morally degenerate cronies Theodor Adorno and Hannah Arendt.[27]

The illustration I have given from my personal experience, just above, is typical of the importance of choosing the Classical humanist approach to classroom education, and also, toward the conduct of that greater portion of any successful Classical education, which must, of necessity, occur in the private, personal activity of the student, apart from the classroom.

The Classical education program, as conducted in the classroom itself, could provide no more than a good partial map of extant knowledge; the broader significance of the in-classroom program, is that it provokes the student to explore, on his own, the larger physical reality which the map attempts to represent, a map which is merely an approximation. A good Classical education, if constantly reenforced by an active, cognitive form of experimentally oriented self-education of that quality, develops in one the ability to make clear distinctions, as I did in my reaction against ivory-tower geometry, between a mere map and the physical reality which it, at its best, merely symbolizes.

The dialogues of Plato, the scientific writings of Archimedes and of his contemporary Eratosthenes, and the founding of mod-

---

27. Theodor Adorno, et al., *The Authoritarian Personality* (New York: Harper, 1950).

ern experimental physical science by Cardinal Nicholas of Cusa, with his *De Docta Ignorantia* and relevant later writings in this field, the notebooks of Leonardo da Vinci, and the writings of Johannes Kepler, especially his *New Astronomy,* are, if combined as one experience, paradigmatic for any serious student today. All great scientists, and all truly promising students, as children and adolescents, are those training themselves, primarily, in the role of becoming ever better performers as original thinkers, discoverers of experimentally validatable universal physical principles, first, and pedagogues only as a subsumed part of the work of ongoing attack upon, and sharing of ever new discoveries.

As I walked readers through the successive steps of the process of such discovery, in sundry earlier publications, there are *three crucial implications of making, or communicating a series of validatable original discoveries of universal physical principles.*

First, what is the process by which a discovery of an experimentally validatable universal physical principle is made, and communicated, as such communication should occur between teacher and pupil in a competent form of education? I summarize here, what I have presented many times in earlier locations on the definition of *ideas.*

Second, what is different about such discoveries of principle, on the one side, and the objects we believe that we have experienced directly through the means of our sense-perceptions, on the other?

Third, when we take into account the ability to generate and communicate the experience of valid discoveries of universal physical principle among the members of society, what is the fundamental difference, on principle, between relations among animals, and among human beings? What happens to the notion of "race," once that difference is taken into account?

It is upon those three considerations that the notion of a Classical humanist mode of primary, secondary, and higher education is premised. It is in such a mode of education, that the otherwise infectious bestiality of notions of "race" is avoided.

Lately, we have been presented with paleontological relics, which anthropologist Maeve Leakey claims to represent human life in Africa from several millions of years ago. I would not insist that she is mistaken in saying that those relics are representative of the human species, but the ideology of the school of anthropology with which she is associated, does not permit us to trust her on the matter of defining the nature of the strict difference between human beings and what are classed as "the higher apes."

Her argument, as I witnessed it on a televised interview broadcast by Britain's *Sky News,* is highly provocative, because of some among its more plausible features; but, the argument I heard from her is not definitive.[28] Perhaps there are physiological characteristics of man as a cognitive species, which should indicate to us, as Leakey claims, even in the case of fossils, whether or not the fossil is human. We know that that kind of distinction has not yet been determined scientifically, *since the crucial question defining the relevant experiment has not yet been recognized among the relevant peer-review establishments.* Meanwhile, what we can classify as human fossils, are cases in which the site in question is conclusively associated with products of distinctively cognitive activity, of which, despite Wolfgang Köhler's use of the term "insight," higher apes are not capable.[29]

As a wag might put the point: "Teacher! Don't you monkey around with my children!"

---

28. Meave Leakey and her daughter Louise announced on March 21, that they had discovered a new species of hominid, dubbed *Kenyanthropus platyops,* which they say lived 3.5 millions years ago. Their claim is based on analysis of a skull found in 1999 in Kenya. What is clearly plausible, is the existence of humans in that part of Africa as early as three to four millions years ago, or even earlier, since the biogeochemical preconditions for human life have pre-existed for not less than approximately two millions years of recurring cycles of glaciation on much of the land-mass of the northern hemisphere. Obviously, the Indian Ocean region and its African coastal region are likely places to find human traces during, for example, the period of massive glaciation of the Eurasian and North American land-mass. However, it is one thing to know that human cultures' existence that early, or earlier, is plausible, and another to assume that a fossil is human, rather than a relic of some higher ape.

29. Wolfgang Köhler, *Gestalt Psychology* (New York: Liveright, 1992, reprint of 1947 edition).

This distinction goes to the heart of my original discoveries in the science of physical economy. What I personally, have to add to the extensive literature on the otherwise known principles of Classical humanism, is the effect of my discoveries in enabling us, today, to resolve certain previously unresolved issues of that topic. It is those resolutions which have made possible the fresh argument on education for freedom which I present here.

Now, focus on the three points I have listed a short space above. I turn now to the first of those topics, the subject of the act of discovering and communicating a valid discovery of universal physical principle.

Discovery and Its Communication

As I have elaborated this definition in locations published earlier, there are three distinct steps in any valid discovery of a universal physical principle. As I have summarized the point in those locations, the most appropriate presentation of that process of discovery references the practical significance of what Leibniz termed *Analysis Situs,* a notion which Riemann addressed explicitly, or otherwise, in all of his leading work. The most rigorous form of recognition of the need to effect a new discovery of universal physical principle, is the following.

Given an assumed set of definitions, axioms, and postulates, which have been assumed to best represent, mathematically, the consistent understructure of our prior knowledge of the physical universe. In the case, that an experimental, or equivalent experience, described strictly in those mathematical terms, produces a certain type of clash of represented results, we must regard that conflict as of the form of what we call an *ontological paradox.* Take as an example of this, Fermat's introduction of the notion of a contradiction between the notion that action occurs along a pathway of shortest distance, and the physical evidence, that refraction of light occurs along a different pathway, that of quickest time.

This discovery, as pursued further by Huyghens, Leibniz, Bernouilli, et al., required the overturn of that Aristotelean-Euclidean notion of mathematical physics which subsumes the neo-Ockhamite variety developed as English empiricism by Paolo Sarpi, Sarpi's house-servant Galileo, et al. That discovery did not provide the accomplishment of that task; it posed the need to develop a solution for that paradox. The combined effects of Kepler's and Fermat's discoveries, thus foredoomed the conventional classroom doctrine of geometry used in the usual mathematics and physics classrooms. The search for a solution for these paradoxes, led, as through the definitions of an anti-Euclidean geometry by Leibniz follower Abraham Kästner, through the work of Monge, Gauss, et al., to the discovery and development of modern hypergeometry, successively, by Gauss and Riemann.

To restate and emphasize that point in broader terms of reference: As I have indicated, in earlier locations, during the middle of the Seventeenth Century, this paradoxical experimental discovery by Fermat, juxtaposed against the paradoxes posed by the revolutionary discoveries by Kepler, set into motion all of the subsequent principal progress in physical science and mathematics, through the circles of Christiaan Huyghens and Leibniz, through the work of Riemann and beyond. Leibniz's originality in discovering the calculus, and his continuation of that discovery as his monadology, contrary to the later frauds by Leonhard Euler, Augustin Cauchy, et al., is a central feature of that process of development. This would be a pivotal feature of any competent secondary program of education in mathematics and physics.

In any truthful, Classical secondary educational program, the student should relive Kepler's, Fermat's, Huyghens', Leibniz's, and Bernouilli's related work, as a mandatory exercise, prerequisite to certification as a secondary-school graduate.

The kind of mutually contradictory, pairwise statements, such as those of Fermat's experimental comparison of reflection and refraction of light, provide an example of the way in which a pre-existing ivory-tower form of mathematical physics often collapses when one attempts to extend it to previously unknown, or overlooked physical realities. The juxtaposing of a pair, or more, of such mutually contradictory statements, as formulated within some existing mathematical-physics doctrine, typifies an ontological paradox, as Plato, for example, addressed such phenomena. The juxtaposition of the contradictory elements of such an ontological paradox, typifies a statement in the form of *Analysis Situs*.

For example, in the history of arithmetic as such, there are ontological paradoxes among the notions of arithmetic, algebraic, and transcendental numbers. Plato addresses the first pair in his dialogues, and implies still higher cases, as in his *Timaeus*. These paradoxes and their implications, are addressed in one way by Kästner and his student Carl Gauss,[30] leading Gauss and his successors Lejeune Dirichlet and Riemann, to develop a new kind of mathematics and physics.[31] In physical science as such, we discover two pertinent things about this. First, that all meaningful paradoxes introduced by higher categories of number, are phenomena which reflect some, underlying, corresponding function within physical science; and, second, that the existence of number itself originates in, and is controlled by the way in which the universe is organized according to physical principles, rather than the simply aprioristic notions of numerical ones, as

---

30. Carl Gauss, *Disquisitiones arithmeticae*. An 1889 German translation from the original Latin is available in a reprint edition: *Untersuchungen über höhere Arithmetik*, H. Maser, trans. (New York: Chelsea Publishing Co., 1981).

31. On Gauss, Dirichlet, and Riemann. Lazare Carnot and Alexander von Humboldt had been closely associated as members France's Ecole Polytechnique during the first decade of the Nineteenth Century. Humboldt continued an active relationship to the functioning of the Ecole, in Paris itself, until about 1827. During the interval following the Restoration monarchy's pro-British ouster of Monge and Carnot from the Ecole, Humboldt had worked both to maintain the Monge-Carnot legacy, and to build up Germany's science through support of the Monge-Carnot line of development of the Ecole in Germany. Dirichlet, one of Humboldt's leading protégés from the Ecole, moved to Berlin under Humboldt's patronage of both Gauss and Dirichlet. Dirichlet, a sometime teacher of Gauss protégé Riemann, succeeded Gauss in Göttingen, and Riemann then succeeded Dirichlet in that position. Notable features of the interconnections of the collaboration among Gauss, Dirichlet, and Riemann, are Riemann's emphasized reliance on what he termed "Dirichlet's Principle," and Riemann's superseding the work of Dirichlet, in continuing Dirichlet's correction of Euler's attempt to define a prime number series.

the latter are typified by the assumptions of Bertrand Russell and such acolytes of his numerological cult as Norbert Wiener and John von Neumann.[32]

The first step in a well-organized process of discovery of some valid universal physical principle, is to define such an experimental quality of ontological paradox, by showing that the paradox must reflect a systemic flaw within (for example) the existing doctrines of mathematical physics as a whole. Such a paradox is stated most usefully in the form of a paradoxical statement in the form of *Analysis Situs*.

At that point in the investigation, the second step takes over. The ivory-tower pedant's classroom blackboard is banned from the continued proceedings, until an hypothetical solution is found. The solution to such a paradox will be found only in the domain of what is defined by Plato as *hypothesis*. This hypothesis must be in the form of a revolutionary change in the kind of mathematical physics used to state the paradox. This hypothesis has, and must have, the form and other quality demanded by the notion of a universal physical principle. Such an hypothesis is purely a creation of the sovereign cognitive powers of the individual mind of the thinker who generates that hypothesis. This is the most crucial fact about all valid methods of education, especially education for freedom.

The third step, once an hypothesis has been generated as a credible kind of proposed possible solution for the paradox, is to craft a design of experiment, which will test for two results. The first such result, must be to demonstrate that a real basis for the assumed effects of the hypothesis can be proven. The second result, must be to show that the hypothesis succeeds not only in some cases, but must be of the quality of *unique experiment* whose results can be regarded as a universal principle of any future mathematical physics.

If those conditions are satisfied, the solution to the paradox

---

32. Bertrand Russell, *Principia Mathematica* (Cambridge: Cambridge University Press, 1994, reprint of 1927 edition). On this see Kurt Gödel on the fatal flaw in Russell's system: *On Formally Undecidable Propositions of Principia Mathematica and Related Systems* and *Discussion on Providing*

is apparently valid. The immediate next question posed is, there-fore, how could the act of discovering and validating *the relevant hypothesis itself* be caused to occur in the mind of other persons? Now, we have touched the most essential question of all educa-tion. On the answer for this question, the very meaning of educa-tion itself depends entirely. *We have thus, now, reached the pivotal issue of our study of the subject of education as such.*

Given two students within a class, who are given a statement of facts corresponding to an ontological paradox as I have de-scribed it above. Let each student withdraw from discussion with the teacher and other pupils for a time. Let each student attempt to solve the riddle, and put any proposed solution into the form of a plausibly arguable hypothesis.

That phase completed, let the class reassemble. Let each of the students who thinks he or she has discovered a solution for the riddle, now observe the teacher's demonstration of each among the students' proposed solutions. Assume that two among the students have solved the riddle, and that, therefore, the exper-imental demonstration shows that, at least, their proposed solu-tions are experimentally plausible. Now, the question becomes, which, if any, of those experimentally plausible solutions meet the standard of a universal physical principle?

Let us redefine that situation, as follows.

In this report so far, I have made reference to various cele-brated discoverers and some part of their original discoveries. Now, instead of merely presenting the class with a riddle, let us make the subject of the riddle historically concrete, referencing one or more of those, or other discoverers. Let us take Archi-medes' cry of "Eureka!" as the point of reference. What was Archimedes yelling about?

We have a place. We have a date, or at least an approximate one. We have a name. We have relevant facts concerning his background, and his previous work. We have portraits which are putatively representations of Archimedes himself. We have a topographical and political map of the area of modern Italy

---

a Foundation for Mathematics, Collected Works, Vol. I (New York: Oxford University Press, 1986).

and of the relevant portions of the Mediterranean, at the time the Sicilian Archimedes was about to be butchered by the invading Roman soldiers. We have also a general picture of the quality of Archimedes' accomplishments and of his relationship to the Eratosthenes, the world's greatest astronomer of that period, then living and working in Egypt, the latter a man of Cyrenaic origin, educated at Athens as a member of the Academy founded by Plato. Give the students the riddle of specific weight which Archimedes solved, by situating him as a real-life person in real history, in their minds, thus efficiently personalizing the task of replicating Archimedes' solution for the riddle. Don't give away the solution for the riddle, but, short of that, box the solution in, factually and historically, as much as possible otherwise.

This is the approach employed in a Classical humanist education.

Let us imagine the case in which two bright pupils, who have obviously been through similar experiences earlier, produce a plausible solution for the riddle. Then, after the demonstration experiment before the entire class, we have the following social situation.

The two relevant students from that class, have experienced a discovery of an hypothesis which is at least an approximation of Archimedes' success. Now, review the dramatis personae of the drama within the classroom as the demonstration is completed.

The teacher knows. Two of the students have each more or less replicated what happened within the sovereign cognitive processes of Archimedes; now that the demonstration experiment has been conducted, they are elated by the fact that they now really "see" the solution. The cry of "Eureka!" is now in order. Other pupils who have not solved the riddle, see a connection between the riddle and the demonstrated result of the discovery, and also see that fellow-students have been able to re-create a living moment from the mind of the great Archimedes within their own minds!

Meanwhile, inside the mind of each of the two students who produced fairly approximate hypothetical solutions for the

riddle, there is a recognition of something of fundamental importance, *something uniquely human.*

There were three distinct, successive actions in the model
case outlined. First, the paradox, then the hypothesis, and, finally, the validated discovery of principle which solves the paradox. It is the second of those three actions which is crucial: the
act of *hypothesizing* a plausible, or entirely valid solution. Here
lies the essential principle of all competent educational policy:
the principle of cognitive hypothesizing of validatable discoveries
of universal principle. Focus on the two successful students, and
their state of mind in the aftermath of the demonstration and
its discussion.

Focus on the fact that the relevant act of hypothesizing has
occurred, independently, within the sovereign cognitive processes of each, a mental act whose occurrence is *intrinsically
invisible* to sense-perception. Yet, that act of cognition was not
only efficient action upon the real universe in which that event
occurred, but, the application of the validated hypothesis to
human practice will alter mankind's relationship to nature, a
definite physical effect. The evidence generating the paradox was
a matter of effects visible to the senses.

The concluding demonstration, was a matter of effects
visible to the senses. However, the connection between the first
and the last, however impassioned Archimedes' cry of "Eureka!"
might be, is not "visible" to the senses. Therefore, how could
the mind of John, one of those who replicated the experience
of the discovery by Archimedes, "see" the thought of hypothesizing in the mind of the other student, Robert? Here, in this
illustration, we have the germ of Plato's use of the term *idea.*

To the degree that John and Robert have experienced the
act of hypothesizing in this case, they each have an experience
which they know to be in correspondence with the relevant
experience of the other. To that degree, Robert can "see" the
act of hypothesizing within the mind of John, and vice versa.
To avoid confusion in terms, let us, for the purpose of this report,
call this not "synthetic judgment *a priori,*" but *Platonic insight.*
Both can each see into that moment in the mind of the living
Archimedes, in the same way. This cognitive connection among

those three figures of this illustration, represents the germ of the truly human quality of social relations, and of the quality which sets the human individual, and species, apart from and above all other living species.

That is, of course, a very simple approximation of what an idea actually represents. Nonetheless, it is a good beginning; we shall improve upon it, step by step.

Plato's Cave

A close collaborator of both Gauss and Riemann, Wilhelm Weber, who was a gifted designer of scientific experimental apparatus, as well as a leading discoverer in the field of electromagnetism, made a very precise measurement, in connection with proving the Ampère angular-force principle, which was, in fact, the first successful modern intervention into sub-atomic microphysics.[33] It was also an idea produced as a part of the overthrow, as also by Ampère's collaboration with Fresnel and Arago, of not only the Newtonian doctrine of propagation of light, but also the general mathematical-physical dogma of the French Bourbon Restoration's "Newton freaks" Coulomb and Poisson.[34]

The advent of atomic, nuclear, and related microphysics, has the categorical experimental implication of showing that, at the very least, certain crucial sorts of sense-perception-observable macrophysical effects, are determined by efficient action located in a domain beyond direct access by human sense-perception.

Thus, Chicago University's Manhattan Project veteran, Professor Moon, speaking in support of the argument I had presented earlier, on the subject of controlled thermonuclear fusion,

---

33. Laurence Hecht, "The Atomic Science Textbooks Don't Teach: The Significance of the 1845 Gauss-Weber Correspondence," *21st Century Science & Technology,* Fall 1996; Jonathan Tennenbaum, "How Fresnel and Ampère Launched a Scientific Revolution," *EIR,* Aug. 27, 1999.

34. Laurence Hecht, "Should the Law of Gravity Be Repealed?," *21st Century Science & Technology,* Spring 2001; Jacques Cheminade, "The Ampère-Fresnel Revolution: 'On Behalf of the Future,' " *EIR,* Aug. 27, 1999.

set before me his affirmative evidence for that same conclusion, that on one afternoon back during the mid-1970s. Moon explained to me (and, repeatedly to others among our collaborators), that the work of Ampère-Weber et al., is evidence in support of ny insistence on the dubiousness of the assumption, that the purely arbitrary presumption, that repulsive "Coulomb forces" are extended simply infinitely, into large and small, is only arbitrary, and not very intelligent, ivory-tower speculation, rather than sound physics. This proof, as set forth by Professor Moon, of the absurdity of such taught dogma as the so-called "Coulomb" principle, exposes the folly of the presumption by some, that a "Coulomb barrier" constitutes a principled barrier to any development of controlled thermonuclear fusion power production for society.[35]

This brings us directly to the crucial topic of "Plato's Cave." Plato's pedagogical allegory was, that what our senses present to us, must be assessed as analogous to the shadows appearing on the irregular surface of the wall of a dimly-lit cave, rather than the objects responsible for that projection of those shadows. Microphysics is an obvious case of such an *ontologically paradoxical quality* of sense-perception.

However, the rule is, that the basis for Plato's argument is not the absurd argument of the Bogomils and also the empiricists such as Locke, Bernard Mandeville, François Quesnay, and Adam Smith, that unseeable little demons, whether called "invisi-

---

35. My own argument had been the much more modest argument, that it was fraudulent to presume that a Newtonian conception, such as that of so-called "Coulomb forces," could be neither arbitrarily extended into the "infinitely small" and "infinitely large," nor assumed to be linear. I had argued, as a matter of our policy, that the matter of "forces at work" on the scale of the nuclear fusion must be left to relevant experimental work. Thus, until Moon's presentation of the crucial implications of the Ampère-Weber principle, our policy had been based on those negative considerations or principle alone; Moon gave us the positive basis needed for the policies respecting controlled nuclear fusion, then formulated on behalf of what, soon after that, became the Fusion Energy Foundation.

ble hands," or "Maxwell's demons,"[36] are the prompters of visible effects. The crucial point is, that each and every discovery of an experimentally validatable universal physical principle, shows that the universe is not controlled by aprioristic kinds of statistical principles; it is controlled, essentially, as Kepler discovered the universal principle of gravitation, by those objects of cognition which we know, as my story's John and Robert did, as the kinds of *ideas* associated with the human *act* of making such discoveries. In physical science, such *ideas* are otherwise known by the name of experimentally validated universal physical principles.[37]

These are *ideas* in the sense indicated by the way in which Robert is able to look insightfully into the mind of John, in

---

36. The Massachusetts Institute of Technology's Professor Norbert Wiener, premised the core of his argument for the founding of the irrationalist cult of so-called "information theory," on citing J. Clerk Maxwell's speculation, that phenomena such as "negative entropy" could be explained by assuming the presence of an invisible little "demon" operating within the cracks of the infinitesimally small. Although this is the same argument made, for theology, by the neo-Manichean cult known as the Bogomils, and, explicitly, in support of "free trade," by Bernard Mandeville, François Quesnay, and Adam Smith, Wiener's citation of Maxwell reflects Wiener's and John von Neumann's conditioning as one-time acolytes of Bertrand Russell. This doctrine, shared by the latter two, provided the basis for the 1970s development of the "Third Wave" cult of Newt Gingrich, Alvin Toffler, Al Gore, et al., and it also supplies the supernatural doctrine of "The New Economy" derived from that "Third Wave" cult.

37. The formal denial of the existence of universal physical principles, so defined, is traced to the famous series of *Critiques* of Immanuel Kant. Modern cult-doctrines of "information theory" and "artificial intelligence" are radical derivatives of the argument, against knowable discoveries of universal physical principles, first published by Kant in his *Critique of Pure Reason* (Garden City, N.Y.: Doubleday & Company, Inc., 1966, translation of 1781 edition). That argument is used by neo-Kantians, such as the positivist followers of Ernst Mach, Boltzmann, et al., as the premise for efforts to reduce the mathematical practice of science to linear statistical methods of the so-called "radical empiricists," as the devotees of Wiener and von Neumann do.

the case of the shared cognitive experience of discovering an experimentally validated universal physical principle.

This connotes, that our sense-perception is not merely something as trivial, and false, as a faithful image of the real universe, but presents us with the mere shadows of physical reality. It is the business of the mind, as the mind is typified by the cognitive action, which generates validated discoveries of universal physical principle, in response to ontological paradoxes. It is the business of the mind, acting in this cognitive way, to discover the reality which corresponds to the effects projected upon our sensorium.

At this point, I summarize the relevant elements of an argument made, with included reference to the work of the founder of the branch of science known as *biogeochemistry*, Vladimir I. Vernadsky, in earlier published locations.

Vernadsky divided the phenomena experienced in the universe among three categories of what he termed *natural objects*.[38] The first is the category of natural objects of non-living processes, the second of living processes (the *biosphere*), and the third of cognitive (*noëtic*) processes. In each case, the distinct difference of these types of natural objects, within the overlapping action among the classes, is defined empirically by the evidence of the changes which living processes successfully impose upon non-living ones (such as the body of natural objects constituting the *biosphere*), and the higher order of changes which human cognitive processes impose upon the functions of the biosphere (the *noösphere*).

Since these differences are measured as the natural effects of those physical principles as causes, they are called by Vernadsky *natural objects*. Physical science is properly defined as the discovery of the principles expressed in the form of the process of production of such natural objects. The differences in effects of

---

38. Vladimir I. Vernadsky, "On the Fundamental Material-Energetic Difference between Living and Non-Living Natural Bodies in the Biosphere" (1938), Jonathan Tennenbaum and Rachel Douglas, trans., *21st Century Science & Technology*, Winter 2000-2001; reprinted in the Appendix, this volume, p. 256.

action among such classes of objects, such as the distinction between non-living and living, cognitive and non-cognitive, are measured in terms of the successively higher orders of *anti-entropy* characteristic of that succession, and are properly defined as of the quality of universal physical principles. This definition, as described by Vernadsky, among others, is based upon the experimental evidence of the corresponding uniqueness of the physical effects associated uniquely with each category of action.[39]

Within each of those three general types of ideas, there are experimentally defined, distinct ideas of valid universal physical principles. My discoveries in the field of the science of physical economy, have the effect of being an insertion into the internal features of the cognitive functions defining the *noösphere* as man's successful transformation of the biosphere, a biosphere which, in turn, is transforming the non-living processes of our planet by such means as creating oceans and atmosphere.

My own original discoveries in the field of physical economy, were prompted by attention to the role of technological progress in increasing the implied power of mankind to exist in our universe, as this could be measured per capita, and per square kilometer of normalized surface-area of Earth. I recognized this as a reflection of the same principle of *anti-entropy*[40] which leading biologists had recognized as the characteristic, marginal

---

39. This is in opposition to the quietly hysterical reference, implicitly against Vernadsky, to so-called "aperiodic crystals," in the "What Is Life?" essay by Boltzmann follower Erwin Schrödinger. Schrödinger hysterically avoids the fallacy of composition underlying his own argument, that the Clausius-Grassmann-Kelvin notion of entropy is a product not of physical science, but of the hereditary implications of the a priori assumptions of Boltzmann's mathematics.

40. My use of "anti-entropy" parallels Kästner's use of the term "anti-Euclidean geometry," and Gauss's and Riemann's following Kästner's teaching of this principle. I was, however reluctantly, obliged to abandon the use of "negative entropy," which had had an excellent record in the field of biology earlier, because of the massive propaganda in support of Bertrand Russell acolyte Norbert Wiener's vulgarization of the term "negative entropy."

mathematical distinction of living processes from non-living ones.[41] My discoveries along that line of inquiry, led, in turn, to my subsequent recognition of both the importance of Riemann for interpreting the application of my discoveries, and the importance of Vernadsky's discoveries for situating the result within the universe at large.

The idea of such measurements had been prompted, in large part, by my adolescent studies of the work of Leibniz, in which his notions of physical economy, as he developed those notions over the course of the 1671-1716 interval, radiate from the pores of his work in general. The essential feature of Leibniz's work reflected in my own attack on the problem of physical economy, was Leibniz's notion of a *monadology*.

There are in the universe, objects such as planetary orbits, as Kepler was the first known to us to define the meaning of a planetary orbit as a *cognitively* distinct object. It was Leibniz's continuation of the combined work of Kepler, and of Fermat on "quickest-action pathway," which led to both Leibniz's uniquely original discovery of the calculus, and, thence, beyond the calculus as such, to those principles of physical science set forth as his monadology.

The effect of the orbit is always distinct, as Kepler showed the harmonic ordering of relative values among the planetary orbits; the caused effect is always a definitely measurable one, but the cause of that effect can not be simply reduced, on

---

41. This is not to argue that the non-living aspects of the universe are characteristically entropic, but only that there exists a characteristic margin of *relative* anti-entropy, distinguishing living processes from non-living ones of comparable chemical composition. The notion of universal thermodynamical entropy, as associated with the reading of the work of Clausius, Grassmann, and Kelvin, is derived from a dubious imposition of a radically reductionist set of axioms upon the model of the work of Sadi Carnot. The resulting mathematical notion of a universal principle of kinematic entropy is, from its inception, an hereditary implication of the dubious axioms pre-embedded in the mathematics applied to the study. The resulting error is a faithful copy of the common, fatal blunder of ivory-tower mathematics, which Kepler exposed in the cases of Claudius Ptolemy, Copernicus, and Tycho Brahe.

principle, to the same exact (constant) form of simple numbers under all circumstances in general. Put most simply, anything which exists, is interacting with larger processes. It is not only interacting with other processes, but is acting within, and acted upon by a manifold expressing the universal physical geometry within which all of these processes are situated, and by which they are controlled. The role of harmonics for Kepler, in determining the relations among the planetary orbits, expresses this principle.

Therefore, in considering any such subject, we must distinguish between the notion of its existence as an existence, and the relative value that existence expresses within a relevant physical-space-time geometry, such as a Riemannian hypergeometry.

I emphasize, that we must not limit our attention to pairwise interaction among other systems of events; we must recognize the efficient principle of action represented by the physical manifold as such, within which all apparently pairwise interactions occur. In other words, we must adduce the notion of a specific physical space-time (hypergeometrical) "curvature," not only as a physically efficient form of action upon all within it, but as a curvature upon which the individual action is itself acting, as if reciprocally. This is implicit in Kepler's discoveries, but becomes explicit only through the work of such followers of Leibniz as Gauss and Riemann. An object so situated and defined, is what Leibniz signifies by the term *monad*.

On the condition that we define objects from the standpoint of cognition, rather than naive sense-certainty, we have, as Leibniz emphasized, a vast plenum of such objects, and also categories of objects. For example, there are the relatively simpler objects of non-living processes, also planetary systems, living processes, and the cognitive processes of the individual person. Each belongs to the class of monads, but each belongs to a distinct class, and is distinct within its class. Each has an identity as a non-Aristotelean form of existence, and also a definable, relative notion of the measurable, relative, non-Aristotelean characteristics of the action associated with that existence.

All such monads are associated with the notion of a Platonic idea, ideas akin to the relatively successful mental (cognitive) act of hypothesizing by our John and Robert. It is as such *ideas,* that the applicable meaning of the term monad is to be defined.

Our knowledge of such ideas is essentially practical in form. *The discovery of any valid universal physical principle, typifies the sole means by which a characteristic increase in man's power to exist within the universe is effected.* By that, we should understand man's increased *(anti-entropic)* power to exist, as a species, into an indefinite number of future generations, as improvement of this existence can be measured per capita and per square kilometer of surface area. That consideration is the primary experimental basis for any science of physical economy.

The shaping of the physical-economic policies of a society, to bring about that combined result, for the benefit of both present and, especially, future mankind, is of a quality which I have defined, in earlier locations, as a scientific intention, following Kepler's use of *Mind* and *intention* as synonyms for efficient forms of universal physical principles. Physical economy is the science of physical intentions, as these are to be embedded in a nation's laws and related policies, for the increase of mankind's per-capita potential relative population-density into a generation ahead, and beyond.

In the rather common case, the design of a successful experiment which proves the validity of an hypothetical universal physical principle, must contain, by its nature, as if hereditarily, some included feature of design which corresponds to the principle being tested. The application of the results of such a feature of such an experiment, to the designs of products and processes, for example, is a result which we recognize as a *technology.*

It is the knowledgeable application of science and technology, so defined, to man's action on the universe, per capita and per square kilometer, which is the determining basis for the physically defined productive powers of labor. Thus, the higher the level of educational development of the person, through related cognitive experiences, the relatively higher the *relative* productive powers of labor of that quality.[42]

That point restated: the combination of the level of development and maintenance of the basic economic infrastructure of the general area and the conditions of the general population, with the levels of knowledge practiced in design and production of useful products, expresses a relationship between the characteristic curvature of that society considered as a Riemannian sort of physical space-time, and the act of production or consumption within that space-time setting. The relative value of a productive act, lies not merely in the internal quality of the intention expressed by that act, but the relative "curvature" of the physical space-time represented by the physical economy in which that act occurs.

Here so far, we have considered only those ideas which are associated with conventional notions of the subject of physical science. This brings us to the third consideration identified above: the social process.

Human Relations

In his work founding modern experimental physical science, *De Docta Ignorantia,* Nicholas of Cusa included report of his work correcting an error by Archimedes, in the matter of the quadrature of the circle (and, implicitly, the parabola). Cusa's report on that matter is the original discovery of a class of geometric numbers subsequently known as *transcendental*.[43] The

---

42. This is also relative to the level of development of basic economic infrastructure. Labor of equal skill, situated in a relatively poorer general level of development of basic economic infrastructure, will be of poor quality in its result, even catastrophically so. As I defined the point in earlier locations, basic economic infrastructure is to be seen as a part of the function of the biosphere, as the quality of that biosphere has been enriched with natural products of cognitive activity, such as products of science and technology.

43. Although, it should be clear that this is already implied in the treatment of the Plato Academy's proof of the uniqueness of the Platonic solids, as reflected and elaborated within Plato's *Timaeus,* and as this feature

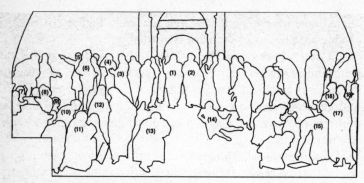

Diagram of Raphael Sanzio, "The School of Athens" (1509): Personalities gathered together by Raphael: (1) Plato, (2) Aristotle, (3) Socrates, (4) Xenophon, (5) Æschines, (6) Alcibiades, (7) Zeno, (8) Epicurus, (9) Federico Gonzaga, (10) Averroes, (11) Pythagoras, (12) Francesco Maria Della Rovere, (13) Heraclitus, (14) Diogenes, (15) Archimedes, (16) Zoroaster, (17) Ptolemy, (18) Raphael's self-potrait.

further implications of this line of development, as to mathematics generally, were broadly settled by the continuing work of Gauss on the implications of bi-quadratic residues.

This case implicitly puts us into the middle of a process of the unfolding of the development of a plenum of cognitive ideas, from Thales and Pythagoras, through Plato, Eratosthenes, Archimedes, Cusa, Kepler, Leibniz, Gauss, and Riemann, and also including all the ideas implied in that succession of discovery. In any competent program of secondary and higher education, the pupils have, like the students John and Robert of our story, relived the cognitive act of original discovery of some of the crucial discoveries of universal physical principle, by each and all of these and comparable historical figures of scientific progress.

Moreover, these ideas are not ideas which exist in isolation from one another; there is a qualitative interdependency of the existence of the discovery of any idea, upon the situation presented by the accumulation of an ultimately enormous array of actual, or merely alleged cognitive discoveries of principle by predecessors. Some years ago, in a featured article, I compared

---

of the work of Cusa, Pacioli, and Leonardo occupies a central place in the work of Kepler.

Look at Raphael's great painting, "The School of Athens," and work through the exercise suggested in the text, identifying the historical figures there represented, mapping the Mediterranean and its littoral, indicating the place and dates of each figure, and then locating each figure in terms of the leading ideas which bear upon the irrecon-cilable dispute between the cognitive Plato and the reductionist Aristotle.

such an array of predecessors to the historical figures assembled by Raphael Sanzio in his *The School of Athens*.[44]

Focus upon that historical class of ideas as subjects of the replication of the cognitive act of the historically original discovery, rather than merely learning. Compare the cognitive relationship to these discoverers, of any student who has successfully relived the experience of discovering those principles, principles known to the student by the name and historical setting of each of those earlier discoverers. Compare the relationship of the student to each of those discoverers to the relationship among John, Robert, and Archimedes, in the illustration provided above.

---

44. Lyndon H. LaRouche, Jr., "The Truth About Temporal Eternity," *Fidelio*, Summer 1994.

Look at Raphael's *School of Athens*. I propose that the reader work through the following exercise.

Make a list of each of the historical figures represented. Take a map of the relevant area of the Mediterranean and its littoral for the period from the time of Homer through the entirety of the Classical and Hellenistic phases of Greek and related culture. Locate the place and date of existence of each figure on that map. Then, identify the relationship among these figures in terms of those leading ideas which bear upon the irreconcilable dispute between the cognitive Plato and his opponent, the reductionist Aristotle. Ask yourself, is the gloomy figure in the foreground, perhaps the Classical Platonist Raphael's recognition of the Romantic tendencies in his contemporary, Michelangelo?

In this collection as a whole, there are sequences of time, and sequences of ideas, or beliefs, such as Aristotle's, substituted for ideas. In the painting, these figures are represented as contemporaries, as if the entire period represented by these figures' mortal lives, had been compacted into a kind of simultaneity of eternity. Yet, when one considers the medley of interacting ideas and other beliefs represented by the whole assembly, there is an order defined in terms of action among both kinds of notions treated as principles by the user, either ideas or substitutes for ideas, or a combination of both.

Ask: What is the meaning of Raphael's resort to such a portrayal of a simultaneity of eternity? Is it not the case, that that painting corresponds to the way in which a well-educated student's mind, even a graduate of a decent sort of secondary education, sees such figures from that period of history? His mind is a simultaneity of eternity, but there is also an ordering, in the sense of sequences, among the elements of that otherwise timeless eternity.

In other words, by introducing the notion of *change as such*, in the form of continuing, superseding generation of ideas, the time during which the changes unfold is collapsed into a relatively very short lapse of time within the bounds of what is otherwise a simultaneity of eternity.

Now, amplify this memory of history, to include virtually

all that pertains to physical scientific knowledge, and to the known aspects of the history of cultures, and of the geography in which they dwelt. We will have then amplified Raphael's example, to approximate the functional elements of the memory of ideas by a well-educated individual mind of today. If that memory is organized around the efficient interaction among ideas defined in Platonic terms, we have imagined thus, the case which I wish to call to your attention here.

The relationship of the students John and Robert to Archimedes, in my pedagogical story, is to be recognized as an expression of the truly essential nature of human relations *per se*, as distinct from the quality of relationship among lower forms of animal life (as mimicked by such as the empiricist devotees of Hobbes, Locke, Mandeville, Quesnay, Adam Smith, Jeremy Bentham, and Bertrand Russell, implicitly profess themselves to be). *Truly human relations, are expressed as relations in terms of a Platonic notion of ideas.*

To emphasize the crucial point here, when we shift the notion of events, from mere sense-experiences as such, to the development of ideas, everything believed about the nature of experience changes accordingly. We then contrast the relative clock-time associated with sense-experience as such, to the relative time expressed by the rate of progress in ideas, that relative to whatever physical process we are measuring in terms of rate of progress. We shift the notion of human relations, from the sensuality of mortal sense-experience, to the passion of the universe of cognitive transmission of development of ideas.[45]

Pause at this point, to reflect on the importance of naming discoverers, of naming the time and place in history in which

---

45. It was the inherent inability of a thorough Aristotelean, such as Padua's Pietro Pomponazzi, to accept that distinction, which impelled him, and all of like persuasion, such as the empiricists, to see human existence in any but strictly *mortalist* terms. Only in the realm of cognitive processes, which, like life as such, does not exist in Aristotle's system of only animal life, of *anima*, does the mortal individual have an efficiently continuing relationship to a pre- and post-mortal past and future. Hence, the Christian, in contrast to Pomponazzi, makes a distinction between the mortal being and the cognitive being made in the image of the Creator, the soul.

each discovery is believed to have occurred for the first time. There is an essential function which requires naming ideas in that historical way, rather than the way in which the worst among today's textbooks and classroom instruction tend to do. As my story of John and Robert illustrates the point, *the most essential feature of all ideas, is the historical relationship expressed in the communication of those ideas in the cognitive form they assumed as hypothesis.*

This is the most essential principle of all competent educational policy of practice, as the Friedrich Schiller-Wilhelm von Humboldt program of Classical-humanist education typifies such competence.[46] Without that notion of the historically determined, functional relations among the discoveries and rediscoveries of ideas in their Platonic form, no scientific rigor can be achieved; worse, no rational comprehension of the existence of society is possible.

---

46. Friedrich Schiller wrote his seminal piece on education, *Letters on the Aesthetical Education of Man,* during the several months in Jena, Germany, beginning in 1794, when he was in the almost daily company of Wilhelm von Humboldt. Schiller's *On Grace and Dignity,* begun in May 1793, is his first major published work to decisively criticize the perspective of Kant on aesthetics. Schiller's inaugural lecture at Jena University, "What Is, and To What End Do We Study, Universal History," delivered on May 26-27, 1789, shows what Schiller's philosophy was, as a teacher.

Von Humboldt captures Schiller's impact, in his essay "On Schiller and the Course of His Spiritual Development" (1830). Von Humboldt was appointed Privy Councillor and director of the Section for Ecclesiastical Affairs and Education in the Ministry of the Interior of Prussia in 1808, and remained there for 16 months. Two key memoranda, produced in this period, outline his philosophy of education: the "school plans" for Königsberg and Prussian Lithuania. Humboldt's ideas were put into practice in Prussia during his ministry, and continued to influence German education until the 1970s "reforms" of Willy Brandt's government. The founding of the University of Berlin, beginning in September 1807, was Humboldt's crowning achievement.

All the writings by Schiller and Humboldt referenced here have been published by the Schiller Institute in *Friedrich Schiller, Poet of Freedom,* Vols. I-III (Washington, D.C.: Schiller Institute, 1985, 1988, 1990), and are available from the Institute (www.schillerinstitute.org).

The way in which societies, such as the U.S. today, degrade the personalities of their individual members into an Orwellian condition like that of human cattle, is through the substitution of popular opinion, as Romantic tradition and Walter Lippmann have defined it, for truth. To this end, explanations of the type often referred to today as "spin," and outright, especially official and academic lies, as well as wicked fables and mythologies, are supplied to the credulous as a substitute for knowledge. The case of so-called "religious fundamentalist" beliefs, is among the best examples of the way official and quasi-official, lying mythologies, are used to control the minds and behavior of large strata of populations, "Big Brother" fashion.[47] Any well-educated person in study of history, recognizes the way in which synthetic religions and other mythologies have been used, as a principal method of effectively dictatorial control over large portions, even the virtual entirety of entire populations, even entire cultures.[48] Much of what passes for education in science

---

47. There should be standards, akin to "pure food" criteria, or labels warning credulous consumers, against the acceptance of the claims of many curious sects, such as those of Rev. Pat Robertson and Jerry Falwell, to the name of "Christianity." The crucial feature of the latter variety of pseudo-Christian cults, is that they claim that "God's intention is to be found in an ordinary individual's reading of the text of passages from the Bible," a variety of the same argument made by the wildly gnostic, self-avowed "textualist," U.S. Supreme Court Associate Justice Antonin Scalia. Typical of the point to be made, is the absurdity of any attempt to apply the "textualist" practice to I Corinthians 13, in which the Apostle Paul defines the meaning of Plato's conception of *agapē* according to a most essential Christian principle. Notably, the type of "Biblical fundamentalist" referenced has no agreement with the literal intent of such authorities as the Apostles John and Paul. Indeed, all such "fundamentalist" doctrines are the clearest examples of wild varieties of anti-Christian gnosticism, with clear affinities for the doctrine of the anti-Christian Bogomil cult.

48. Thus, a nation can be truly a democracy and also truly a dictator-ship exerted by an oligarchy. Such is the nature of the degeneration of the U.S.A., especially since Richard Nixon's launching of his 1966-1968 campaign for the Presidency. The degeneration of the character of political parties as organizations of the citizenry, into a master-client relationship, instead, typifies the role of a pro-"Southern Strategy"-oriented, oligarchy-

and other matters, in today's universities and public schools, is of this degraded nature and wicked intent.[49]

The emphasis should be on the word "intent." The instant one challenges a fraudulent myth of academia, the banshees are unleashed against the offender. Pedants of what ordinarily appear to be of a mind most successfully detached from reality, fly into a mentally deranged state of rage against the violator of what passes for "the code." The phrase from Eugene O'Neill's *The Iceman Cometh* pops into mind: "Hickey, you took the life out of the booze!" Once the hypnotic spell of accepted mythology is broken, as by the mere mention of an embarrassing bit of truth, the enraged reaction to this from the thoroughly conditioned pedant, betrays the fact that the dogma being defended by the pedant is a device concocted to serve, and be enforced as a control mechanism over the minds of the credulous members of the student population. You are the target of his, or her rage, because you have unmasked the magician, and spoiled his magic: you have taken the life out of the booze he was intentionally dispensing for its intended effects.

The essence of what we should recognize today as Orwellian brainwashing of large populations for purposes set forth in Fabian ideologue Walter Lippmann's 1922 *Public Opinion,* is the total substitution of the claimed authority of arbitrary forms of

---

controlled mass media, in crushing the U.S. population into a condition of rule by "popular opinion," a condition akin to the status of the lower classes, plebeians and slaves, of ancient Rome.

49. It is very much to the credit of author James D. Anderson, that, in the 1988 book I have referenced here [Footnote 3], he stresses the conscious intention of Wall Street banker George F. Peabody, 1914 Woodrow Wilson appointee as Vice-Chairman of the New York Federal Reserve Bank, as typical of those who controlled much of so-called "black education" in the U.S. as an intended control mechanism directed immediately against the so-called African-American population. The same methods were used, by interests of the same Wall Street pedigree, to introduce into public schools and universities, mythologies intended to terminate the role of the ideas represented by Rev. Martin Luther King among so-called African-Americans, as in some propagandistic efforts to discredit the memory of Frederick Douglass.

mere *belief* for knowledge. I described such substitution of mere belief for knowledge, in my references, earlier in this report, to the kind of lying which I encountered as dominating opinion among family and school environments during my childhood and adolescence. The use of the modern mass media, notably an entertainment and news media which can no longer be strictly distinguished from one another, to orchestrate a synthetic *vox populi* better named *vox pox,* is exemplary of what we may recognize as the functions of the use of myths and fables for mass social control in former history.

The question posed by today's Orwellian practices to such effect, is, how could a population defend itself against control by the kind of mass-media and related methods of mind-manipulation rampant in the U.S.A. today?

The relevant difference between myth and truth, credulity and reason, is located in the way in which human relations are defined.

If the student has experienced each ancient and other discovery of validated universal physical principle, by means of reliving the historically situated act of original discovery of that principle, the student now knows personally that moment in the mind of the living original discoverer of relevance. There lies the pivotal distinction.

However, competent scientific knowledge is not a mere basketful of separately collected discoveries from the past. Usually, as in the case of the combined impact of the cognitively referenced discoveries by Kepler and Fermat, upon the minds and work of Christiaan Huyghens, Leibniz, et al., the Leibniz calculus, for example, was developed. Knowledge of universal principles, gained in this way, is a highly reticulated, highly interdependent lattice-work of an historical, ongoing process of continuing discovery and rediscovery of ideas of a Platonic form. We should say, that this is a multiply-connected lattice-work, as Riemann signifies by his use of "multiply-connected." The process of knowledge is an organic process, rooted in the principle of cognitive action.

A competent process of education, is organized and conducted according to that conception of the cognitive experiencing of the relevant lattice-work of validated discoveries of universal physical principles, up to the present time. That goal is accomplished, by limiting the core of all educational practices and related experiences, to the experiencing of the cognitive process of generating knowledge, rather than by means of learning. *The primary intent of any good education, is to produce a graduate who embodies the most essential achievements of history, in that way, up to that moment.*

3. 'Science and Culture'

A good education does not end with the subject of the discovery and application of universal physical principles as such. Although we must measure economic performance, and its demographic characteristics, in physical terms, and per capita and per square kilometer of a normalized cross-section of the Earth's surface, the individual does not act solely as an individual, but also as a product of, and functioning part of an entire society. When we consider a society's relationship to the planet on which it lives, it is the ordering of the social relations within the society, which determines the ability of the society to cooperate in ways which make the fostering of discovery of universal principles, and their application, effective, if they are to become, indeed, truly effective.

Stated in terms of the implications of a Riemannian physical geometry, the productive potential of the individual lies not entirely within himself, but in the relationship of his development to the characteristic "curvature" of the society and more immediate circumstances in which his function is situated.

This brings us, now, to the second principal aspect of a competent form of education, the role of Classical culture in determining the relative ability of a society to discover, and to utilize knowledge of validated universal physical principles.

The best way in which to define this second aspect of a Classical humanist education, is to focus, first, on the role of what is strictly definable as a Classical humanist species of artistic culture, as this is distinct from, and also the natural adversary of either Romantic forms of culture, or those so-called popular, modernist, and post-modernist novelties which a jaded Romanticism has concocted, apparently, at least in part, in its desire to escape from its boredom with its tedious self.

Situate what I have said in this report so far, in terms of the referenced discoveries reported by Vernadsky. See the place of human relations within a functional image of what Vernadsky defines as the noösphere.

In Vernadsky's imagery, we have three classes of what I have defined in this report as *experimentally validated universal physical principles*. I restate that argument now:

The first, is a set of such principles as might be assumed to be acting within and upon a non-living universe.

The second, is what Vernadsky defined as the *biosphere*, a principle of life, not derived from the physics of non-living processes, which is able to impose its *intention*, as Kepler uses the notion of "intention," to place the Earth under increasing domination of the effects of action by a principle of life as such, thus producing a *biosphere*.

The third, is the power of willful, cognitive ("noëtic") discovery, unique to the human species, by which mankind is able to impose its will to change the characteristic behavior of both non-living processes in general, and of the effects of the principle of life in general. This creates the *noösphere*.

These three classes of experimentally validated knowledge of universal physical principle, represent, combined, an implicitly Riemannian form of multiply-connected manifold of three distinct types of universal physical principles.

In the study of the efficient role of cognition within the context of the noösphere so conceived, what are those physically efficient forms of relations which define the cooperation upon which man's efficient role within the noösphere depends?

As is reflected most explicitly in the science of physical economy, the ultimate validation of the hypothetical principles governing efficient forms of cognitive relations among the members of society, lies in manifest physical effects produced, or what Vernadsky's argument defines as the natural products of cognitive ("noëtic") activity. That natural product is the increase of the potential relative population-density of the society, or human species as a whole. Since cause and effect express themselves over generations, this subject must be considered over a span of not less than several successive generations. Those changes in the organization of society and its physical economy, which determine such increases, represent the natural products of cognition, as defined in the way consistent with the way in which Vernadsky uses his general notion of natural products.

Thus, the view of a natural science of culture defined by the principle of the sovereign cognitive process of the individual mind, requires that we adduce the principles underlying cognitive relations within society, by a study of the relative superiority or inferiority of forms of culture, as adduced from long-range studies of those changes in culture which are empirically the most characteristic, relative features of multi-generational trends of change within the evolution of society in general.

Since the changes in culture introduced by the revolutionary establishment of the first modern sovereign form of nation-state, during Europe's Fifteenth Century, is, as measured by the standard of potential relative population-density, by far the most successful development in human culture known, we must proceed from a study of the relevant qualities of changes which that revolution has introduced to the preceding phases of both ancient and medieval European civilization. At the same time, we must focus upon those conflicts within European civilization which show us which cultural trends within modern European civilization are responsible for the improvements, and which, as Henry C. Carey showed for the case of slavery, detrimental in their effects upon the society's development as a whole.

In the later sections of the present section of this report, I shall emphasize those issues to be seen from the standpoint of the role of Classical humanist policies of education, in the struggle against slavery and its effects within the U.S.A. itself. In the subsequent section, I shall turn to the role of today's globally extended modern European civilization within the economy and culture of humanity as a whole.

Thus, we continue this section of the report, by beginning now with a restatement of an immediately crucial point.

Where mankind's discovery of universal physical principles

of non-living and living processes as such, deals with the relationship of the individual human mind to the universe, the ability of the human species to accumulate, transmit, and use such knowledge, depends upon discovery of certain universal principles of the human mind, principles upon which society depends for the successful application of what are physical principles of nature, as the latter are considered apart from viewing the problems of individual and society in terms of the measurable effects of mankind's relationship to the universe at large. We must distinguish between the potential relative population-density of society, as measured from the standpoint of the physical universe outside us, and the manner in which society organizes its internal, social relations, to produce changes in society's voluntary relationship to the physical universe.

This involves a crucial point, and must be made clear, even if it costs a bit more effort to do so.

In the usages of Vernadsky, the effective increase of the potential relative population-density of mankind is a *natural product* of a cognition-driven progress in the practice of society, upon the biosphere which it inhabits. This is the form in which physical productivity of society can be measured for its relative success in improving its ability to exist in terms of the world around it.

The making of that natural product, occurs within a different dimension of the process. It occurs primarily as the cognitive production of valid discoveries (or enactments of discoveries) of universal physical principles; but, the fostering of those discoveries and their application, is a reflection of a social process, the process in which mankind defines relations within society.

So, those social processes, especially the social processes associated with the transmission and application of ideas as ideas, are themselves properly the subject of the same methods of investigation used for discovering universal physical principles in the domains of non-living and living processes in general.

To restate that point, we have the following. The cognitive work of scientific discovery must be continued, from the subject of mankind's effective physical relationship to the universe at large, to the subject of the principles governing the way in which man's ability to cooperate for the mastery of nature, is determined in terms of the relations among the cognitive processes of the individual members of society at large. Just as mankind must discover how better to order our species' physical relationship to the universe, the noösphere, in which we live, we must discover those principles needed to better order such task-oriented relations among ourselves.

This signifies that our programs of education, and related activities, must rise above the application of cognition to the narrower purpose of discovery of valid universal physical principles respecting man's direct mastery of the non-living universe and biosphere. We must broaden the inquiry, to focus upon the application of cognition to the discovery of the universal principles governing the efficient consequences of relevant, directly functional relations among the cognitive processes of persons. We must, so to speak, expand upon what is demonstrated as the cognitive relationship among the minds of John, Robert, and Archimedes, to include the generality of such cognitive relations within society.

This application of the principle of cognition to the subject of the functions of the cognitive relations within society, is best named *Classical humanist culture*. The clue leading to solutions to this problem, is study of the way in which self-conscious forms of cognitively creative social behavior in children, determine the possibility of healthy forms of functioning of adult society, or, in the alternative, how the lack of such cognitive development among the young, tends toward descent of the adult society into bestiality. The theme of such an inquiry, must be the subject of policies of education.

The essence of all competent forms of Classical artistic composition, is *the principle of cognitive play*. For example, the person who is not more or less effervescent in impulses for specifically cognitive forms of playfulness, as Wolfgang Mozart expresses that quality so beautifully, or J.S. Bach before him, has little or no capacity for sustained creative work in general, either scientific, or in Classical forms of artistic composition and performance in particular.

I have suggested, in earlier locations, that one might examine more closely the happier instances of play between a boy and his puppy, noting particularly the impulse of the mentally healthy boy for invention of harmless games, which the puppy then happily learns. In that combined symbiosis and difference between boy and beast, a principle of humanism is being demonstrated. Nicholas of Cusa, on this account, referenced the animal's participation in man, as parallelling man's participation in God the Creator. The morally healthy order among living creatures, is the participation of the lower species in the work of the higher.[50]

Perhaps the best way to describe the individual's impulse for cognitive play, is to regard this as the individual's impulse, at least implicitly so, to play with the Creator, as the puppy desires to play with a boy who treats it well. I think that neither Cusa nor Friedrich Schiller would disagree with that. Plato's Socrates is a paradigm for such a playful individual; the dialogues are models of a quality of play which seeks to define forms of behavior which are cognitively pleasing, not only because of the need of the sane human individual to be cognitive, but the desire to choose games in which nothing sordid or unjust ensues.

The characteristic of such cognitive play, is the exercise and development of the powers of cognition themselves. This may be expressed, in approximation, either as the development of the individual powers to rally one's mental powers for making discoveries, which might be termed developing one's cognitive mental muscles, or may emphasize the specific capacities needed for cognitive undertakings in direct, explicitly cognitive modes of cooperation with others.

The study of these matters, from that standpoint, obliges us to focus attention on the relationship between productive

---

50. The boy, as usual, had hitched up his mule, and the day's ploughing was under way. A stallion and a donkey, watched from over the fence. Suddenly, the donkey began braying, ridiculing the mule. "Why are you laughing at me?" said the mule. "Because, despite all your hard work, you will never have a child," the stallion intervened. The mule rejoined, "Who do you think is walking behind me?" From the mule's standpoint, it made perfect sense.

EIRNS/Roger Ham

A child explores solid geometry at a Pedagogical Musem, as her father looks on. The characteristic of such cognitive play, is the exercise and development of the powers of cognition themselves. The study of the connection between productive forms of play in young children, and more developed forms essential to the best performance of adults, is the proper definition of education.

forms of play in young children and the productive role of the more developed forms of play which are essential to the best performance of adults. The study of that connection is the proper definition of education.

Classical Drama as Science

So, ironically, but also insightfully, we also use the word "play" to describe what we may regard as a successful design for a drama. In the emergence of what became known as Classical Greece, the successive emergence of the Homeric epics, the Classical tragedy, and the Socratic dialogues of Plato, represent phases of development, in that form, of what is meaningfully identified as a notion of a Classical artistic principle of composition and performance for today.

From the New Testament, we have the parable of the *talents*.

The impulse for cognitive play, is the talent which must be returned to the Creator enriched by the user. In other words, play as the work of generating anti-entropy for the sake of humanity. In what is called physical science and the practice of physical economy, such a return of the thus-increased talent, is manifest, *as a natural product,* as the increase of mankind's per-capita power in and over nature. In art, it is called play, signifying the importance of the quality of play, which Shakespeare's character Hamlet recognizes, but can not embrace, a Hamlet who is, like his nation, self-doomed by his fear of play, his fear of that realm from which he thinks no traveller might return.

A true Classical drama is never composed for the purpose of providing mere entertainment. Every great drama was composed with irrepressible playfulness, but also in deadly earnest, as were: Dante's *Commedia;* Boccacio's *Decameron,* written as a commentary on the tragic siege of the Black Death, then raging among the leading wealthy families of Florence, across the river below; François Rabelais' *Gargantua and Pantagruel;* and, Cervantes' portrayal of the tragedy dooming the Spain of Philip II, *Don Quixote.* Forms of play such as the Classical tragedies of Aeschylus and Sophocles, the Socratic dialogues of Plato, and the tragedies of Shakespeare and Schiller, were composed in deadly earnest, to provoke the cognitive processes of the actors and audiences, alike, to an awareness of urgently needed adoption of certain principles of statecraft, for the sake of the historically specific, successful solution, for an historically specific problem of that place and time: the successful continuation, and betterment, of the society represented by those audiences.

For example, Shakepeare's plays on English history, reflect the legacy of the studies of the overthrow of King Richard III, as passed down as a tradition through, chiefly, the work of the martyred figure of England's participation in the Golden Renaissance, Sir Thomas More. Thus, from the same vantage-point as that study of the transition from Richard III to Henry VII, Shakespeare composed a dramatic overview of two centuries of the history of England's place within Europe. This was put on stage as a series of dramas, from *King John* through *Richard III.* This series of dramas is devoted, throughout, to a single subject, the actual lessons to be adduced from the history of England, from the accession of the Plantagenet allies of imperial Venice, through the revolutionary change in statecraft established under Henry VII. Schiller's dramas, in most instances, addressed actual historical situations, and, on reflection on the actual history so selected, were accurate representations of the crucial issues of statecraft posed in the real-life history referenced by the stage.

In such great drama as that of Shakespeare and Schiller, the object is not the type of impulse to entertain the vulgar appetites for sensual exhibitions, such as those of the "night club," pagan Rome's Colosseum, or mass spectator sports, nor to provide a vehicle for the narcissistic impulses of the actors like Sir Laurence Olivier, or the sado-masochistic, existentialist impulses of a director toward playwright, actors, and audience alike. The function of great drama, is to make the issues posed by a moment of real history, come to life with great force, within the cognitive processes of director, actors, and audience alike. The crux of such Classical artistic composition and its performance, is the evoking of the specific quality of passion unique to a state of cognitive insight. It is the same quality of passion experienced by one who is engaged in bringing forth a validatable cognitive discovery of a universal principle.

Compare this with the case of the profound superiority of the so-called Negro Spiritual to the banality and superficiality of so-called "gospel" singing, to say nothing of that axiomatic contradiction in terms known as "Christian rock." I am not an expert in the Negro Spiritual, but I have the advantage of being presented with the essence of the matter by experts who have demonstrated their argument to me most efficiently; the case they make has two aspects, both of which are relevant to the point I have just made, above, on the subject of Classical drama.

In its raw form, the Negro Spiritual as I recognize it, expresses the historically specific situation and experience of the slave. On this account, a certain authenticity of presentation is essential for a convincing result. The singer must put himself, or herself inside that slave, and sing in a way which touches the quality which Friedrich Schiller defines as the *sublime*. I compare this quality of the spiritual to the expression of the sublime in Schiller's *Maid of Orleans*.[51]

In the development of Classical drama, we must recognize chiefly two distinct levels of such drama. The relatively inferior form is typified by the Classical Greek tragedy. On this account, Plato was not only critical of the leading Classical Greek tragedians, but presented the alternative in the form of his intrinsically dramatic Socratic dialogues, which must be performed and heard as the drama they are, to master their cognitive content. With Plato's dialogues, we encounter a typification of the transition from Classical tragedy, to the higher principle of the *sublime*.

In reviewing the works of the world's greatest modern dramatists, Shakespeare and Schiller, in their respective entireties, we may trace an upward development in their work, from the level of tragedy, to the sublime. The case of Jeanne d'Arc illustrates the distinction.

In history, Jeanne d'Arc's passion contributes a crucial role to the subsequent freeing of France from the evils of the long reign and ruin under the alliance between Venice and its Norman-Plantagenet partners. Her sacrifice made the existence of a true nation of France possible; also, in fact, she contributed indirectly, but notably, to the proceedings leading into the great ecumenical Council of Florence, which was the central event of the Fifteenth-Century Renaissance. Jeanne d'Arc was not a tragic figure, neither in history, nor on Schiller's stage. Her sacrifice of herself for her mission, was not a tragedy, it was the achievement of the sublime, as Schiller does much to define and refine the notion of the sublime in history and in art. She rose to the sublime in the imitation of Christ crucified. She lived and died for all mankind, not only France, all this, as she insisted repeatedly, for His sake. In the drama, Schiller substitutes a fictional element for the crucial historical event which actually precedes her execution, but, otherwise, the drama is true to history in everything it claims to present.

The great achievement of the Classical tragedy, even as

---

51. Friedrich Schiller, "On the Sublime," in *Friedrich Schiller, Poet of Freedom*, Vol. III, *op. cit.*, p. 255.

tragedy, is that it presents an historically specific moment of crisis in civilization, in which the fatal errors of the prevailing national cultures and leaders of the drama, are placed on stage in such a way that the audience may be induced to recognize the principled nature of the fatal error then reigning in that society and its relevant leading figures. However, although recognition of the moral unfitness to survive of both the culture of Hamlet's nation and Hamlet himself, is a great and useful improvement of the moral and intellectual qualities of the audience, it presents the sickness, but not the solution itself. Its usefulness, is that making the audience conscious of the fact that an avoidable error in moral character of a nation and its leaders was responsible for the catastrophe, inspires the audience with cultural optimism, with the hope that it might willfully free itself from such folly.

With Jeanne d'Arc, both in real life, and on Schiller's stage, she acts in a course, where she spends her life, but does not waste it; she returns her talent to God, enriched. Therefore, she is no tragic figure, but a representative of the principle of the sublime, just as the outcome of Plato's Socratic dialogues, notably Plato's treatment of the figure of the judicially murdered Socrates himself, exemplifies the principle of the sublime in science, statecraft generally, and artistic composition.

See a certain likeness in the slave represented by the Negro Spiritual. Out of that condition, he affirms his humanity and his trust in God, and thus touches the sublime. It is always a song of humanity, of the humanity being crushed by servitude, but a cry of humanity which will not be stilled.

Classical Music as Science

In the first aspect of Classical art, as typified by great drama and poetry, the benefit of Classical art is more directly identified. Persons who have been civilized by saturation with the greatest examples of such artistic composition, have relatively superior powers for competence in statecraft and related matters.

This brings us to the second aspect of Classical art, in which the relationship to statecraft is, with certain exceptions, of a less obviously direct quality. Music typifies this second aspect.[52]

In this second aspect, as through the work of Harry Burleigh and others, as Haydn, Beethoven, Schubert, Schumann, Brahms, and Dvorak applied the relevant principles of Bach's and Mozart's Classical contrapuntal composition to the folk-song of the British Isles and Germany, principally, the great composer employs his musical insight into the folk-song, or folk-song-like compositions, to polish the intention which needs to be released from the encumbering limitations of the original.

For comparison, consider the challenge posed by the attempt to perform either of J.S. Bach's two great passions, the earlier *St. John Passion,* and the later *St. Matthew Passion.* Both address a spiritual subject, the Passion and Crucifixion of Jesus Christ, as defined by the relevant Gospels. The object of the performance of each composition, is to inspire the participants to relive, with cognitive passion, the actual circumstances of the Crucifixion, as a cognitive experience of the sublime. The scores as written, recommend the participation of a musically qualified congregation in singing the parts obviously assigned to them, to such effect that they are not spectators for, but rather participants in the event.

How that functions, and what Wolfgang Mozart and others did, in adducing the principles of Classical contrapuntal thorough-composition of Mozart, Haydn, Beethoven, Schubert, Mendelssohn, Schumann, and Brahms from Bach's discoveries in use of series of Lydian intervals, need not be examined in any

---

52. Notable exceptions include Giuseppe Verdi's operas, as only typified by those which are adopted from the tragedies of Shakespeare and Schiller. Mozart's *Abduction from the Seraglio, Marriage of Figaro, Don Giovanni, Magic Flute,* and *Clemenza di Tito,* and Beethoven's *Fidelio,* are musical dramas which are purely musical, and yet also Classical drama of political relevance to the historical specifics of both the nominal setting of the drama and the audiences for which they were composed. The religious music of J.S. Bach, Mozart, Haydn, and Beethoven also typifies the integration of drama and music in an integrated way, not as a musical setting of text, but a qualitative, creative transformation of the delivery of the text to a higher dimension.

depth in this location. What does need to be stressed, is that Classical composition, most notably that of Bach, Mozart, Haydn, Beethoven, Schubert, Mendelssohn, Schumann, and Brahms, as contrasted with their adversaries, the Romantics, such as Rameau, Liszt, Berlioz, and Wagner, and the hoaxsters Helmholtz and Ellis, was to define the means by which the use of well-tempered counterpoint brings out the quality of cognitive passion, and thus produces a composition which, if competently performed, represents a single unifying Platonic idea as the identity (e.g., the "monad") of the composition as an indivisible unit. In the best result, as typified by Beethoven's Opus 132 string quartet, or the last of Brahms' four hymns, the *Four Serious Songs,* is the achievement of a sense of the sublime.

The origin of this mode of musical composition, lies within ancient notions of Classical (sung) prosody used in poetry composition. It uses the natural well-tempering subsumed by the natural range of human speaking and singing voices, to derive a corresponding polyphony, and a principle of polyphonic development, derived from the principle of the Lydian interval as the pivot of a developmental feature of composition. The difference between Bach's well-tempering and those who seek to degrade it to equal tempering, is the same difference expressed by Kepler's exposure of the incompetence of the mechanistic, reductionist method of Ptolemy, Copernicus, and Brahe.

Similarly, in Classical plastic art-forms, the most important development, is that which existing evidence traces to the Classical Greek developments in sculpture, as distinct from the preceding Greek as well as Egyptian Archaic. Here, the subject is presented to the mind as in mid-motion, rather than as "tombstone" carvings. The revolution in perspective, established by Leonardo da Vinci, has a relationship to Classical Greek sculpture, but is a revolutionary scientific development in art effected during the course of the Fifteenth Century as continued into the beginning of the Sixteenth Century, and as echoed by Rembrandt.

Those background observations now supplied, the point to be made in this report, is that Classical artistic composition is defined as the development of methods for bringing the same cognitive principle required for generating a discovery of a valid

universal physical principle, into its corresponding form of application to the study and representation of those social processes
of cooperation among persons on which the successful promotion of physical-scientific progress depends.

In the literary non-plastic art-forms, notably Classical
drama and poetry, the political side of the social function of
Classical composition is explicit. Similarly, Leonardo's *The Last
Supper,* and Raphael's *The School of Athens* and his *Transfigu-
ration,* are examples of work which is purely Classical art, but
also has a powerful political and scientific importance for statecraft, as I have indicated the general nature of that above.

A few more glances at the case of Classical musical composition, will round out that picture as much as is needed for this oc-
casion.

The subject is now *metaphor.* The example chosen is *Classical thorough-composed song,* as typified by the new form of
song-composition developed by Mozart, as expressed in his setting of a Goethe poem, *Das Veilchen,* as that new approach to
song-composition was continued by Beethoven, Schubert, Mendelssohn, Schumann, and Brahms, most notably.[53]

Metaphor is the name, in literary composition and song,
for a form of poetical *irony* which is termed *Analysis Situs* in
mathematical physics. It is the immediate juxtaposition of two
or more mutually inconsistent statements, or individual terms,
to define an idea which exists outside the bounds of consistency
within the medium of representation employed in communication: *a dissonance.* It is to be compared with the case of Fermat's
counterposing a description of reflection to refraction in terms
of the language intended for representing events in what is imagined to be a Euclidean space-time.

Fermat's exemplary, concise juxtaposition of those two contrasted statements, both in the same form of description, implicitly destroys the credibility of a so-called Euclidean mathematics
of physical space-time. So, Kepler asks, what is the *Mind,* the

---

53. John Sigerson and Kathy Wolfe, eds., *A Manual on the Rudiments
of Tuning and Registration,* Book I (Washington, D.C.: Schiller Institute,
1992).

intention of the planet Mars which causes its orbit to lie in a pathway not calculable within the framework of the Aristotelean notions of space-time commonly used by Claudius Ptolemy, Copernicus, and Brahe. To make that point, Kepler measures the orbit of Mars by means consistent with those of Euclidean mathematical statistics, and gains a result which is implicitly anti-Euclidean.

J.S. Bach approaches the issue of defining the proper tuning of musical instruments in a way which echoes Kepler's *Harmony of the World*. This comparison is demanded by a direct contrast of well-tempered values to those erroneous, so-called equal-tempered values, which a soulless mechanical man might estimate by use of an electronic hand-calculator. As I have already stressed here, the right value of the interval in a well-tempered composition, like the right value for the future velocity and position of a planet in its Keplerian orbit, can not be mechanically predicted as the systems of Copernicus and Brahe would suggest, or the methods of attempts at equal tempering.

The right value for well-tempering arises from the relations among what are called the natural register-shifts of each species of singing voice, among *bel canto*-trained groups representing the standard chest of *human singing voices*. In short, well-tempering is not defined from a so-called instrumental standpoint, but from the standpoint of certain ironies intrinsic to *bel canto vocal polyphony*.

To understand the problem, it is sufficient to throw out all notions of a theory of instrumental composition and performance, and recognize that the Classical performance of the musical instrument, must be an expression of the idea of the human singing voice, that musical instruments are intended to be echoes of the principles of the *bel canto*-trained human singing voice.

This brings us to Wolfgang Mozart's great discovery, as expressed in a series of compositions typified by the Köchel Number 475 keyboard *Fantasy*. This composition represents Mozart's reworking of a celebrated J.S. Bach composition, the so-called *A Musical Offering*. That Bach work, as complemented by the posthumously published *The Art of the Fugue,* is a concentrated expression of one of the most important revolutionary features of Bach's work. Mozart's intensive Vienna study of Bach's work, led him to a discovery which not only revolutionized all Classical musical composition after that, but which is the most frequently quoted musical idea within the work of all leading Classical composers after that; the kernel of the discovery is expressed by that playful K. 475 *Fantasy*. Mozart made explicit Bach's increasing reliance on a principle of musical composition, and play, associated with the term "Lydian interval."

To get directly to the essential point of relevance for this present report, focus upon the role of the method of *Analysis Situs* intrinsic to Bach's art of well-tempered counterpoint.

Take an interval of two tones, and now state that interval in an inverted order. State both of these juxtaposed intervals in the same key signature, and do so in a way which expresses the natural dissonance inhering in such a notion of inversion. If the development of that germ is successful, the attempt to resolve the counterpoint will lead inevitably toward a series of what are called "Lydian intervals," as Beethoven's famous Opus 132 ("Lydian") string quartet illustrates this, or the Brahms Fourth Symphony derived from a germ in the slow movement of Beethoven's Opus 106 "Hammerklavier" sonata.

The implicit dissonance in well-crafted choices of inversions, has the same effect as Fermat's resort, in counterposing reflection to refraction, to what Leibniz later named *Analysis Situs*. These metaphors, whether in mathematical physics or Classical artistic composition, define germ-ideas, as provoking that cognitive "energy" which requires the mind to make the cognitive leap from reductionist schemes, to discovering the cognitive principle which overcomes the apparently insoluble paradox so posed. That, in music, as in practice of mathematical physics, constitutes the identity of a Platonic form of *idea*.

When a great composer employs that principle of inversion, by such devices, to that purpose, his conscience requires him to do nothing which does not introduce and develop that idea in such a way, that the development of the entire composition reaches a conclusion which defines the idea which the composer has chosen to bring into being through the introduction of the root-metaphor generated through inversion. If the composition is well-crafted, then it becomes the performer's duty, to deliver the performance of the composition in a way which never spoils the indivisible unity of the idea embodied in the composer's intention. Such a principle of performance was sometimes termed by the conductor Wilhelm Furtwängler, "playing between the notes."

Such was the stroke of genius expressed in Mozart's pioneering *Das Veilchen*. Instead of setting the poem to the natural prosody supplied by the custom of the language used, as J.F. Reichardt did, follow the advice of the poet Friedrich Schiller, apply the principle on which Beethoven, Schubert, Schumann, and Brahms agreed with Mozart and Schiller, contrary to the argument of Reichardt and Goethe: Discover a single musical idea, which shall control the singing of the poem from beginning to end, and use the implications of the Lydian principle in composition, as a way of making the sung prosody march to the idea which the poem itself is intended to express.[54]

The same intention is found, and made undeniably obvious, in the great artist's performance of the Negro Spiritual, even when the means used by the artist may differ, in a formal sense, from the German Classical *Lied,* for example.

Complement the argument I have just given for music, with frank assessment of the decadence in the art of speaking which usually contrasts literate English speakers of my generation, to the "up-talk" and comparable perversions in habits of speaking, or of reciting text induced by recent or current, immoral idiosyncrasies of public school and university instruction, especially in reciting prose passages or poetry aloud publicly, among those of the "Baby Boomer" or later generations. The loss of the habit of Classical poetry, the Classical dramatic stage, and Classical music, has been a crucial factor in the loss of ability to communicate ideas among comparable representatives of later generations.

The person who speaks in a literate Classical mode, speaks as one *who can be heard actually thinking,* rather than merely

---

54. Ibid., Chapter 11, "Artistic Beauty: Schiller versus Goethe," passim.

engaged in a more or less arbitrarily stylized recitation of what is either written, or memorized text, or a text the speaker is, in effect, writing as he goes along. The modern tendency is comparable to the case of the musician who is so busy interpreting the score itself, that he, while in that virtually schizophrenic state of mind, has no perceptible intellectual connection to the music which the composer intended.

The problem of speech typified by the increasingly illiteracy of manner of speaking among post-war U.S. generations of university graduates, in particular, is comparable as a problem to the case of the trained musical performer, who can play notes, without any understanding of music beyond the conventions which he or she recognizes almost as programmed instructions for note-playing. It is often worse than that; they "improve" the dish by putting tabasco sauce on the raspberry ice cream, so to speak. They read text in such idiosyncratic styles in text-reading; they do not oblige the prosodic utterance of the statement to conform to a process of development of ideas. Worse, they, as the Romantics do, add interpretation to text as such, without regard to the cognitive processes required by the clearly adducible intent of the text itself. They become functionally illiterates of that sort.

The same pathological state of mind is exhibited by the person who, when challenged to debate his, or her statement socratically, responds by repeating the statement more loudly, more angrily, perhaps adding the unsanitary proposal, "Read my lips." The victims of that perversion do this even in the case that the criticism itself exposes the statement being repeated as absurd. Why does that person exhibit such pathological behavior? The explanation is elementary: "It is my opinion!" and therefore has the attributed authority of the believer, of being *self-evidently my opinion.* One is reminded of the state of mind lurking behind the glaring eyeballs of that maniacal pre-middle-aged tail-gater, searching for her own shortcut to Hell, along the Maryland and Virginia highways of the greater Washington, D.C. region.

The relative impairment of the ability to communicate ideas, in the manner a Classical education and practice provide the relevant contrary standard, becomes a loss of the ability to think clearly, a loss of what the poet Shelley describes as the power of "imparting and receiving profound and important ideas respecting man and nature."

Culture as Education

As the case of Classical drama typifies this connection, all knowledge of statecraft is best developed through emphasis upon educating the young in both Classical approaches to physical science and Classical forms of artistic composition. The Classical form of study and practice of physical science, as I have indicated in this report, combined with a Classical artistic education, serves as the foundation for a competent grasp of the general problems and purposes of cooperation in general, and of matters of statecraft more narrowly. To complete the picture: The science of physical economy, properly bridges the roles of both science and Classical art.

The obligation of Classical humanist education, is to employ an historical approach to the cognitive apprehension of the history of scientific and Classical-artistic ideas, to the purpose of building up within the student's memory, his or her own equivalent of the kind of sense of a simultaneity of eternity, as I outlined the case of Raphael's *The School of Athens*. The pupil should relive the history of ideas, historically and cognitively, to that effect.

The intended result, is that the student should locate himself, or herself in a great span of human history, as one in direct communication, cognitively, with the living minds of the greatest original thinkers of that past. The development of the personal character of the student, in this mode of education, tends to ensure a beneficial result which could be achieved in no other way. In brief: As the student defines the student's personal relationship, through the methods of the Socratic dialogue, to living notable persons long since deceased, so the student is impelled to come to see himself, or herself, in respect to those who have yet to be born. It is that manner of development of the moral character, so defined, of the pupil, which is the only proper central aim of education.

The motivation of the pupil must become, concern for the consequences which the present bequeaths to the future, a generation or more ahead. There is nothing arbitrary in this. To transform a newborn child into a young adult, requires approximately a quarter-century of development. During that quarter-century, the expenditure of effort and means on the development of the young individual, brings no net return on that expense. Important projects of development take years before reaching the point of yielding net economic fruit. Yet, what will happen a quarter-century ahead, will be determined, often, by the decisions chosen today. As in the case of Kepler's meticulous measurement of the orbit of Mars, the velocity and position occupied by that planet tomorrow, will not be determined by the statistical trend adduced from its recent movements. Science must always locate the long-term expression of the intention embedded in the process being considered.

It is not possible, except in an oppressively stagnating economic culture, and perpetually decadent society, such as that prescribed by the Code of the Roman Emperor Diocletian, to determine what a young person in school today should be doing a score of years ahead. The choices available then, will depend upon a combination of the decisions made beforehand and in between. What we can know with reasonable certainty, is the degree of general development, and related adaptability we should seek to build into the labor-force as a whole. Rather than training the person to fit the specific form of employment (which, by that time, should no longer exist), develop the economy to make use of the quality of labor-force we are working to develop.

It is the level of development which the present generation will make possible for its successors, which should be the determining consideration in economic policy today.

Beyond all other considerations, educational policies must be conditioned principally by the consideration, that the function of education, is to produce qualified citizens of a true republic, with no substitute for that allowed in defining educational policies of practice. The primary responsibility of the citizen, is not that of an employee, but, rather, a policy-maker for society as a whole. It is to that end, and no other, that goals for the education of the individual are to be chosen. Nothing less than the fulfillment of that goal shall be a minimum standard of education of the future adult member of society.

Once it is agreed, without exception, that that is the universal mission of all education, we can consider other things, but without eliminating, or depreciating any part of the obligation to serve education's primary mission-responsibility.

This does not place an excessive burden on the educational system. The presently practiced modes in education are immensely wasteful of the time and energy of the pupils. Heave out the popularized rubbish, to save time and energy for what is of more durable value.

As I have indicated here already, there are really two essential departments in required forms of education: 1) Mankind's relationship to the universe, in physical terms; 2) mankind's relationship to mankind, and person to person within society. Both departments are, and must be situated in history apprehended cognitively as a simultaneity of historical eternity, as this must be provoked into existence within the mind of the student. Stick to that business, and discard the clutter which is commonly substituted for education in today's educational institutions.

Take astronomy, for example. For many cognitive exercises a pedagogical laboratory capability is needed. Very little is required, by comparison, for an introduction to astronomy. The universe is there, an astrophysical reality which serves as a demonstration experiment relentlessly continuing its motion. It is that, the great demonstration experiment, up there, called astronomy, ocean navigation, geodesy, and so forth, upon which the most ancient of societies, whichever they were, first produced the rudiments of what we recognize as physical science today. "With your bare eyes and some sticks and stones, proceed to construct a calendar. Don't admire the stars; don't waste your time just mooning and gawking, when you might be engaged in beginning to construct a calendar. Don't look it up on the Internet; know what you are talking about; look up to the stars, instead."

Keep what I have identified as the principles of cognitive education in focus. The practice of learning must be superseded,

Claudio Celani

Bush's Attorney General appeals to the Supreme Court.

to a relatively enormous degree, by a thoroughly cognitive, historical approach to education, as my references to the example of Raphael's *The School of Athens* typify the point. The historical, direct and personal link, through cognition, of the minds of the original discoverers from the past, to the students, must be the foundation of all pedagogy. The students must be engaged in the cognitive passions of an endless Socratic dialogue with all notable minds from the past. All knowledge is located in the importance of experimental validation of the hypotheses developed in response to the ontological quality of paradoxes expressed within the bounds of that realm of relative simultaneity of eternity.

On this account, the structure of public and university education must incorporate a relatively great emphasis on the facilities for, and activities of pedagogical proof-of-principle experiments. The notion that any hypothesis must be validated, and that in the direct cognitive experience of the students, must be the rule, whether the replication of a past discovery of universal principle, or testing of the mastery of the lessons of that experience, in pioneering into the experimental domains of fundamental research to the purpose of discovering new universal physical principles, and discovering new kinds of technologies which may be derived from those principles.

This also means a certain upper limit on average class-size, and the training and placement of teachers and other relevant specialists in the amount and quality needed for such a program. In the end, these changes in the program and its budget, will cost the U.S.A. (in particular) less than nothing. The increase of the harvest will vastly exceed the added costs of the program. The principle is, that the only source of increase of the average productive powers of labor in society, is the increase of the rate of production and assimilation of more advanced knowledge of universal physical principle, and of the new technologies spawned as offspring of such discoveries of principle.

This implies a sweeping recrafting of the entire primary and secondary curriculum, and correlated changes in programs for universities, too. That requires a great effort. That effort is not only worth the expenditure; it is now indispensable for the survival of civilization.

4. European Civilization

Up to the present day, we have no reasonable choice of dating available, for the first appearance of the human species on this planet. We can only estimate, that that must have begun in the order of millions of years ago. The best evidence to date, is fairly consistent with the general retrospective picture given by Plato's *Timaeus,* which points toward the conditions under which what we regard presently as historical times, emerged, during the closing, melting phase of the preceding 200,000 years or so of the most recent general glaciation of the land-mass of the Northern Hemisphere.

To supplement that information, we have cave paintings from scores of thousands of years before the present, which show a much higher level of culture than most current cultural anthropologist's standard mythologies would allow to exist, and we also have crucial evidence dating from some hundreds of thousands of years earlier than that, of a cognitive human individual, no mere higher ape, existing in Europe.[55]

On the deeper issues of scientific method posed by this subject, the implications of Vernadsky's case for the "historical" self-development of the biosphere and noösphere, respectively, give us some useful parameters. Two sets of observations to such effect, matters on which I have reported in earlier locations, should be sufficient to situate the way in which we should approach the subject of the recent approximately 2,500 years, since the emergence of European civilization on the foundations provided chiefly by the legacy of ancient Egypt. Look at the matter from this vantage-point, and then turn to the immediate political setting of U.S. education today, the matter of European civilization's development as so situated.

First, as to the existence of the human species as such.

To situate the existence of mankind with respect to the phenomena of both European civilization in general, and globally extended modern European civilization as well, let us box in the issue of the origins of human life, by aid of the following observations, once again, on the implications of the work of Vernadsky.

The issue of tracing the origins and development of human life on Earth, must begin with the fact that the uniquely cognitive form of life, mankind, exists. Not only must human existence have begun at some point in the development of the Earth's biosphere, but certain preconditions, within the biosphere as a whole process, had to have been satisfied for that emergence of man to have occurred.[56] Inevitably, for many, the most shocking, even stunning implication of Vernadsky's portrait of both the

---

55. See Renate Müller De Paoli, "Die Höhlenmalerei der Eiszeit," *Neue Solidarität*, Feb. 23, 2000; Hartmut Thieme, "Lower Paleolithic Hunting Spears from Germany," *Nature*, Feb. 27, 1997, pp. 807-810; Robin Dennell, "The World's Oldest Spears," *Nature*, Feb. 27, 1997, pp. 767-768.

56. I do not mean evolution in the empiricist's sense. I mean the existence of man as a cognitive species, requires preconditions, knowledge of which has yet to be determined, within the biosphere as a whole process.

biosphere and the noösphere, is that what he cites as his experimental evidence, points implicitly to the appropriate dating of
the occurrence of a principle of life, and also of a principle
of cognition, as located in whatever might be considered the
beginning of the existence of the universe.

To restate that crucial last point, if life is not derived, in
fact, as by evolution or otherwise, from a universal physics of
non-living processes, and if *life is,* as Vernadsky argues experimentally, *a demonstrably efficient, universal physical principle
in its own right,* then, *life always existed* as a principle of our
universe. *The same kind of experimental proof applies to the
principle of cognition,* which, among all perceptible phenomena,
was, from the beginning, unique to those human forms of life
which emerged later.

Then, the appearance of the existence of a living species
which is characteristically cognitive, the human species, signifies
that the preconditions for the appearance of the already waiting
principle of human life, had then been realized, that in a certain
degree and quality of the development of the biosphere in general. It also indicates, that within the specific features of organization of that living process which is the human individual, there
exists something to be discovered, which corresponds to the
appropriateness of the human species for cognition, an appropriateness which is lacking in the higher apes.

Moreover, it follows from this, that since, as our national
"melting-pot" experience in education exemplifies this, all human beings have the same kind of cognitive potential, then, on
this account, it follows, that all human beings are of the same
species, and, when defined by that specific cognitive distinction,
are of the same race.

These distinctions, among three respectively unique classes
of universal physical principles, are associated with the corresponding, specific ranges of relative anti-entropy, as expressed
among each of those three classes of universal physical principles.
This is demonstrated, with relative great emphasis, by the effect
of human intervention in accelerating the anti-entropic development of the biosphere, as this is shown by including the human
species and its specific activity as a biological part of that bio-

sphere as a whole. This entails the consideration, that the durability of the existence of a species, depends upon its enjoying *the level of rate of attributable relative anti-entropy associated with, and required for the perpetuation of its own existence.*

In the case of the only known cognitive species, the human species, its superior anti-entropy is expressed by those cognitive aspects of formal and other education, which transmit accumulated discoveries of principle, as from the past, into the mental processes of the living.

Meanwhile, to understand what this anti-entropy represents, and to shape policies to the effect of promoting it, we must discard the Clausius-Kelvin mythology, respecting thermodynamics. We do this on the basis of what should be the obvious, conclusive epistemological evidence, that the root argument in support of their claims, does not actually reflect crucial scientific evidence as such. Rather, as the reductionist's axiomatic fallacies of Grassmann's and Boltzmann's mathematics illustrate the point, it reflects the superimposition upon the physical evidence, of the hereditary influence of purely arbitrary, reductionist types of axiomatic mathematical assumptions. They made the same hereditary type of reductionist error which Descartes perpetrated on the matter of *vis viva,* and Ptolemy in astronomy.

In that case, our view of what we regard as the non-living aspects of our universe, must define development in the alternative terms of the emergence of relatively higher orders of anti-entropic *organization,* as primary, and the phenomena of relative energy-flux density are to be judged as derived from a universal physical principle of organization, as Leibniz's principle of the monadology expresses this conception, rather than the ideological reductionists' insistence on interpreting the experimental evidence the other way around.[57]

---

57. In knowledge, as cognitive generation of the ideas of universal physical principle are generated, a paradox of the type of *Analysis Situs* always defines the fact of experience from which knowledge of universal principle is derived. When such knowledge is configured as Riemann's principle implicitly requires, physics, so defined, presents us with a multi-connected architecture of the universe, its *organization* as to matters of principle. It is the view of the universe as a self-organizing process, from

In that latter case, the notion of universal entropy, is discarded into the black museum where all superstitions and other biological freaks should repose, there to warn future mankind against repeating such follies. Instead of axiomatically reductionist thermodynamics, we must regard as primary, the different orders of relative anti-entropy to be considered in assessing the relations and distinctions among apparently non-living universe, life, and cognition. In that case, the universe we inhabit, then becomes, to say the least, much more interesting.

So much for situating a discussion of the preconditions for human existence. Now, turn to the second point, as to the emergence of modern civilized forms of human life.

The earliest evidence of the existence of what we call scientific culture today, is passed down to us in the form of ancient astronomical calendars, such as those known to us from the period of the building of the so-called Great Pyramids of Egypt. The study of these calendars from the standpoint of modern science, shows that these include cycles which reflect cultures of far greater sophistication than can be explained as products of relevant known cultures dated from early within historical times. That is to say, that much of the astronomical and related traditions known from early within historical times, is, like the lunatic contemporary fads of astrology, demonstrably a vulgarized and superstition-ridden parody of actually scientific work from within earlier, so-called prehistoric times.[58]

---

this standpoint, which shows us what the evidence as such permits us to consider as "elementary," and what not. Hence, organization-as-such, so defined in principle, must replace notions of self-evident discrete magnitudes. Then, consider Planck's discovery as correlated with the notion of a monadology, rather than self-evidently elementary particles as the reductionists define them. Notably, as emphasized implicitly by Kepler's success over the reductionist methods of Claudius Ptolemy et al., the attempt to derive physical principles from within the bounds of a mathematics based upon reductionist assumptions, is the hereditary principle which separates all constructs in formal logic fatally from science.

58. Typical is the case of the hoax perpetrated by the Roman Empire's Claudius Ptolemy, who fraudulently reworked the heliocentric constructions of his Classical Greek predecessors, in service of the method of Aris-

We must not underestimate such scientific achievements from within the so-called prehistoric times of the last great ice-age on the Northern Hemisphere's land-mass, but we must not overrate the moral qualities of the cultures of those times, either.

As the case of ancient Greece attests, some ancient societies have contributed a rich legacy of intellectual contributions, at the same time they treated the majority of the related human population, as Sparta did, among others, as actually or virtually human cattle. Chattel slavery in modern European civilization, is but a specific expression of the bestiality of man to man which was characteristic, in more severe or relatively milder degree, of every historically known society from every part of the world. The myth of the "noble savage," or of the moral "beauty" of cultures which actually never existed outside classroom and other mythologies, must be relegated to the same black museums in which the existence of deadly diseases and past experience with oligarchs and biological freaks, is kept on record as a warning to future times.

For these reasons, combined with considerations I have addressed in earlier locations published in the course of decades, the earliest traceable civilizations are to be found among trans-oceanic maritime ("Peoples of the Sea") cultures, such as the Dravidian language-group's maritime culture, which introduced civilization, as its colony of Sumer, into lower Mesopotamia, and the trans-Atlantic cultures whose Indo-European language-group branch settled in post-glaciation Central Asia, and contributed its cultural legacy to areas including Iran and the Indian subcontinent of today.

During the latter phase of the melting of the great glaciation that had sat for so long upon much of the Northern Hemisphere's land-mass, the oceans had risen by 300-400 feet above their earlier levels, the great periods of devastating flooding had come to a close, and a process of civilizing parts of the more accessible coastal and major riparian areas then proceeded. As the maritime

totle. Repeatedly, societies based upon the oligarchical model, perverted the results of earlier astronomy, as a matter of producing myths used as instruments of social control over the minds of the population.

traits of certain calendars indicate, civilization did not move from inland to the oceans, but the reverse. Even to this day, as the condition of the so-called "Great American Desert," Central Asia, Africa, and the heart of South America attest, the process of making inland areas of continents as accessible to the development of physical economy as coastal and major riparian regions, has been far from completed.

Those two considerations, the one scientific, the other representing some relevant, broad-best estimates, situate the emergence of the history of civilization in a general way. However, one additional point must be heavily emphasized, before taking up the emergence of European civilization upon foundations which were supplied, to a large degree, from Egypt.

The Indomitable Human Spirit

The best examples of the Negro Spiritual as such, express that essential quality of all mankind, on which a competent education policy must be premised, as if axiomatically. As long as mankind exists, the essence of human nature, the cognitive principle, can not be stilled. Thus, as history affirms Plato's calling attention, as in his *Timaeus,* to the verifiable fact of many cases of destruction, or self-destruction of cultures before his time, there has arisen, repeatedly, from within mankind, the force of that indomitable spirit of cognition, to give a new birth to the hope of achieving a durable civilization.

In fact, as Plato emphasizes, entire cultures have been swept away, either by natural catastrophes beyond mankind's control at that time, or by a tragic error embedded within the self-doomed culture itself. The case of the super-Krakatoa-like explosion which demolished ancient Thera, is but one example of natural catastrophes. The self-destruction of the Mesopotamian and Roman empires, typifies cultures which collapsed because they lacked the moral fitness to survive. Yet, after such catastrophes, the impulse to give society a new birth, has expressed itself somewhere, sooner or later, sometimes with manifest, if but partial success. To give the best examples of successful renewals of a failed culture, a scientific name, call these, exhibitions of the universal principle of the renaissance.

The Fifteenth-Century, Italy-centered Renaissance, which created a revolutionary new form of society, the modern sovereign nation-state premised upon the principle of the general welfare, is the most important example of the universality of the indomitable human spirit in action.

In history, there is usually an essential conflict between the influences welling up from the human spirit, and the contrary characteristic impulses of the culture which that population inhabits. The cognitive principle is a natural human impulse, naturally specific to the individual member of our species. It is the principle of goodness, the quality which defines all newborn persons as intrinsically, redeemably good by nature. However, in every form of society known, even within the U.S. today, for example, the prevalent tendency of the culture is that expressed by the degradation of a very large part of the population to the condition, and sense of personal identity, which is fairly described as characteristic of human cattle. There sits the principle of evil.

The innate goodness of the individual person, his or her cognitive potential, is, generally speaking, always there, and will express itself if the cognitive impulse is not suppressed, or corrupted in other ways. From case to case, such spontaneous expression is more or less difficult. Some oligarchical cultures are less unfavorable to cognitive expression than others. Those poets and scientists who express the Classical approach to composition, rather than the opposing Romantic approach, or something like it, are a measure of the degree to which the spirit of freedom, otherwise called cognition, has found moments of escape from the oppression which otherwise prevails in that culture, that society.

The case of the development of Classical Greek culture, Plato and his Academy most notably, typifies the relatively happier developments to such effect.

Sometimes, all the noted evidence suggests, that some admirable piece of creative expression, such as the Negro Spiritual composed amid the conditions of slavery, springs into being without any connection to the work of some earlier period of Renaissance. However, we know that no creative thinker works without a strong impulse to reach into the more or less distant past, or some distant place, in search of predecessors or contemporaries with whom he might identify in a way akin to our John's and Robert's study of the discovery by Archimedes. So, ancient, medieval, and modern European civilization maintained connections of that sort to Classical Greece's legacy.

So seek in all distant and past places, likely spoor of the good, but also attempt to situate the place of the occurrence of that good in its appropriate, actual place in the historical process as a whole. This brings us to focus upon the unique global historical significance of the successive impact of the cultural revolution which occurred in Classical Greece, and, its successor in that Fifteenth-Century European Renaissance which gave birth to a revolutionary new kind of institution, the modern sovereign nation-state premised upon that principle of natural law called the general welfare.

In Plato's Socratic dialogues, and in the Christian view, the combat against that evil of oligarchism, is the imposition of what is properly called *natural law* upon government, to serve what is called by such names as "the common good," or "the general welfare." That Socratic principle, called *agapē,* was adopted from the Classical Greek of Plato by Christianity, as typified by the Apostle Paul's I Corinthians 13. Although that term, translated into Latin as *caritas,* and thence into English as "charity," is often degraded into the giving of kindnesses, such as forbearance, by the ruling oligarchs to the human cattle of society, such as British ladies teaching the Irish poor to hang lace curtains in their windows, Paul's contrary meaning of the term is clear, as is Plato's.

However, despite the principle of Christ and His Apostles, it was not until the Fifteenth-Century Renaissance, that a putatively Christian Western Europe acted to create a new form of state, the sovereign nation-state, under that rule of natural law known as the general welfare. Even then, the oligarchical faction in Europe, typified by the far-flung imperial maritime power of Venice and its instrument, the Habsburg oligarchy, drowned Europe in orchestrated religious warfare, during much of the 1511-1648 interval, in the effort to eradicate the pioneering forms of nation-state first introduced as that of France's Louis XI and England's Henry VII. Since the close of the Seventeenth Century, within globally extended modern European civilization, the newly established British monarchy and the legacy of the Habsburg faction, has continued its efforts to eradicate the principle of the general welfare, and to turn the world back, forever, to modern echoes of ancient and medieval oligarchical imperial models of world government, as over the course of the Twentieth Century, and still today.

In the U.S., past and present, the anglophile alliance of Manhattan-centered predatory finance-capital and the tradition of the Southern slaveholder interest, usually acting so in concert with the British monarchy, has maintained the oligarchical tradition to the degree it has been able to do so, both inside the U.S.A. and in our nation's foreign policy of practice. This continuing struggle between good and evil, the republican commitment to the general welfare, and the anglophile commitment to the evil of oligarchical interest, has been a dominant feature of educational policies and practice within the U.S.A. itself.

That is what must be changed. Reforms of the usual this or that will accomplish virtually nothing good in the end. The evil can not be tamed with meliorative reforms; it must be uprooted. To uproot it, we must impose an appropriate form of what is for today, a revolutionary change of governing principle in national educational policy of practice. To accomplish that, we must know what we are doing. That means that we must locate the unique significance of the modern sovereign form of anti-oligarchical nation-state, as summoned by the 1776 U.S. Declaration of Independence, in history as a whole.

To understand that, we must know how good conspiracies work.

The Christening of the Idea

Nothing constructive in shaping history could be brought into being without a good conspiracy.

Among literate people, "conspiracy" means what a strict etymological-historical reading of the term suggests. People who agree to act in concert according to certain common axiomatic kinds of assumptions, are conspiring in the most literal meaning of the term. The U.S. Declaration of Independence and Preamble of the Federal Constitution define active conspiracies. However, be cautioned, that to agree to do an act, would be a crude and inelegant literary pretense, which would not in and of itself, meet the standard for literate use of the term "conspiracy." The term should be used to signify the case in which people agree to cooperate, chiefly in actions yet to be determined by them, but in service of the realization of some set of axiomatic-like principles, such as those, once again, reflected in the 1776 U.S. Declaration of Independence and the 1789 Preamble of our most fundamental constitutional authority on law, the U.S. Federal Constitution, with its included "general welfare clause."

So defined, conspiracy as such is neither good nor bad, and may be either good or bad. There is nothing bad in conspiracy as such. Judges and prosecutors often conspire against defendants, for example, and sometimes, in cases well known to me from my studies, the defendant's attorney shares in that conspiracy. That is bad; but, conspiracy is also an indispensable way of bringing about all public good.

The most relevant historical example of a good conspiracy, is the manifest transformation in the image of man, which is traceable from the beginning of the Homeric epics, through the full-blown emergence of Classical Greek culture in the work of Plato and his Academy. The most significant changes are of an axiomatic quality, changes in the set of axioms expressed as ideas about man in the universe.

The most interesting phase of that process of change, begins some centuries before the judicial murder of Socrates by the Democratic Party of Athens, in the sponsorship of the Ionian Greeks and the Etruscans, as allies of Egypt's combat against the so-called Phoenicians. The long alliance of the Babylonian and Persian Empires with Tyre, against Egypt, the repeatedly unsuccessful efforts of the Persian Empire and Tyre to crush Greek civilization, and the destruction of both Tyre and the Persian Empire by forces led by Alexander the Great and his advisors from the Platonic Academy, are the pivot of a great conspiracy, on which the definition of the emergence of European civilization, as European civilization, depends.

Think of the emergence of European civilization as a prime example of a true conspiracy. This conspiracy does *not* take the form of the planned attempt to impose some "blueprint" upon reality, but like the *Odyssey* of Ulysses, expresses *an impulse for a certain direction of successive changes in axiomatic assumptions of practice respecting man, his conception of the reigning gods, and his relationship to nature.*

For the world as a whole today, the most interesting mythic figure of the ancient Greek epic as a whole, is the ironical role of a putatively Egyptian goddess imposed upon the Olympic pantheon as the figure of reason, Athena. The direction of those successive changes, approximately culminating in the establishment and work of Plato's Academy, is the emergence of the Classical humanist conception of man.

The impelling force of this process of change, was the insurgency of what I have identified as the indomitable, cognitive human spirit.

This was not a mere epiphenomenon of those we know retrospectively as the ancient Greek population. It was a conspiracy within that population, a conspiracy which was able to impose its mark on the ancient Greek heritage for later times with such force, that many people forget that those who introduced those changes were, like the circles of Benjamin Franklin, revolutionaries within their own times and among their own people. These changes were, like all truly good changes, revolutions of the type associated with the validated discovery of a universal physical principle by the initiative of an individual and the support for that by a relatively small group associated with the work of that individual. This is as appropriately a model of the best creative artists as of physical scientific discovery.

Great good conspiracies are of the type to be recognized in the relationship of Leibniz follower Abraham Kästner to his student and collaborator Gotthold Lessing, and the close collaboration of Lessing and Moses Mendelssohn, as defenders of the work of both Leibniz and J.S. Bach, against the circles of Voltaire and Leonhard Euler of the Berlin Academy. The same is true of the continuation of the German Classic, as organized in that form by the initiatives of Kästner, Lessing, and Mendelssohn, which gave the world the German Classic of Goethe, Schiller, the Humboldts, Scharnhorst, Mozart, Beethoven, Schubert, Heine, et al. These changes occurred within societies which were, otherwise, predominantly expressions of the anti-Classical Romanticism of Immanuel Kant, G.W.F. Hegel, Novalis, et al., just as the evil, oligarchical Delphi cult of the Pythian Apollo, typified not only Lycurgan Sparta, but many among the contemporaries of Greece's greatest and noblest Classical figures.

The central feature of the centuries-long process leading into the establishment of Plato's Academy at Athens, was a struggle against, and within the grip of the existing pagan religious beliefs of that time and place. Two overlapping expressions of evil, are of the greatest relative importance: the cult of Olympus and the Delphi cult of the Pythian Apollo. It is important to capture a sense of the revolutionary character of the figures of both Ulysses and Athena, relative to the setting of the Olympian myths.

Like the mind of the majority of the U.S. electorate today, the minds of most of the populations of known societies have been controlled by the use of fraudulent kinds of religious superstitions. These have been superstitions of a frankly religious character, such as the Olympus cult and Apollo cult, or in ostensibly secular disguises for religious belief, such as British empiricism, existentialism, astrology, the escapist mystique of mass popular entertainment, and "the market." All taken together, they constitute a body of *ideology*. By ideology, I signify a system of belief which is adopted by learning or kindred, axiomatically irrational methods, such as the belief that humanity's fate is controlled by the whims of supposed gods of Olympus.

In conventional U.S. practice, ideology is expressed typically by a certain way of using the pronoun "they," as to signify some eerie "establishment," of which it is said, "they will always decide." Granted, as long as 80% or more of the U.S. population continues to behave in that superstitious way, as it has in recent general elections, for example, as virtual human cattle herded into the allotted pens, a relatively small number of people, operating through their lackeys, will rule the U.S. pretty much as the most pathetic true believers among the ancient Greeks believed in the absolute power of the ever-whimsical gods of Olympus. It is useful to see the U.S. population today, as exhibiting the most pathetic features of the subjects of the *Iliad*.

It is useful to compare the *Iliad* and *Odyssey* on this account, and to trace the changes in man's conception of himself as expressed by Solon's reforms at Athens, by the Classical tragedians, and by Plato's figure of Socrates. Such false gods rule only as long as the people allow this state of affairs to prevail, as long as the people fasten the shackles of humility toward such would-be, or even purely imaginary gods, such as "The Invisible Hand," upon themselves.

What emerges in this progression from the Homeric epics to Plato, is the shift to the concept of what becomes, in Plato, the *idea*, as the adducible principle of Classical Greek sculpture's difference from the Archaic, presents the image of the idea as reflected in the language of stone, the idea of *becoming-in-motion*. The figure of Ulysses already introduces a willful evocation of an idea in the hearers of the song of the *Odyssey*.

The poem of Solon presents the idea of the idea with great force. The Classical tragedians Aeschylus and Sophocles, are most notable. Plato and his figure of Socrates, represent the pinnacle of this Classical Greek achievement. The notion of *agapē*, as elaborated in the *Republic,* for example, goes to the heart of the matter.

Throughout the span from Homeric epics to Plato, there is an unfolding process at work, a process which returns always to the issues of justice and truthfulness, these as the alternative to credulous submission to belief in "they," the alternative to submission to "popular opinion," to submission to a reigning ideology. In the end, the work of the Socratic dialogue, in defining the Platonic form of ideas as the standard of justice and truthfulness, becomes, ever since, the quality which sets the emergence of European civilization apart as the birth of a distinct culture, and which provides the foundations for what became the characteristic distinctions of the Fifteenth-Century Renaissance.

The destruction of the Persian Empire by the hand of Alexander the Great, established the leading position of the Platonic legacy within the Hellenistic culture of the eastern Mediterranean and its associated regions, which continued until the Romans had defeated the Greek states in Italy, and moved on to conquer, and largely enslave Greece itself.

Pagan Rome, which expressed both the legacy of the syncretizing cult of the Pythian Apollo and of ancient Babylon's oligarchical model, became the long nightmare of European civilization, from which Europe could escape only through an affirmation of the Classical Greek alternative to Romanticism. This affirmation occurred through the embedding of the Classical Greek legacy of Plato within Christianity, to an effect typified by the Fifteenth-Century Renaissance.

So, in the form of a continuing conflict, over thousands of years, between the Classical Greek and Romantic legacies, the continuity of European civilization has been established as of a distinct type, up to the present day. It is impossible to achieve any effective comprehension of the internal history of today's now globally extended European civilization, except from that standpoint. The Classical Greek legacy was thus christened to become the most powerful form of culture known to date, not merely by some standard of raw power, but on account of the power expressed by the use of the method of the Platonic idea.

The corollary is, that the world was fated to bear the burden, and the advantages, spilling over from the continuing, millennia-long, great conflict between the Classical and the Romantic within European civilization. Such has been the christening and the aftermath of the *idea*.

The Birth of the Sovereign Nation-State

Now, to sum up with the following crucial, concluding point.

To understand the now globally extended history of European civilization over the past two millennia, it is sufficient to begin by recognizing, that the terrible conflict within European civilization could be overcome, only by eliminating the oligarchical model. That means, today, uprooting the Venetian model of an imperial financier-oligarchical form, in which the reign of a policy sometimes called "shareholder value" degrades virtually all of mankind to the condition of herding, consuming, and culling, the great mass of the population as human cattle, as has become the increasing practice inside the U.S.A. since the Richard Nixon "Southern Strategy" campaign of 1966-68.

For this end, of freeing humanity from an oligarchy's degradation of the mass of the population to the status of the virtual human cattle which the great majority of the U.S. population suffers today, it has been necessary to impose a specific principle of universal law which, by implication, outlaws oligarchical practices. That law has two features. First, that the authority to rule over a nation must be given only to sovereign governments of nation-states. Second, that no government has the moral authority to exist, except as it efficiently promotes the general welfare of all of the people and their posterity: the common good. In all matters, that principle of the general welfare must be accorded the authority of the highest law applicable to the case at hand.

This was the great change sought in the battles fought by the Emperor Frederick II against Venice and Venice's Plantagenet allies. This was the great end sought by Dante Alighieri's proposed reforms. This is the great fruit of the Fifteenth-Century Renaissance. This is the principle under which Louis XI's reform of France occurred, and Henry VII's uprooting of the evil represented by the Plantagenet legacy of Richard III. This is the source of the unique quality of the intention applied by Benjamin Franklin and his collaborators to the creation of the U.S.A. This reform is modern European civilization. This is the unfinished business, which we must bring to a conclusion.

In this unfinished business inside the U.S.A. itself, policies governing the general practice of education, form a leading, crucial part. For historic and related reasons, the policies of education and related perspectives for employment of our so-called African-American families are a kind of acid test. Often embittering, and bloody experience of our nation shows, that if we are either unwilling, or incapable, to bring about a reversal of the legacies of chattel slavery and so-called "Jim Crow," as it applies to education, the nation and most of its people will continue to walk, as they have done lately, like serfs or slaves, bearing their shrunken heads on their shoulders.

The power of a nation's real economy lies entirely in the combination of the development of the cognitive maturity of its people, and in the provision of those forms of organization and conditions of life and work, which are the circumstances required for production and for general life by any level of advancement of the scientific and technological capabilities of the minds of the individual members of the labor-force and their families. The higher the level of development, and latitude for expression of the cognitive powers of the individual, the greater the average power of the economy as a whole, the greater the rate of progress of the human condition.

Do not fit the development of the people to the perceived requirements of forms of employment deemed available. Rather, transform the policies of investment in employment, to set priorities on the utilization of the greatest feasible development of the labor-force and its family households.

Indeed, it was never the lack of opportunity to upgrade employment opportunities, which prompted racists to condemn African-Americans into tracking (of most among them) for menial employment and worse education. They were racists, because they were oligarchs, who understand that if a people is not stupefied in relevant ways, it will not endure rule by oligarchs. Therefore, the oligarchs prefer to keep people dumb and deluded, and also culled as much as is deemed convenient, even if that means a much poorer performance for the economy, because it is more important to them to be oligarchs, than to allow that far more successful form of economy, in which free, thinking men and women, will not tolerate being human cattle for oligarchs.

The object of sane economic policy, is to develop the cognitive powers of all the citizens to the highest possible level they are willing to achieve, and to compose the conditions of production and distribution to keep pace with the progress achieved through such policies of reliance on Classical humanist education for each and all.

We must give priority on this approach to education and employment prospects, and to developing the means to conduct such a policy of practice. Only when all means "all," in these terms, will the legacy of racism dwindle away. Only when we do this for ourselves, and reflect this in relations with other nations, will our nation's prolonged gut-pain of racism pass away.

Benjamin Franklin: part of—an originator of—that American intellectual tradition which, throughout its history, has been inseparable from an ecumenical foreign policy, one based on the notion of a community of principle amongst nations.

"I write here as a spokesman for what is sometimes called 'the American intellectual tradition,' that European Classical tradition expressed in the writing of our 1776 Declaration of Independence and the Preamble of our Federal Constitution. . . . The leading founders of the United States, and their forerunners, such as Benjamin Franklin and Cotton Mather, would have agree with my emphasis upon philosophy."

A Philosophy for Victory: Can We Change the Universe?[1]

February 11, 2001

This piece first appeared in the March 2, 2001 issue of Executive Intelligence Review *magazine.*

Foreword

At a Washington, D.C. meeting in mid-February 1983, I warned the Soviet government, and also relevant high levels of our own, that unless President Reagan were to offer what the President later did announce as a Strategic Defense Initiative (SDI), and unless the Soviet government were to accept such an offer, the Soviet economic system was doomed to collapse in about five years. I repeated that forecast many times, publicly, during the course of the 1980s. The President made that offer,[2] and the Soviet government rejected it peremptorily. The consequent collapse of the Soviet economic system took about six years, not five.

In a Berlin press conference of October 12, 1988, which was nationally-televised in the U.S. shortly after that, I forecast the imminence of a chain-reaction collapse of the Soviet economic system, an already onrushing collapse, which would lead

---

1. The author is a registered candidate for the 2004 U.S. Presidential nomination.

2. National TV network broadcast, March 23, 1983.

toward the probable reunification of Germany in the short-term period immediately ahead.[3] I proposed a policy for dealing with that crisis.

My policy of October 1988 was later elaborated as the "European Productive Triangle" program of 1990,[4] and expanded and promulgated as the "Eurasian Land-Bridge" program crafted by my associates during 1992-1993.[5]

Unfortunately, by the combined decision of Britain's Prime Minister Margaret Thatcher, France's President François Mitterrand, and President George Bush, a policy was adopted, which was directly opposite to what I had proposed at Berlin in October 1988. As a result of the 1989-2001 continuation of those policies, aimed at ruining the economies of both Germany and the former Comecon states, which were jointly launched by Thatcher, Mitterrand, and Bush during 1989-90, not only has the former Soviet power collapsed, but the world's economy as a whole is presently at the brink of the most disastrous economic collapse in modern history.[6]

In my warnings, during the 1982-1983 period leading up to President Ronald Reagan's March 23, 1983 announcement, I had emphasized that the military side of my proposal for strategic ballistic-missile defense, was only the surface of the strategic policy I was proposing. Both the U.S. and Soviet economies were then already far advanced in their decay, down from the levels of long-term physical vitality both had commanded until about

3. This forecast proved entirely correct.

4. Jonathan Tennenbaum et al., *Das 'Produktive Dreieck' Paris-Berlin-Wien: Ein europäisches Wirtschaftswunder als Motor für die Weltwirtschaft* (Wiesbaden: EIR Nachrichtenagentur GmbH, August 1990); "The Economic Geography of Europe's 'Productive Triangle,'" *EIR*, August 3, 1990.

5. Organizing around this report began about 1990. A full report was issued June 9, 1991, as an *EIR* Special Report, "Can Europe Stop the World Depression?"

6. LaRouche's "Ninth Forecast" was published in *EIR*, June 24, 1994, under the title "The Coming Disintegration of Financial Markets." For the policy implications of the confirmation of that forecast by subsequent events, see also Lyndon H. LaRouche, Jr., "Trade Without Currency," *EIR*, August 4, 2000.

the mid-1960s.[7] Without a "crash" kind of science-driver program, akin to the economically successful Kennedy space-program, both the U.S. and Soviet economy were self-doomed to that collapse inhering in their respective, current policies of economic practice. The most notable difference in their situation, was that the risk of a Soviet collapse, was relatively more immediate at that time, than the prospect for an ensuing U.S. economic collapse. The only feasible medium- to long-term alternatives for such collapses, was a "crash program" type of science-driver upturn, which would be intended, and gauged to reverse the damage already done to the world's physical economy by the policy-changes of the 1966-1983 interval.

Thus, I had argued, since even two years earlier than my strategic-defense proposal of Summer 1979, that the need of both super-powers for economic recovery vastly outweighed the adversarial issues between them. Yes, we should free the world from the grip of strategic-missile blackmail, but we should use the need for such a defense as the pivot for a global "crash economic-recovery" effort, from which both sides would benefit.

The essential difference between the 1989-1991 collapse of the Soviet system, and the presently onrushing collapse of the world economy of the Anglo-American powers, was chiefly in their timing. Both have been on the road to collapse since about the time of President Richard Nixon's 1966-68 election-campaign.

Looking back to my Washington, D.C. discussions of February 1983, the correct view of the world situation today, is expressed by saying that "Two economic systems have collapsed. Russia is now struggling to rebuild itself out of the wreckage left by the collapsed and carpetbagger-looted Soviet system; the Anglo-American system is now at its fag-end." Still, after all that, the ruling monetary powers of today's world are, chiefly, engaged in desperately defending a post-1971 world monetary system which was always foredoomed to fail, and has now reached the advanced stage of the crisis, under President George

---

7. A useful date of reference, would be British Prime Minister Harold Wilson's pound sterling collapse of Fall 1967, and the ensuing March crisis of the U.S. dollar.

W. Bush, that that world system could not be saved in its present form, even for a relatively short-term period.

So, today, we are assembled here, under the auspices of the written word, to consider, *not* whether the continued existence of the United States is still possible; the question is, whether it is possible that the United States might choose the available road to survival. Classical philosophy, properly defined, is the only branch of science in which possible solutions to such a crisis in decision-making can be rationally discussed.

The leading founders of the United States, and their forerunners, such as Benjamin Franklin and Cotton Mather, would have agreed with my emphasis upon philosophy. Sometimes, to survive, one must know how to swim. The problem today, is the relatively vast numbers from recent crops of university-trained professionals, in or outside high positions in government, who, like the "Ozymandias" from Shelley's poem, neither know how to swim in the waters of Classical philosophy, nor would be willing to learn, even if the survival of their nation depended upon it.

As in many other matters, today's universities, and their textbooks, have degraded what is taught under the rubric of "philosophy," into the categories of teachings which are, usually, disgustingly trivial when they are not actually evil. Thus, as Shakespeare's Doll Tearsheet spoke of Ancient Pistol's title of "Captain," so she might have spoken of the name of philosophy today: "God's light, these villains will make the word as odious as the word occupy; which was an excellent good word until it was ill-sorted."[8] It were often necessary, as today, in dealing with serious matters at hand, to substitute another term for the misused name of philosophy: *epistemology,* the matter of the often hidden axioms of assumption which underlie the entirety of specific systems of thought. In the alternative, we might do as I do here, to use other ways to make the relevant distinctions sufficiently clear, that we have no need to seek a substitute for the name of philosophy.

---

8. i.e., "fell into bad company." William Shakespeare, *King Henry IV: Second Part,* Act II, Scene IV.

So, if we are to understand the real universe in which cultures, even great empires, destroy themselves, we must begin, as I do here, by making a sharp, uncompromising distinction between my own choice, of historically rooted, Classical use of those terms, and that contrary, trivial or worse, use which is commonplace among the intellectual "bottom feeders," the existentialists, pragmatists, empiricists, and logical positivists, of today's academic life.

Despite all else, the term "philosophy" ought to be recognized as signifying the most important conception to be mastered, in attempting to deal with the menacing reality of current world history, even in the short term. The possibility of a continued existence of civilization, even in the relatively near term, depends absolutely upon leaders who govern themselves with obligatory attention to the practical significance of thinking philosophically, as I define philosophy here.

Thus, the following pages address a subject-matter which must be resolved as a philosophical problem of great urgency, a subject which must be addressed, as I do here, for the sake of the possible survival of the recently existing global civilization. For purpose of this review, I emphasize the form which the crisis assumes for the specific type of *globally extended modern European civilization,* focussing chiefly upon the immediate, short-term interval of the escalating global crisis currently in progress.[9]

The most important, and most fundamental of the issues

---

9. The distinguishing characteristic of European civilization, is the combination of the Classical Greek cultural legacy, especially that of Plato, and Christianity. This is extended through the spread of Islam, which shares with Christianity, and the Mosaic tradition of Philo of Alexandria and of Moses Mendelssohn, the conception of man and woman as made equally in the image of the Creator of the universe, and as specifically empowered to rule over all things within that universe. Other cultures, especially among those in Asia, do not necessarily proceed from that image of the nature of man specific to the European expression of the Judeo-Christian-Islamic current deeply embedded in globally extended modern European civilization. However, since European civilization is the world's most powerful culture, as measurable in per-capita terms, the fate of the world as a whole

posed to us by this onrushing catastrophe, is: *As a matter of principle, to what degree, in what manner, and by what means, can man gain foreknowledge of the method by which to willfully change the current direction of his society's destiny, for the better, in specific ways? Even to overcome, thus, the worst sort of impending, seemingly inevitable catastrophe, such as the presently onrushing one?*

Threatened by the present, overwhelming likelihood of a collapse of civilization, into a planetary new dark age of humanity, how might *we* change what I shall define here as the presently characteristic behavior of mankind, to bring this civilization to safety, even within the relatively short term?

I write here as a spokesman for what is sometimes called "the American intellectual tradition," that European Classical tradition expressed in the writing of our 1776 Declaration of Independence and the Preamble of our Federal Constitution. Those institutions I defend, and see any proposal to consider superseding them, as far worse than useless, at present, or during the foreseeable future. The cause for our nation's current self-afflictions lies in influences which have been contrary to that American intellectual tradition.[10]

The root of our current crisis, lies in the way in which policies contrary to that American intellectual tradition, have been brought to hegemonic positions, where they have lately ruled and ruined our national policy-shaping institutions. It is those superimpositions, alien to that tradition, which are ruining

---

is set in the context of the crisis within globally extended modern European civilization.

10. A notable example is former Secretary of State Henry A. Kissinger, who described himself explicitly as a proud foe of that "American intellectual tradition," in a London Chatham House keynote address of May 10, 1982, "Reflections on a Partnership: British and American Attitudes to Postwar Foreign Policy, Address in Commemoration of the Bicentenary of the Office of Foreign Secretary," as he had represented himself similarly in his *A World Restored: Metternich, Castlereagh and the Problems of Peace 1812-1822* (Boston: Houghton Mifflin, 1957). He stressed that this had been his position while Secretary of State and National Security Adviser to Presidents Richard Nixon and Gerald Ford.

us. Therefore, no action possible within a framework limited to the currently hegemonic, errant policy-making assumptions of our government and most other influential institutions, could have any net effect but to ensure, even worsen, the presently onrushing catastrophe.

I denounce not only the present policies of our government, or political parties, for example. Under lately corrupting, even implicitly treasonous trends, especially those of the recent thirty-five-odd years' rise of Nixon's "Southern Strategy," our nation's policy-shaping errors have become *systemic*. Our nation's presently threatened doom, is neither accidental nor cyclical; it is systemic, as merely typified by increasingly demented qualities of public utterances by the presently panic-stricken Federal Reserve Chairman Alan Greenspan.[11]

By *systemic crisis,* I mean that we must uproot and replace many among the implied set of axioms which currently govern the selection of the kinds of changes in policy which those institutions, and prevailing public opinion, would be presently willing to tolerate. The possibility of surviving this crisis, depends upon selecting the right answers to the question: *Which adopted or implied axioms of present policy-shaping behavior of our government, and citizenry, must we replace, and replace with what, to bring about the needed, early change in direction toward survival and recovery of both the U.S.A. and civilization generally?*

1. The Issue of Historical Method

Given the fact, that man is a creature distinguished from the beasts by his free will, nothing is "in the cards." In a truly sane society, there is no place of influence over policy-making, given to crystal-ball gazers, contemporary astrologers, "Biblical prophecy" windbags, or the like. So, the doctrine of "historical

---

11. The most appropriate documentation of Greenspan's tendency to disintegrate before TV cameras, appeared after the foregoing lines were written, in his appearance before the Congress on Tuesday, Feb. 13, 2001. In the popular vernacular of today, "This man has really lost it!"

objectivity" preached by socialists such as the early Twentieth Century's Kautsky and Plekhanov, for example, in claiming a certain kind of fatal, so-called "objective," so-called "anti-voluntarist" ordering of history, never produced anything but ultimately catastrophic results for their followers, during that time. A similar outcome awaited such later followers of the same, virtually mechanistic doctrine of "historical objectivity," as Soviet leaders Brezhnev, Andropov, and Gorbachov.

Once we acknowledge, that man is distinguished, *systemically,* from both the non-living and the beasts, by free will, there are, nonetheless, bounds which define what nature will, or will not tolerate from man's free will. Free will is not the right of individuals, or even majorities of entire societies, to make arbitrary choices. As I shall present the case in the following pages, free will is a higher principle of law, otherwise called *reason,* or *natural law.*

There are special, higher qualities of universal lawfulness, operating at a higher level than the non-living aspects of our universe, or even higher than living processes other than the human species. These higher qualities of universal lawfulness, govern the way in which man is variously allowed, or punished for attempting to change the universe in which our species exists. It is that higher lawfulness, which we must adduce, if we are to become capable of foreseeing the most important of the consequences which our decisions, or lack of changes in habits, might bring about. Therefore, my use of "free will" is a qualified one; in my hands, it means that form of "free will" which coheres with that higher lawfulness which I have defined repeatedly, in published locations, as *a universal principle of physical-economic anti-entropy.*

Such were the issues of the Classical controversy between the heroic Prometheus, and tragic figure of the doomed, satanic oligarch Zeus and his gods of Olympus, in Aeschylus' *Prometheus Bound.* That is the underlying nature of the crisis, which threatens to bring about the early doom of our United States under President George W. Bush, today. That latter, is the determining, underlying issue referenced by the subject of this report.

How shall we, then, select only those aspects of implicitly

revolutionary, *"free will"* changes in the axioms governing policy-making, which represent a positive factor in the shaping
of history?

Thus, the direction being taken by a society, is often flanked
by the swamps defined by such lunatic extremes as either arbitrary, existentialist kinds of choices, or capitulation to fatalism.
There are discoverable pathways, leading upward from such
perilous terrain, as that into which careless opinion has presently
misled most nations. The point is, to know how to instruct
free will in selecting society's appropriate, *axiomatic* choices of
historic pathway.

This view and practice of the making of history, is what I
have defined as a scientific basis for the application of the *voluntarist* method. It is the use of that method, so refined, which
must be mastered, and applied, if civilization is to escape the
horror which presently besieges us. In this report, I situate that
voluntarist method, from the vantage-point of Leibniz's development of his notion of *monadology*.

At a time when all influential policy-shapers who are *not*
philosophical voluntarists, will tend to behave as bunglers, the
following question is posed: *by means of what voluntarist intervention, by the rest among us, can the necessary change in direction be brought into play?*

The Problem of Historical Specificity

Whenever that discussion touches the matter of stated or
implied claims to knowledge of universal principles, we should
focus sharply upon a certain special problem, that of *historical
specificity*. For our purposes here, we shall define and re-examine
this question of historical specificity from the vantage-point of
Gottfried Leibniz's notion of monadology.[12] That topic of
method, so situated, is the following.

---

12. See *Gottfried Wilhelm Leibniz: Philosophical Papers and Letters*,
Leroy E. Loemker, ed. (Dordrecht [Netherlands]: Kluwer Academic Publish-
ers, 1989), pp. 592-721. References are implicitly to Leibniz's *Theodicy*
and posthumously published *New Essays*, the latter refuting John Locke
in terms which played a decisive role in shaping the concepts and language

For reasons which I have defined extensively within earlier writings, any discussion of this topic, must situate itself by efficiently implied reference to the accumulation of knowledge possessed by mankind, and, more narrowly, by any specific culture, up to the time of a current discussion. In other words, the investigation of matters pertaining to the question of method set forth at the outset of this report, must adopt its empirical basis from the history of the efficient effects of the previous development of *ideas, as Plato defined the term ideas,* and *as Leibniz defined the Platonic idea of a monadology.*

Such is the setting, in which a specific culture, at a specific time, is faced with a specific challenge to its continued existence. That challenge must be seen as that culture is situated not merely within the context of the world's geography, but also the legacy of that society's cultural development, accumulated from all human history, up to that time. This retrospective view defines the broad meaning of *historical specificity.*

For example, that great artist and historian, William Shakespeare, proceeding from the legacy of England's Sir Thomas More, located the immediate historical specificity of Sixteenth-Century England in a series of historical dramas, culminating in the accession of Henry VII (Richmond) as the great reformer who created a modern England to match the model provided by the kindred, successive achievements of Jeanne d'Arc and Louis XI in France.

Thus, from that portion of Shakespeare's work, we have the unfolding of English history under the impact of imperial Venice's orchestration of the role of the Norman oligarchy throughout Europe and the Mediterranean region more broadly, over three centuries, from the time of King John (during the time-frame of the Second through Fourth Crusades), through the Hundred Years' War and the Wars of the Roses. This is a very specific chunk of English history, as also of France and of Europe and the Mediterranean region as a whole. To understand that history, we must recognize it as having a specifically coherent

---

of the 1776 U.S. Declaration of Independence. See Philip Valenti, "The Anti-Newtonian Roots of the American Revolution," *EIR,* December 1, 1995.

character, a specific character which must be brought to bear, if we are to become capable of understanding the development occurring in that setting over the sweep of centuries, and impacting relevant parts of the world, in historically specific ways, still today.

The characteristic feature of that three centuries of history, is the *relative* inevitability of such catastrophes as the mid-Fourteenth-Century New Dark Age, resulting from the defeats of the opponents of Venice's imperial maritime rule during that entire period. The Hundred Years' War and the Wars of the Roses in England, represent the continuing calamity for Europe as a whole, inhering in that continued Venetian influence.[13] Thus, the coincidence of the role of Jeanne d'Arc with the preparations and outcome of the great ecumenical Council of Florence, the subsequent victory of Louis XI in France, of Henry VII in England, and the launching of the great transatlantic voyages of exploration, such as that of Christopher Columbus, which was organized by Nicholas of Cusa's circles from the great Council of Florence, typify a revolution against the evil inhering in the preceding centuries' use of Norman puppets by Venetian thalassiarchs: the Fifteenth-Century Renaissance, the revolution against the Venice legacy on which all of modern European civilization's achievements have been premised ever since.

The dramas of Friedrich Schiller, as the transmission of the heritage of Shakespeare into the German Classics, was influenced, through the work of Kästner and Lessing, represent today a still higher standard of historian's skill than Shakespeare, although both are typical of the heirs and spokesmen of the Fifteenth-Century Renaissance. Schiller's studies of the Spanish war against the Netherlands, the Thirty Years' War, and of the case of Jeanne d'Arc, show the power of the great poet-historian to bring forth the essence of the true history of a people by the devices of the Classical stage.

This is the same principle expressed in any performance of

13. By "relative inevitability," I signify the consequences inhering in stubborn adherence to a defective set of implied axiomatic beliefs and the practices associated with them.

J.S. Bach's *St. John Passion* and *St. Matthew Passion,* which is conducted as Bach had intended the organic participation among composer, soloists, chorus, and congregation. The intention is that all, composer, soloists, chorus, and congregation, might *participate in reliving that passion within their own cognitive experiences.* Mozart's *Great Mass,* his later *Requiem,* and Beethoven's masses, express the use of art to bring about a truthful cognitive experience of the reliving of history, shared among composer, performers, and audiences. These are not fiction, not entertainments, but the adducing of the cognitive reality of history, as distinct from a reductionist's dumb reading of the shadows on the wall of a dimly firelit cave, or, as seen darkly in a mere sensory mirror of reality.[14] The superior truthfulness of great Classical art, on this account, is that it accomplishes the essential function of enabling the audiences, among others, to relive the cognitive experience of the historical subject to which the art, or an appropriate form of religious service, refers.

As I have elaborated on this point in published locations, the truthfulness of Classical artistic compositions, such as those of Shakespeare and Schiller, lies in their insight into the uses of the Classical stage, as a domain distinct from the panoramas outside. The idea presented on the Classical stage, must be a truthful representation of the idea underlying the sensory experiences of the panorama, but, the panorama and the stage are different media, differing to that effect, that, to present the idea of certain events on a vast area and lapse of time, *compactly* on the stage, the composer must, as Schiller did with the figure of Posa in *Don Carlos,* create onstage the *idea* which may not correspond exactly, in every detail introduced, to the actual history, but corresponds, with historical truthfulness, to the essence of the historical reality referenced. The truth remains the same in both cases, but the media upon which the truth is staged, differ. There is no excuse, for writing tragedy as fiction, nor for interpreting Classical tragedy as the writing of fiction. Thus, no great tragedian would ever compose a work in response to some arbitrary choice of subject-matter; he would always choose a

---

14. I Corinthians 13.

subject whose treatment was faithful to real history, and would choose only subjects for which he had first discovered a truthful representation of the real-life tragedy, a truth demonstrable, on stage, by the means available to him.

To understand the flaws and accomplishments of all Classical tragedy, from the Homeric epics through Schiller's dramas, real history must be read, and portrayed with the eyes of Plato's dialogues, as an exercise in the search for cognitive discovery of important truth.

Together with Plato's devastating moral criticism of the greatest Classical Greek tragedians before him, Schiller's historical studies, as reflected in his dramas, typify what should be understood by the term "Classical philosophy." The comparison of Schiller's treatment of Jeanne d'Arc, to Shakespeare's tragedy of Hamlet, shows that higher level in Schiller, as Plato's dialogues supersede the methods of such great artists as Aeschylus and Sophocles.

By the very nature of the subject-matter, much of the actual history of mankind in general, even our own nation, is unknown to us; however, despite that shortfall, we must and can, nonetheless, reach conclusions which have a relatively universal authority, relative to the recent millennia of the emergence and development of today's globally extended European civilization, especially six centuries of modern European civilization, and, also relative to those conclusions which have bearing on effects which might be projected for a period as long as several generations into the future.

Schiller's greatest achievement, beyond what Shakespeare accomplished at his best, lies in Schiller's degree of emphasis upon the principle of the *sublime*.[15] This distinction is shown most efficiently in his treatment of Jeanne d'Arc. Classical tragedy tends, too often, to show how a society destroys itself, often by the deep-going moral defects of those it has chosen to place in positions of great authority, as we might be worried about

---

15. See Friedrich Schiller, "On the Sublime," in *Friedrich Schiller, Poet of Freedom*, Vol. III (Washington, D.C.: Schiller Institute, 1990), p. 255.

the newly inaugurated President George Bush, today. That is useful, and uplifting for the audience which recognizes the possibility of a willful choice of alternative to tragedy. However, it were better to affirm the alternative, which, as in the real-life case of the Jeanne d'Arc treated by Schiller, locates the higher meaning of life and purpose of action, as in Beethoven's Opus 132 string quartet, in the sublime.

What we may claim, or might strongly suspect to have been known, from such an actual history of *ideas*, must be defined in two quite distinct, but connected categories.

In the first, straightforward case, there are some things which we can show from the past, as having been both explicitly known at that time, and able to be known to us today, as either relatively valid, or clearly mistaken beliefs, as each are encountered in such specific, earlier, cultures and times. We can thus adduce corresponding, necessarily underlying assumptions of principle which are implied in the work of an historical predecessor.

Then, in the alternative, we have the muddier waters, in which the actions considered express relevant, underlying, adducible principles, which the relevant representatives may, or may not have explicitly claimed to know, or, cases in which, those who apparently claimed knowledge, left us, today, without indications of desired forms of proof which we might presently replicate.

Heraclitus and Plato, For Example

Typical of the problem of supplying presently relevant distinctions of this type, are matters posed to us by implied attributions of certain essential ontological notions, for example, to pre-Socratic thinkers such as Pythagoras, Thales, Heraclitus and their predecessors. As an illustration of that point, compare what we know of an apparent convergence between the views of Heraclitus and Plato, respectively, on this account.

For example, in the work of Plato, we encounter a definite, knowledgeable clarification of an argument, defining the essential nature of the quality of existence as *becoming*, as axiomatically, universally opposed to the reductionists' naive reading of fixed objects such as those of sense-perception. A similar argument by Heraclitus, is referenced by Plato himself, but the surviving fragments of Heraclitus's writings tease us, as if to tempt us into making extrapolations which may or may not be valid ones. Plato appears to admire Heraclitus' notion of becoming, but, as we may be limited to the fragments of Heraclitus more or less known to us, we can not be certain, as a matter of knowledge, that Plato's concurrence with Heraclitus on this point is thorough-going, is admissible for extrapolation of it as universal in quality. I mean, in the sense that we must attribute functional universality, to any validated *idea* defined in the strict, cognitive sense of the term *idea*.[16]

Plato's method in treating of existence as *becoming*, as implied in the famous allegory of Plato's Cave, shifts the question of the nature of existence, away from the illusory inferences of ignorant sense-certainty, up and away from what is sometimes termed "vulgar materialism." The primary empirical expression of existence, is located by Plato, where it must be situated, as *a universal ontological principle of change*, rather than those deductive, or kindred relations among the sense-certainty-like objects so greatly esteemed by the reductionists. Although Heraclitus pointed toward a similar alternative to reductionism, with his "nothing is constant but change," it is only from Plato that we first obtain the dialectical form of exposition which enables

---

16. Autobiographically: During 1951, the puzzle posed by the similarities and differences between the import of the known fragments attributed to Heraclitus, and the clarity of Plato's argument on the ontological implications of "becoming," prompted a crucial turn, at that time, in my own approach to the problems of a science of physical economy. The qualitative differences among the Homeric outlook, the pre-Socratic thinkers, that of the Classical tragedians, and Plato's dialogues, must be appreciated if any useful knowledge for modern use is to be adduced from the study of the work of any among them. If a reader were curious as to where I developed the passion for historical specificity which I stress here, the answer is implicitly provided him in the present location.

us actually *to know that principle, from a cognitive standpoint,* as a physically efficient, universal one.[17]

For example, some of the most important of the practical ideas on which the actual achievements of modern civilization depend, meet the requirements of expressing necessary ideas, but we can not show, with certainty, that the author we reference, in each case, was conscious of that implication of the way in which we may wish to adduce that idea from a modern stand-point in scientific method: as if it were an idea apprehended from a dialectical statement in terms of a *geometry of position.* That latter method, named *"Analysis Situs"* (Geometry of Situa-tion) by Gottfried Leibniz, and known otherwise as "geometry of position,"[18] was later developed by Gauss, Abel, Riemann, et al. into the general form for expressing experimentally-defined ontological paradoxes, that, in mathematical terms, not possible within the framework of a conventionally deductive mode of mathematical argument.[19]

The distinction I am making here, is, admittedly, a fine one, but, nonetheless, like Kepler's discovery of astrophysics, in opposition to the blundering method of Copernicus, or the devastatingly infinitesimal difference between Leibniz's defini-tion of the calculus, and the fraudulent version concocted by Leibniz-hater Leonhard Euler, Lagrange, and Cauchy, it is a crucial difference for science as a whole. Therefore, we must be certain that we understand one another clearly on this matter of seemingly fine points of distinction.

Sometimes, we know, with certainty, that the source refer-

---

17. See discussion of "ideas" known "from a cognitive standpoint," later in the course of these prefatory remarks. This concept of *ideas* is a central feature of all of those of my ideas which I consider important ones. It is pervasive in the writing of these pages. See Plato, *Parmenides.*

18. Loemker, op. cit., pp. 247-248.

19. Bernhard Riemann, *"Über die Hypothesen, welche der Geometrie zu Grunde liegen"* (1854), *Bernhard Riemanns Gesammelte Mathematische Werke,* H. Weber, ed. (New York: Dover Publications reprint edition, 1953), pp. 272-287; *"Theorie der Abel'schen Functionen"* (1857), op. cit., pp. 88-144; and other locations, in the same collected works. It is from the standpoint of the first cited work, the 1854 habilitation dissertation,

enced did *not* make a discovery of the form which wishful thinking might attribute to that source.[20] At other times, as in certain
cases, such as Plato's reference to Heraclitus' notion of an ontological principle of universal change, we can not be certain that
Heraclitus intended fully what Plato intends as the universality
of an ontological principle of change; we simply lack the quality
of evidence adequate to support the conclusion that Heraclitus
intended the kinds of universalist implications which we can,
and must adduce from Plato's conception. The need for caution
in this comparison is underscored by the implications of *the
historical specificity* of the lapse of time between the life of
Heraclitus and the work of Plato. Similarly, in using the term
"Christian Platonism," we must take into account the historical
specificity of the lapse of time between the death of Heraclitus
and the birth of Christ.

This is a fine distinction, but not so fine that it can be
competently overlooked. *It is a distinction which we must make,
whenever the matter at hand involves staking the future of society
upon a correct, historical appreciation of some deep universal
principle,* as I am doing in these pages.

---

that the physical basis for Riemann's work on the implications of Abelian
functions and topics of hypergeometry must be located.

20. For example, Isaac Newton did not discover a principle of universal gravitation; he produced a bungled effort to plagiarize the available,
published edition of Kepler's *New Astronomy,* which Newton and his
associates had available to them in England at that time. Furthermore, as
Newton's three-body paradox illustrates this fact, Kepler's principle of
universal gravitation can not be adduced from what Newton et al. vulgarize
from their reading of Kepler as "Kepler's Three Laws." Similarly, Copernicus did not "discover" the Sun as the center of the Solar system; this was
ancient Greek knowledge, long before the hoaxster Claudius Ptolemy, and
was emphasized by Nicholas of Cusa during the Fifteenth Century. Kepler
showed that Copernicus' method could not have produced such a conclusive, original discovery of principle.

The Use of Analysis Situs

In such cases, where fine distinctions are obligatory, we can be certain of the author's intent, only if the author's work presents the idea in the form of the method of cognition expressed by Plato's Socratic dialogues. In modern terms, that is the method which I reference here by such terms as "Analysis Situs" and "geometry of position." That is the mathematical method of physical science, as opposed to the deductive, "ivory tower" constructs of the "Euclidean" geometries and related constructs of the reductionist mathematicians.

In physical science, as the example of atomic and nuclear physics underlines this fact, knowledge is never defined as empiricists and some others imply, by sense-certainty. Rather, as Plato illustrates the point by his allegory of the Cave, sense-certainty is like the irregular surface of the wall of a dimly lit cave, on which the movements of the shadows reflect real action, but do not show us directly the action itself. Thus, in physical science, we know something only to the degree we are able to demonstrate that existence of the real action, and its efficient characteristics, through experimentally verified cognitive insight. To the extent that we recognize an object solely by means of our senses, we do not actually know that object. We actually *know* only that which we know with the quality of scientific rigor, in the cognitive, anti-empiricist, anti-Kantian, way which the method of Analysis Situs reflects.

That dialectical method of Plato, on which Kepler and Leibniz relied, is reflected in modern scientific practice in the rigorous form identified by the terms "Analysis Situs" and "geometry of position." It is the method demonstrated, pervasively, in Plato's Socratic dialogues. It is the method of Carl Gauss, as Riemann, as in his 1854 habilitation dissertation, brings Gauss's work on this to general form of expression for physics as a whole.

Rather than say, simply, "ideas," let us qualify that, by stating that I mean both the process expressed by the original discovery of an idea, and also the process of the communication of that idea, *as an idea*, from one person to another. The principles of original discovery of an idea, as typified by the original discovery of an experimentally validated universal physical principle, are identical to the means by which such an idea is communicated, as actual knowledge of that idea, from the cognitive processes of one mind, to the cognitive processes of another person.

On this account, when we use the term "idea," as Plato, Kepler, or Leibniz would, we mean, either the quality of idea associated with a universal physical principle, such as Kepler's original discovery of a principle of universal gravitation, as Kepler details this, step by step, in his *The New Astronomy*,[21] or the idea of communication of such an idea to another individual person. Or, we mean the notion of an idea common to both such discoveries of a validated universal physical principle of non-living processes, or of living processes, and also the idea of the communication of ideas of that *specifically cognitive quality, as ideas are defined by Plato,* from one person to another.

In the first of the foregoing classes, we are pointing to ideas concerning the reciprocal relationship of the "normalized" case of the individual representative of humanity to nature. In the second class of cases, we are referring to that lawful, functional aspect of social relations (e.g., communications), in which ideas respecting either man's individual relationship to nature, or ideas of man's communication of ideas, are themselves communicated as ideas. These latter are communicated to other persons, that in the form of specifically cognitive qualities of knowledge. In the second class of cases, we should be judging such communicated ideas as in the form of hypotheses, subject to a principled

---

21. Johannes Kepler, *New Astronomy* (1609), William Donahue, trans. (Cambridge: Cambridge University Press, 1992). The reader is cautioned against the hoax featured in the translator's and Owen Gingerich's fraudulent disregard for Kepler's explicit condemnation of the incompetent method employed by Claudius Ptolemy, Copernicus, and Tycho Brahe, the condemnation of those persons for a falsification of what is, in fact, what Kepler identified as the crucial characteristic of his revolutionary accomplishments in this work taken as a whole. Reading that foreword and the translator's introduction, one might imagine a detective pointing to a freshly killed body lying bloodily on the living-room floor, and the witness's responding, "I don't see any body!"

form of experimental validation. The validation is defined, as to be measured in terms of society's increase of its power to exist, in and over the universe, in physical terms. Typically, this validation is to be measured per capita and per square kilometer of a normalized cross-sectional area of the Earth's surface.

In that modern case, we can say that we know the subject author's intent, because he obliges us, in that way, through that *specific faculty of cognitive insight,* to replicate the discovery of the intent of the experimentally verifiable idea in our own cognitive processes. This principle governs the way in which communication of ideas, as Plato defines *ideas,* occurs among living persons; it is also the way in which ideas are communicated, as *ideas,* from the past to the present, and to the future.

In opposition to that single step of perception, through which we learn to recognize objects in the form of sense-perceptions (e.g., the empiricist's brutish notion of "sense certainty"), the individual act of knowing an *idea* requires three steps. First, there must be the recognition of a true paradox of an ontological form, in judging observed phenomena from the standpoint of what were previously considered universally valid ways of interpreting such apparent types of phenomena.[22] Second, there must be an act of *hypothetical* discovery of some universally efficient principle, a discovery which solves the paradox. Third, there must be an experimental test of the discovery. That must be a test designed, not merely to show that the hypothetical principle works in some cases, but must work as an integral part of knowledge as a whole. In other words, the test must show that

---

22. The same function is performed in Classical poetry, and in literate forms of written and spoken speech, by irony in general, and metaphor in particular. Notable is Galileo-trained Thomas Hobbes' hatred of metaphor. Metaphor, which is the literary expression of the same principle as Analysis Situs, is the use of language in which cognition is expressed. Since Hobbes, in the footsteps of Galileo's master Paolo Sarpi, is committed to denying the cognitive nature of the human individual personality, as distinct from the beasts, he, like his professed admirer and follower Henry A. Kissinger (op. cit.), is obliged, by his hatred of both man and reason, to demand the exclusion of human behavior from the composing of literature.

EIRNS/Susan Bowen

France's Jeanne d'Arc—Joan of Arc. Jeanne's role, coupled with the impact of the great ecumenical Council of Florence; the founding by Louis XI in France, of the first modern nation-state; and comparable developments in England under Henry VII, ensured that a new kind of political institution was created in Europe in the time of the 15th-Century Renaissance. And, as a result, there came the greatest improvement of the conditions of human life ever recorded.

the hypothetical principle is either universal, or not. If not, it is not a principle.[23]

Since the first and third steps are both demonstrated experimentally, a second person who repeats those steps recognizes the successful nature of the thought which engendered the hypothetical discovery in the mind of the original discoverer, as recreated in his own. It is in that way, that the imperceptible is known, because the existence of that idea is efficient in controlling the shadows on the wall of Plato's Cave. This sharing of the act of discovery of an experimentally validated principle, defines an *idea* of the Platonic type. Ideas of principle generated and validated in this way, thus represent communicable, and also efficient ideas for practice, even though the idea itself is not visible to the mere senses.

Thus, the subject of history, properly apprehended, is the history of ideas, as that is to be defined in the terms which I have just summarized. Thus, the only valid idea of history, is the history of ideas.

In Analysis Situs, the evidence of a contradiction is stated within the terms of a pre-existing, referenced set of ideas of principle. Such a set of ideas might be the notion of the physical universe consistent with a so-called Euclidean model, as in the case of the paradox which prompted Fermat to discover a principle of quickest time governing the propagation of light. By stating the case for reflection, as in contrast to the case for refraction, Fermat defined an ontological paradox existing within the so-called Euclidean domain of then widely-taught ideas of the physical universe. The experimental validation of Fermat's discovery, as by Huyghens, and by the anti-Newtonians Leibniz, Bernouilli, and Fresnel later, defined the principle of universal least action as not merely an hypothesis, but a validated idea corresponding to a universal physical principle.

Thus, to summarize what I have just said:

In all cases, the efficient generation and communication of ideas occurs, as I shall show at a later point in this report, solely in the paradoxical form of *Analysis Situs,* or *geometry of*

---

23. This is sometimes known as the principle of "unique experiment."

position, each mutually contradictory pair of elements of which, expresses the typically underlying form of crucial statements of a Socratic dialogue. For the simplest valid classroom presentation of the point, consider again Fermat's contrast of reflection to refraction, as a paradox which defines a universal principle of quickest time, as superseding the mistaken conception of shortest distance. This is a typical example, as a statement, of the way in which a validatable discovery of universal principle is generated, by stating the relevant paradox in the form of geometry of position.

The communication of an idea occurs in the same, three-step way just summarized.

This explicitly Platonic dialectical method, as employed by such as Plato, Nicholas of Cusa,[24] Kepler, Leibniz, and Riemann, is, contrary to the hoaxster G.W.F. Hegel, et al., the only meaningful use of the term "dialectical method." This is the method by which all discoveries of validatable ideas are prompted, and the basis for the design of experiments which test the universality of the hypothetical principles generated within the mind by the prompting statement of an ontological paradox in the form of geometry of position.

These ideas are not images of sense-perception, but experimentally demonstrated discoveries of solutions for paradoxes which inhere in the flawed nature of sense-certainty as such. The discovery of principles, beyond the reach of sense-perception, in the domain of microphysics, typifies the notion of experimentally validatable ideas of universal physical principle, which are prompted by paradoxes which have been presented in the rigorous form of statement required by geometry of position. Max Planck's definition of the quantum of action, typifies this, as does his defense of scientific method against the fanatical followers of the positivist Ernst Mach.

---

24. In the founding of modern experimental physical science, in Cusa's *De Docta Ignorantia,* the point of origin of the work of Luca Pacioli, Leonardo da Vinci, William Gilbert, and Johannes Kepler, and such as Leibniz, Gauss, and Riemann after them. This method was known, as during the Sixteenth Century, as the Socratic method of *docta ignorantia.*

It is the discovery and experimental validation of those ideas, beyond sense-certainty, generated by the prompting action of a paradox stated in the form of geometry of position, which we are able to recognize as *knowledge,* as the strictly defined use of that term, knowledge, is to be distinguished from both merely fantastic illusions, such as symbolism, and naive interpretations of literal sense-perception. It is only such ideas, so defined, which constitute *knowledge,* as distinct from *mere learning.*

How To Use History

Even in the case, in which the replication of a relevant physical experiment, demonstrates, dialectically, the feasibility of the application specified by an author, if we lack access to a specified cognitive exercise, as might have been provided by the referenced source, we are left with a certain degree of uncertainty respecting that source's intent. By observation, we might conclude that the result is a plausible one, on the surface; but, we do not recognize the way in which the author reached that conclusion. In other words, we witness the result, but we do not actually *know* the process, *from that source,* by which the supposed discovery of the result was accomplished.

In other words, the minds of discoverers from the past are able to communicate with our minds, even if that discoverer were long deceased, through the three-step method outlined above. So, we, too, are empowered to communicate to the minds of persons who will be conceived and born long after we are dead. This relationship, defined in terms of ideas, among past, present, and future, is the equivalence of the idea of history to the history of ideas. It is not through learning rooted in sense-certainty, but only through the cognitive communication of *ideas* of a Platonic quality, that we are in efficient relationship to humanity as a whole, to our predecessors, our contemporaries, and our posterity alike.

This carries us a very important step, above and beyond the elementary, three-step process of discovery and communication summarized above. When we act as individual cognitive beings, rather than like beasts, rutting like pigs in the trough of sense-certainty, the powers of cognition which we bring to bear upon anything like an ontological paradox, reflect the full weight of our individual cognitive experience of previous generations, implicitly all humanity which has existed to date. So, the mere existence of the development of language typifies such a cumulative impact of the cognitive experience of the past upon the individual in the present.

This points to the indispensable role of a Classical-humanist mode of universal primary and secondary education for all members of our society. The primary goal and function of education, must be to enable the young, in particular, to relive the important cognitive experiences of past generations, especially the great discoveries and the great crises of earlier cultures and peoples. It is in the seeking of cognitive truth, in such Classical-humanist modes of education of the young in ideas, that education provides a foundation for the moral development of the character of the young person, and, hence, also the adult.

The superior moral character of the individual enjoying the benefits of a Classical-humanist education, in contrast to today's more popular practices, expresses itself not only in the development of persons who are usually more moral, more sane than in other parts of the population, but endowed with superior qualities of intellectual achievement in whatever profession takes them up. Thus, the idea of an historically so-defined generality of cognitive development, points to an induced state of mind described as the expression of a principle of higher hypothesis, expressed, typically, as the individual's power to generate entire families of discoveries.

Thus, in the cases in which our access to the intent of reported ideas is not in the form suited to cognitive communication of past with present generations, we can not be confident that we actually know the idea of that earlier generation merely from the facts transmitted to us. Where such doubt arises, we can neither claim that that author's intent in the matter corresponds to our own cognitive insight into the matter, nor, as in the referenced case of Heraclitus, can we disregard the efficiency of the experimental evidence which might support that author's pertinent, apparent conclusion. We could never understand history, and the making of history, until we have adduced the reliable principles involved in such crucial cases of shadings of difference in interpretation.

We can not ignore the influence of apparent ideas of principle, even in the case we remain uncertain as to whether or not a certain people understood efficiently the idea by which their shaping of their history was influenced. Even provably false ideas, if they command that practical relevance, such as the provably false and poisonous notions of empiricism, can not be ignored, but must be given critical consideration, if not implicit trust, in our accounts.

Thus, in our efforts to account for what we presently know, from our familiarity with some relevant aspects of the earlier existence of mankind, we actually know, chiefly, only certain slices from that relatively tiny span of human existence which we study as that portion coinciding with so-called recorded history. Even from much of that record, our available evidence is fragmentary and otherwise imperfect.

On account of such imperfections in the record available to us, we must pay special attention to the possible implications of what we do not know, and also to those border-areas, in which our knowledge is imperfect, as in such cases from Greek history as Pythagoras, Thales, and Heraclitus. The achievement of the degree of rigor we must apply, to be justified in stating, "I know," depends upon our sensitivity to the possible implications of that which we do not know.

This precaution, as it applies to study of the past, is the indispensable training of the mind in the kind of discipline required for work in areas in which history has yet to come into existence, in the effort to present reasonable forecasts of the future. Without this rigor, we could not trust our estimates of the consequences of the choices of change in axioms we are considering for implementation.

Therefore, it is only through acquiring the habit of studying history as the cognitive history of the production of ideas, that we might develop what is best labelled an epistemological sense about ideas. It is when the term "philosophy" is used to point toward a matured, richly developed "epistemological sense" of history, as the history of ideas, that the competent forecaster emerges.

On that account, there is little that pleases certain epistemologically matured discoverers more, than to discover that turning up the kind of evidence from what had been previously considered to be unknown patches in history, which shows that one was right, or wrong, in his attitude toward the possible significance of topical areas in which he had previously lacked knowledge. In science, we must make great leaps into the realm of the hypothetical; but, those leaps are permitted only to the degree we are epistemologically circumspect respecting opinions in areas from both past and future history, yet unexplored, as I have illustrated this warning in the foregoing remarks on the exemplary case from Heraclitus' fragments. You shall discover below, why I place that repeated emphasis on that illustration.

With the modern followers of Plato, Nicholas of Cusa, Leonardo da Vinci, Kepler, Leibniz, Gauss, and Riemann, most notably, modern science is defined as a realm, in which the matter of the author's conscious intent to claim a universal principle, is made known to us through the author's reliance on experimental modes of demonstration of what are claimed as discovered universal principles. All topics within this specific realm, are immediately situated within the bounds defined by Plato's work; on this account, we can not disregard relevant work which preceded that of Plato, but neither can we be certain that Plato's predecessors saw these matters as we are able to adduce the clear intention of Plato and his indicated modern followers. Plato's explicit reference to Heraclitus is a model case in point.

Before turning to the subject of the monadology itself, conclude this introductory section of the report with the following summary of the most crucial points we have presented thus far. To summarize that experimental method to which we have referred here, we have the following.

Discovery of a valid universal physical principle, begins with a set of facts recognized as as an ontological paradox. Such an *ontological paradox* must be, then, rigorously restated, in a mathematical or quasi-mathematical form, exactly as Fermat showed the paradoxical relationship between reflection and refraction. From this paradox, Fermat adduced a universal principle of quickest action, rather than shortest distance for refraction of light.

Thus, prompted by the combined impact of Kepler's discovery of a principle of universal gravitation, and Fermat's principle, Huyghens, Leibniz et al., proceeded, through a series of relevant, well-crafted experimental designs, to Leibniz's development of the original differential calculus, and to his later formulation of a general principle of universal least action. It was the latter formulation which led him directly, to his most crucial contribution to physical science, his monadology.[25]

So, I went from defending Leibniz's monadology, against Kant, during my adolescence, to my discoveries of the 1948-1952 interval, to Riemann. From there, I went to the "pre-Socratics" and Plato, and on from there, back to Plato and Leonardo da Vinci, and, thence, back to Nicholas of Cusa! So, I, too, like Leibniz, after Fermat and Huyghens, traversed the ironical pathway of the quickest time.

2. Monadology

The philosophically *voluntarist* method by which individuals might willfully bring about axiomatic changes in the direction of future human history, can not be efficiently defined as an undertaking, except from the standpoint implicit in Leibniz's discovery of a *monadology*.

At this point, we must confront a problem, concerning the relationship between mathematics and physical science. Most modern university graduates in mathematics have, so to speak, stumbled and broken their intellectual legs, over this problem. The reason for those failures, is not that the subject of geometry, as we have to consider it here, is so terribly complicated. The problem is the impossibility of understanding what is actually an elementary proposition, which I am about to address here, without asking the reader to give up a certain commonplace prejudice, which spills over from the day-to-day beliefs of igno-

---

25. See note 2.

rant people into the secondary and university classroom, still today. To continue with our presentation, we must, at this point, pause amid the argument I have been developing, to make clear what is actually meant by so-called Riemannian geometry.

Prior to the introduction of the institution of the modern sovereign nation-state, which was first established during the course of Europe's Fifteenth-Century, Italy-centered Renaissance, all known forms of society treated the majority of mankind as human cattle, hunted, or used, herded, and culled, like beasts, that by ruling castes and their armed and other classes of lackeys. This form of society was known as *the oligarchical model* of Babylon. Such was the tradition of ancient Babylon, the Sparta of the Delphi cult of the Pythian Apollo, ancient Rome, and feudalism under the hegemony of the combined forces of the imperial maritime power of Venice and its Norman allies.

This model was directly contrary to Christian belief. It was a violation of the Christian definition of human nature; but it persisted, nonetheless. It was not until the period of the great ecumenical Council of Florence and its aftermath in Louis XI's France and Henry VII's England, that the anti-oligarchical principle of the *general welfare*, or *common good*, was introduced as a condition for the legitimacy of government. The history of globally extended modern European civilization, since that time, has been a continuing conflict between the persistence of the old oligarchical model, as typified by the British monarchy, and the sovereign nation-state, as typified by the British monarchy's leading adversary, the American intellectual tradition. Every major war within European civilization since the Fifteenth Century, including the religious wars of the interval 1511-1648, has been an expression of the efforts of the oligarchical faction to stamp out the existence of the sovereign nation-state and the principles of economy associated with that nation-state model.

This principle of the general welfare, first introduced to government during the Fifteenth-Century Renaissance, is that expressed by the 1776 U.S. Declaration of Independence and the Preamble of the 1789 Federal Constitution. The typification of those principles of economy of a sovereign nation-state, is the anti-"free trade," so-called American System of political-economy, as most widely recognized in connection with the names of Treasury Secretary Alexander Hamilton, Friedrich List, and Henry C. Carey.

The cases of France's Dr. François Quesnay, Lord Shelburne's lackey Adam Smith, and Immanuel Kant, are typical expressions of the kind of ideologies which the oligarchical faction has thrown up, in its attempted ideological counterattacks against the influence of the emergence of the modern sovereign nation-state. That is a problem whose typical effects are to be addressed, as a crucial interpolation, at this point of the report. Although man is naturally endowed with those creative powers of reason, cognition, which set man apart from and above the beasts, and although this principle of cognition is characteristic of Christian belief, as I Corinthians 13 and other sources emphasize, feudal society and its legacies sought to suppress those forms of cultural development which did not abort the development of the cognitive powers of the individual human mind.

That same anti-Christian campaign by European civilization's oligarchical interests, has been often conducted through the use of pseudo-Christian cults. Such was the tradition of the slaveholder class in the relevant Southern U.S. states; such were the dogmas of economic and social policy of the Physiocrats and Shelburne's Adam Smith; such was the central feature of the argument made by Leibniz-hating, pro-irrationalist Imannuel Kant, on behalf of the anti-Classical German Romantic movement of the late Eighteenth and Nineteenth Centuries. Such was the Romantic, irrationalist basis for Nazi doctrine, for example.

Take Quesnay's Physiocratic doctrine of *laissez-faire,* for example. Quesnay, whose ideology was in the tradition of the notorious, pro-feudalist, Norman *Fronde* and the legacy of the pagan worship of the Delphic Apollo under France's self-anointed *Pontifex Maximus,* King Louis XIV, preached that the wealth of the feudal estates was a product of the landlord's aristocratic title to that land, and the peasants on the estate merely cattle whose labor made no contribution to the gain of output over costs. Adam Smith's doctrine of "free trade," which was chiefly a plagiarism of the doctrine of Quesnay and other French Physiocrats of that time, makes the same argument. Such was the doctrine of John Locke, whose teaching, under the rubrics "Life, Liberty, and Property," was the fundamental law of the Constitution of the Confederate States of America, and the basis in taught slaveholders' law for the maintenance of the system of chattel slavery, and prohibition against allowing literacy to "those of African descent," under the Confederacy and its tradition since, to the present day.

Among the victims of such pro-oligarchical teachings and practices, the serfholders, slaveholders, and their like fostered a curious form of pseudo-Christian belief, sometimes called "Christian fundamentalism," which was spread throughout much of what is called "The Bible Belt" today. Call it the "religious beliefs of those who are proud to consider themselves human cattle." Consistently, the sundry varieties of this pseudo-Christian belief, with their notorious "single issue" style in grievances, were often lumped together under the rubric of the lowest of the "low church" cults, as the so-called Pentecostalists typify the more extremely irrationalist examples of this. Not surprisingly, the hard core of those "low church" fanatics is found in the same localities of the U.S.A. in which President Woodrow Wilson's sponsorship of the revival of the Ku Klux Klan (KKK), and the influence of the so-called Nashville Agrarians, have been spread inside the U.S.A. during the course of the Twentieth Century.

These populist varieties of religious cults, and their echoes into secular society, are found typically among those unfortunates who view themselves, in practice, as an underclass, that of virtual human cattle. By the so-called "logic" of reaction-formation, they made a god in their own image, a god made in the image, not of man, but of human cattle, or the "golden calf."

As the spread of the policies associated with Nixon's Southern Strategy campaign of 1966-1968, turned the formerly industrialized regions of the U.S., on which the nation's prosperity chiefly depended, into what became known as a "rust belt," and as the skill-levels of employees, and number of jobs held, and hours worked or spent in commuting increased, the emphasis upon cognitive self-development in personal and family life dwindled, increasing thus the ration of the total labor-force which viewed its virtually unchangeable condition as that of almost slave-like human cattle, like the Southern "poor whites" under the rule of those slaveholders in whose interest the Confederacy was established.

As trends in popular culture, so called, plunged downward, during the recent thirty-five years, the almost brainless irrationalism of the lowest of the low-church types, the most human-cattle-like types, spread and worsened. The result of that has been the reaction-formation in which our nation's life is polluted, more and more, by those religious and kindred expressions of anti-cognitive irrationalism typified by the lowest of the low-church cults, such as those of Rev. Pat Robertson and Rev. Jerry Falwell. This trend is complemented by the soaring incidence of mental disorders within the population as a whole.

The result is, inevitably, both the spread of pseudo-Christian cults, echoing the Flagellant hordes of Europe's Fourteenth Century, and a growing hostility to everything rational in science and culture generally. The result has been, as in the moral and intellectual degeneration of Eighteenth-Century England under the House of Hanover, the transformation of a large and growing ration of our population into "Yahoos."

The popular ignorant prejudices among the victims of that populist disorder, read matters of science as curious religious sects usually misread the Bible. The ignorant populist insists that "God wrote the Bible so that ignorant people like me" ("human cattle") would automatically have a perfect understanding of what is written in the translation "which we use in our church." They believe that everything can be explained in terms of simple sense-perceptions, and that this means that all objects perceived by their senses are floating about, moving in a kind of infinite "soup," of empty space, which has four, mutually independent senses of direction: up, down, sideways, and time. They believe that each of these senses of direction is infinite in length. In other words, today's populist varieties of religious belief are fairly described as either "Religion for Dummies," or, simply, "religion suited for the beliefs of those proud to be human cattle."

For that reason, if we put aside some of their wild-eyed

notions about such exotic matters as "Bible prophecy," they believe in statistics and, therefore, in luck (e.g., gambling, mutual funds, etc.). Their idea of statistics, is based on the assumption that God designed the universe in such a way that it could be perfectly understood by dummies: everything one needs to know, can be discovered and proven by seeing, hearing, smelling, and touching. From the sermons in their churches, and their prayers, we observe a religion centered upon bargaining, at God's back-door, for personal favors, chiefly in matters of health, sexual gratification, and wealth. Their religion reminds us of dutiful slaves begging for hand-outs at the back door of the master's big white house. They believe that everything that the human senses can observe, can be understood by drawing more or less straight lines among dots on paper.

Put the son or daughter of such a populist type in school, and the student's family background will have prepared that student to accept the beliefs of Seventeenth-Century ideological types known as "empiricists," such as Galileo Galilei, Thomas Hobbes, René Descartes, John Locke, and Isaac Newton. In short, their ideas of physics are based on what is often called a "Euclidean" model of space, time, and matter. Their religious-like family traditions cause them to reject any idea about the real world which is not consistent with the empiricist's pro-oligarchical doctrine of "God for Dummies."

It happens, of course, that the real world does not work in the way that so-called "Euclidean model" requires. Unfortunately, often, the mass of evidence which proves that the world does not work that way, does not convince the believing populist to give up his unworkable model of reality. Instead, he or she adopts, even invents superstitions, which pretend to explain away the evidence that the "Euclidean model" does not work, and places his confidence in a form of prayer which does not differ from black magic, turning to witchcraft, in the effort to compel a deity to bestow upon him benefits which reason and reality would never allow.

As an expression of the popularity of those superstitions, university students have often heard the professor instructing students to the following effect.

"Euclidean geometry is the logical form for the application of mathematics to describing of physical phenomena. This geometry consists of a collection of self-evident definitions, axioms, and postulates, all of which are given to us by a purely intuitive interpretation of nature and its phenomena."[26]

The fraud in that professor's argument, is identified most efficiently, by pointing out that he pretends that the paradox of Plato's Cave never existed.

His geometric model (or its algebraic parody) assumes that cause and effect move between points along straight lines, pretty much in the same way as the usual financial accountant argues that *profit* is *income* less *costs and expenses,* instead of the more sensible approach, of considering the *physical actions reflected as some* costs and expenses as the causes of both income and profits, and attempting to discover which of them does what. Worse, the accountant who reads his accounts all to literally for his client's good, will regard as a profitable "cost-saving," the elimination of expenditures on which the continued maintenance and improvement of output and profitability depend—as "deregulation" has done to many sectors of the U.S. economy, in such a devastating degree, especially during the recent quarter-century since the inauguration of President Jimmy Carter.

In a real economy, the increase of output over the costs and expenses incurred to produce that output, is the result of the application of *physical action* to the process by which the output is produced and distributed. These actions express physical principles, most of which can not be competently represented in so-called "Euclidean," or analogous arithmetic or algebraic terms.

26. Even worse than this "Euclidean" dogma, is the case in which the professor and his textbook fly from geometry into a more or less purely abstract algebra, or arithmetic, which contains all of the foolishness of the "Euclidean geometric" view, but does not remove the "Euclidean" dogma's flaws, but merely hides them from view, as Bertrand Russell acolytes such as Norbert Wiener ("Cybernetics") and John von Neumann ("systems analysis") did.

In real economy, contrary to such pseudo-economists of the stopped-up kitchen-sink-drain variety as Senator Phil Gramm, economy means, essentially, physical economy. Physical economy, my specialty, is the discovery of physical principles and the technologies derived from those discoveries, which enable mankind to produce an output in excess of the *physical* cost of the efforts required for that production. What is shown on the wall of the financial accountant's dimly lit cave, are only the shadows of the reality which the all-too-typical financial accountant, by choice of profession, and by affinity for the class of dangerous lunatics known as monetarists, refuses to see.

For that reason, all real physical science is axiomatically non-Euclidean, and not a matter of a formalist interpretation of the "postulate of parallels." This does not mean that the Nineteenth-Century treatment of the matter of parallels, as by Janos Bolyai and Lobachevsky, was not useful. These discussions are to be viewed as scrutiny of propositions stated in the form of Analysis Situs, in the same sense as Fermat's overturning the fallacy of assuming that light follows always the shortest pathway, instead of the quickest pathway, which may not be the shortest distance.

It is always through the exhaustive exploration of paradoxes, such as the paradoxes of the attempt to prove the existence of a parallel postulate, that the alert, cognitive mind is prompted to discover higher principles which overturn all of the intuitive assumptions of what are still today, prevalent guises for generally accepted classroom varieties of mathematical physics. Critical treatments of the "parallel postulate," were neither the meal, nor the fuel by which it was cooked; those treatments were the oven in which the cooks were attempting to test the recipes with which they were experimenting.

The confusion over "non-Euclidean" geometries arises, only when the mathematician gets no further than developing a statement in the form of Analysis Situs, and never reaches the next step, as Riemann did, of discovering the geometry which replaces entirely the paradox-ridden debris of so-called "Euclidean" geometry's cultish application to physics. Typical of the incompetents, are those who attempt to compare Riemann's habilitation

Gottfried Wilhelm Leibniz. He invented the original differential and integral calculus, and formulated the adequate scientific conceptions of a monadology *and of universal least action, to the effect of situating in scientific method and practice the* voluntarism *which makes human history.*

dissertation to some aspect of the discussion of the parallel postulate by others. *With Riemann's approach, the parallel postulate, as such, enters nowhere in the formulation of the design.*

The Riemannian solution is resisted, chiefly, because the empiricists, who dominate the academic classroom still today, usually refuse to allow anything on campus which might prove offensive to those same, populist traditions which I have identified as also turning up prominently in the heathen delusions expressed as "Religion for Dummies."

In real science, formal, intuitive classroom mathematics is left behind. All intuitive forms of definitions, axioms, and postulates are discarded, simply because they are intuitive, rather than being the required universal principles, validated as such by appropriate qualities of experiment. Therefore, put aside the mathematics of "Religion for Dummies," and adopt instead, the notions of physical geometry consistent with the crucial experimental evidence.

The pivotal feature of the argument to this effect, involves the implications of Leibniz's notion of *characteristics,* as, about a century and a half later, Riemann employed that conception as central to his habilitation dissertation.[27] Leibniz's notion of such characteristics, on which his definition of the differential of the calculus was premised, reflected Kepler's proof of the incompetence of the method employed by Copernicus, Tycho Brahe, and others, and also reflected the development of the notion of quickest time as introduced by Fermat.

Thus, Riemann's work implicitly defines the essential feature of the existence of a distinct *natural object,* as Vernadsky defines a "natural object,"[28] by its characteristic, as Kepler defines a planetary orbit as a characteristic. So, the differential of the Leibniz calculus (contrary to the Euler-Cauchy hoax commonly

---

27. Cf. Riemann, habilitation dissertation, Sec. III, op. cit., pp. 283-288. Anyone who has examined Riemann's work more closely, and taken into account the political situation in post-Carlsbad Decrees Germany at that time, will recognize the references to Archimedes, Galileo, and Newton, in this dissertation, as politically dictated references to a Galileo and Newton, whom Riemann already regarded at that time as little better than hoaxsters.

28. See Vladimir I. Vernadsky, *"On the Fundamental Material-Energetic Difference between Living and Non-Living Natural Bodies in the Biosphere"* (1938), Jonathan Tennenbaum and Rachel Douglas, trans., *21st Century Science & Technology,* Winter 2000-2001. This was the first full translation into English of this crucial 1938 paper by Vernadsky, offering the best insight into a body of ideas otherwise known from the work of the great founder of biogeochemistry. It was earlier work of Vernadsky, along the same lines, but less thorough than the 1938 piece referenced here, which I employed, in Spring 1973, as part of the core argument for a science of physical economy, upon which the subsequent founding of the Fusion Energy Foundation (FEF) and its influential *Fusion* magazine, was premised. For a recent biography of Vernadsky, see Kendall E. Bailes, *Science and Russian Culture in An Age of Revolutions: V.I. Vernadsky and His Scientific School, 1863-1945* (Bloomington: Indiana University Press, 1990).

taught in universities today) is, from the standpoint of "ivory tower" mathematics, an axiomatically incommensurable magnitude, comparable to the distinctiveness of the unique characteristic of a specific Keplerian planetary orbit.

Here lies the difference between physical science taught as mathematics-at-the-blackboard, and real physical science: as Riemann emphasizes that crucial distinction in the concluding portion of his habilitation dissertation. This is the crucial argument already made by Kepler, against the connect-the-dots method of Ptolemy, Copernicus, and Tycho Brahe, in his *New Astronomy*. It is the crucial difference between the competent physics of Leibniz's definition of the calculus, and the fraudulent alterations in that calculus made by the "ivory tower" ideologues Euler, Cauchy, et al. The existence of different natural objects in the universe, each with distinct characteristic, including the human mind, defines a *monad*. Hence, Leibniz's *monadology*. Hence, Riemann's leading contributions to physical science.

Therefore, the first step now to be taken, is to situate that topic of monadology in the form relevant to that specific argument.

In forecasting the results of man's efforts to willfully change his future, we encounter two connected classes of challenge.

The first challenge, is to discover how man exerts control over nature, to the effect of maintaining and improving man's ability to maintain the numbers and quality of life of our species' existence. In the science of physical economy, we measure the result in terms of changes in demographic characteristics of both entire populations and typical households, and per capita and per square kilometer of our planet's normalized surface-area. We emphasize those ideas, both ideas of physical principles of non-living processes, and those of living processes, through which increased mastery of the universe, per capita, is effected on behalf of our species.

In this first case, therefore, we are estimating a normalized expression of man's per-capita relationship to nature, a relationship expressed as a function of ideas.

The second challenge, is to define those principles of social relations, by means of which, ideas of the first class are transmitted to the effect of enabling society to coordinate its efforts for effective use of principles through which man's increased power, per capita, in and over nature, is accomplished. These principles are exemplified by the principles of invention and performance of Classical artistic compositions in plastic and non-plastic forms, and in the application of the same Classical artistic principles to the comprehension of history and statecraft.

The two sets of conceptions, taken today, represent the development of the human intellect, as a Classical-humanist form of education best serves that end.

Now, consider examples of the first of the two classes of discoveries.

What Are Physical Principles?

Taking into account all the relevant matter that is to be considered here today, we have included, for special consideration, a comprehensive form of modern mathematical physics, which was begun with the crucial discoveries made by the founder of that branch of science, Johannes Kepler. The pivot of Kepler's most crucial discovery, was his discrediting of that childish, connect-the-dots method commonly employed by the malicious Romantic hoaxster Claudius Ptolemy, and also by the well-meaning, but systemically erring Copernicus and Tycho Brahe.

By recognizing the Platonic implications of the paradoxical curvature of the orbit of the planet Mars, together with related evidence, Kepler freed science from the suffocating grip of "ivory tower" varieties of mathematics, and located the identity of a planetary orbit in a characteristically incommensurable value corresponding to a universal principle of harmonics, that specific to an orbit which is not necessarily of uniform curvature. In other words, Kepler defined the orbit as measured in terms of a constant, but not necessarily uniformly curved, but measurable effect of *Platonic* change.

He met that challenge of the individual orbit, by defining the Solar system, considered, functionally, as an harmonically unified whole, as a subsuming (in Riemann's terms), *multiply-*

connected manifold of such change. So, Kepler was first to discover, thus, that principle of universal gravitation which would-be plagiarizers intellectually crippled by the influence of empiricism, such as Isaac Newton, could never even begin to grasp as a cognitive conception of principle. [29]

So, Kepler's founding of the first competent form of modern astrophysics, defined certain crucial problems of universal physics, which he relegated to the attentions of future mathematicians. When Kepler's such discoveries were matched with Fermat's discovery of an "anti-Euclidean" geometrical principle of quickest time, as in paradoxical contradiction of the so-called "Euclidean" notion of shortest distance, a generalized form of development of modern physical science, was set into motion, by such followers of Nicholas of Cusa, Leonardo da Vinci, and Kepler, as Christiaan Huyghens and Gottfried Leibniz.

On this basis, Leibniz developed the original differential and integral calculus, according to the combined prescriptions and implications of Kepler's and Fermat's seminal discoveries.

---

29. See Kepler, *The Harmony of the World*, E.J. Aiton, A.M. Duncan, and J.V. Field, trans. (The American Philosophical Society: 1997), passim. Note the way in which the "equal areas" phenomenon is applied to the distinction of the relative values among the characteristics of the various orbits. This is the root of the way in which Newton, et al., formally incurred the "three-body paradox." It is the exclusion of Kepler's emphasis on the crucial principle of harmonics, from the Newtonians' bowdlerization of Kepler's work, which leads the Newtonians and the credulous fools who follow them, into the pits of the "three-body problem." To attempt to separate the well-tempered harmonics embedded in Kepler's treatment of "equal areas," must necessarily create the "three-body paradox" in elementary classroom physics, as it tends to foster bad musical composition and interpretation among the Romantics. In noting the general case of hysterical denial of such a connection by the Newton devotees generally, note the exemplary relevance of the hysterical denial of such a connection in Kepler's astrophysics, over which H. Helmholtz and his accomplice Ellis had their fits (*Sensations of Tone*) against J.S. Bach et al., on the subjects of *bel canto* voice-training and on the related matters of well-tempering. This and related implications of the connection between the work of Kepler and that of Bach, is a special topic of historiography in itself.

This calculus is to be contrasted with the fraudulent, but popularized classroom definitions, as the latter are supplied, with the mere appearance of the Leibniz calculus, by such malicious figures as Leibniz-hater Euler, Euler's follower Lagrange, and the plagiarizing (e.g., of Abel) hoaxster and Laplace creature Cauchy.

Out of Leibniz's accomplishments in this direction, came his discovery of a principle of *universal least action,* and the still higher principle known as his *monadology.* Through the work of, chiefly, Kästner and his student Gauss, and with important contributions by Monge, Carnot, et al., we have the crucial and unique contributions to the founding of a true and comprehensive anti-Euclidean geometry by Bernhard Riemann.

Riemann's 1854 habilitation dissertation, marks the first act freeing physical science completely, and mathematics, too, from the grip of those "ivory tower" fantasies which had crippled, more or less severely, most of modern scientific work up to that time. This accomplishment, by Riemann, provides the Gaussian foundations for the development of my view of what Vladimir Vernadsky defined as the *noösphere.*[30] It is in my situating that notion of the noösphere within the framework of my own discoveries in the field of a science of physical economy, that the connection of Leibniz's principle of *monadology* to solving that problem of *voluntarism* set forth here, can be rendered more fully comprehensible today.

I situate this latter subject by summarizing, as follows, what I have described in earlier locations, as those implications of the concept of noösphere which are brought into their necessary focus by my work in physical economy.

1. *By a physical principle, I signify an experimentally validatable, discovered principle, whose application generates a human effect within, and upon the universe, a quality of effect not otherwise predetermined, than by the impact of the willful human application of that discovery of a universal physical principle.*

---

30. Op. cit.

The specific quality of difference between that, my preceding definition of universal physical principle, and the usual classroom definitions, is more easily recognized by reference to Vernadsky's definition of the noösphere.

Already, as in 1938, Vernadsky supplied a rigorous definition of the noösphere. The human *noëtic* will,[31] transforms the functionally definable relationship of the biosphere to the universe it both inhabits and reshapes. The question left unanswered by Vernadsky, is what function defines the way in which mankind may acquire *foreknowledge* of how to take the next step in transforming mankind's action on the pre-existing noösphere?

This is a proposition of the same general type, as Kepler's response to the evident non-uniformity of the curvature of planetary orbits. Where does the determining *intention* lie, by means of which the present moment of action already contains the immediate next turn in a trajectory of not necessarily uniform curvature? This was, contrary to Euler and Cauchy, Leibniz's requirement for the "infinitesimal" interval of the differential calculus. In Kepler's usage: How do we define the *Mind* of the planet; how do we define that stubbornly persisting expression of the *intention* of the planet which can not be attributed to simply mathematically defined uniform cycles? *How is the mind of man able to adopt a successful intention to change the course of history from its present trajectory?*

The known features of the demographic characteristics of human populations, as reflected from both history and pre-history, show that the development of the potential relative population-density of the human species is not random in any sense of that term. There is an expressed *intention,* especially in the long-term rise, since the Fifteenth-Century, Italy-centered Renaissance, of the potential relative population-density of globally extended modern European civilization's impact on the demographic characteristics of the human population as a whole.

This factor of intention, corresponding to Kepler's notion of the *Mind* of the planet, is what is expressed, typically, in the form of explicit intention, as those changes associated with the

---

31. Hence, Vernadsky termed the result a *noösphere.*

establishment of the modern (e.g., anti-"free trade," anti-"globalization") form of sovereign nation-state economy, and with the correlated emphasis upon both development of basic economic infrastructure, and investment in capital-intensive modes of scientific and technological progress. This accomplishment depends, also, in a more or less crucial degree, on the extent to which a Classical-humanist form of education dominates elementary and secondary education of children and youth.

Thus, although Vernadsky is explicit, in emphasizing the unique quality of noëtic function of mankind, in transforming the biosphere to higher states of anti-entropy, *his argument does not yet define that specific quality of human intention, by means of which that noëtic impulse is expressed as a "trajectory" of such transformation of the biosphere.* This omission is addressed, and corrected, by introducing the *voluntarist* definition of "physical principle" described above. *Here lies our debt to Vernadsky, and, also, the debt of his legacy to us.*

The existence of such a principle, is determined solely by the method identified as, variously, *Analysis Situs,* or *geometry of position.* Recall the three-step process of discovery outlined here earlier.

Given a known, existing array (i.e., *manifold*) of experimentally validated universal principles; given an effect, which that manifold prescribes as necessarily predetermined; and given a description of an experimentally definable effect, the which contradicts, paradoxically, that prescription, that by a significant margin of error. What is the universal principle which must be added to the manifold to bring the manifold into conformity with the thus-expanded view of universal reality? Such a "model" illustrates the general principle associated with geometry of position. Such is the way in which physics, as defined by Riemann's habilitation dissertation, supersedes deductive forms of mathematics in all competent practice of physical science, including the science of physical economy.

The result of such change, as Gauss laid the principal foundations for the discovery featured in Riemann's habilitation dissertation, is a recognition of the experimentally measurable effects of the efficient existence of such principles, in terms of the related change in curvature of the physical space-time defined by the inclusion of the newly discovered principle. Hence, the core argument of Riemann's dissertation. Here lies the essential contribution to all science by Riemann; here lies Riemann's indispensable contribution to the fuller comprehension of the nature of the Keplerian orbits and the deeper implications of the work of Leibniz and Gauss.

How, then, can such an experimentally validated discovery of such a physical principle, be applied willfully to produce a new quality of behavior of the observed manifold considered as a whole?

Exactly the same principle of geometry of position, is expressed by J.S. Bach's discovery of a well-tempered system of tuning, and of his method of counterpoint, inversion, based upon a musical expression of the same principle of geometry of position employed by Fermat for the discovery of a principle of quickest time. Bach's use of inversion, whose lawful ordering is reflected characteristically by the *Lydian principle* celebrated in Beethoven's Opus 132, is a perfect example of the principle of Analysis Situs, and of the manner in which that principle generates, in this case for music, a principled notion of musical idea. This is the notion of musical ideas, based on the work of Bach, which defines the absolute separation of the methods of Classical thorough-composition of Haydn, Mozart, Beethoven, Schubert, Mendelssohn, Schumann, and Brahms, from the irrational sensationalism of such Romantics as the silly Rameau, Liszt, Berlioz, and Wagner.

Fermat's argument for a principle of quickest time, in refraction of light, typifies such a paradox of universal import. Kepler's appreciation of the paradoxical implication of the Mars orbit's elliptical form, is also such a paradox. The statement of such paradoxes in the form of contradictions within the manifold of reference in which they erupt, is the conceptual prototype of what is representable by the method of *Analysis Situs* or *geometry of position*.

If the proposed *hypothetical* solution, the new universal principle, is demonstrated, by appropriate form of experiment, to be valid *universally,* that principle is to be added to the manifold. *It is the willful application of such a newly discovered principle of nature, to nature, which causes the relevant change within the manifold as previously extant.* It is the resulting transformation of the manifold, by deleting false assumptions, and adding needed principles, on which the Leibniz notion of characteristic action (i.e., least action) is premised. This notion is already implicit in Kepler's original development of modern astrophysics, and in Leibniz's undertaking the corresponding challenge which Kepler bequeathed "to future mathematicians."

It is the willful action of the individual human mind, in making such a valid discovery of *a pre-existing universal principle* in the universe, which, *by willfully applying that same principle, changes the universe from which that discovery has been adduced.* It is as if to say, that *"In the beginning was the Logos..."* This point of principle, already introduced a few pages earlier, has yet much deeper implications, to which I shall come shortly here, in due course.

I must restate this point just made, for both emphasis and clarity.

The characteristic form of action, which distinguishes the human species, from all inferior forms of life, is those discoveries of universal physical and congruent principle, by means of which the quality of man's functional, demographically expressed relationship to the universe as a whole, is raised to a higher level. These discoveries have the effect, of transforming the entire manifold of man's implied knowledge of universal physical principles.

What I have said here, so far, signifies this. It is not so much the individual such discovery, in and of itself, which is characteristic; it is the transformation of the manifold as a whole, from its state prior to the discovery, into its state after the incorporation of the discovery. It is this transformation of the manifold, which supplies a validated discovery of principle its universal character. It is that change in the universality of the manifold, which is the subject of the characteristic form of human cognitive action. It is that characteristic which defines the role of human noëtic activity in effecting those transformations which elevate man's existence within the biosphere, to man's dominant role in the noösphere.

It is this role of the thus-informed human will, so informed, which is the pivot of our concern in this report as a whole.

Manifolds so expandable are implicitly of the general form of Riemannian manifolds, as typified by Riemann's 1854 habilitation dissertation.

2. There is an hierarchy of three known, respectively distinct types of manifolds which conform to that definition of universal physical principles: a) The manifold of *non-living processes* in general; b) The manifold of *living processes* in general; and, c) The manifold of *cognitive processes*. The general nature of the experimental distinctions, and interrelations among the three classes of manifolds, is that defined, from the standpoint of bio-geochemistry, by Vladimir I. Vernadsky. The three, combined as multiply-connected, constitute what Vernadsky terms a *noösphere*.

Look briefly at these distinctions, using the standpoint set forth by Vernadsky.

There are several types of evidence to be considered as either crucial, or relatively so, in distinguishing life as a universal physical principle, from those notions of universal physical principle associated with non-living processes. In other words, what is the evidence, in support of Vernadsky's insistence, that living processes are not derived, by "spontaneous" evolution, from non-living ones?

In each case, as with Louis Pasteur's empirical distinction, in chemistry, between non-living and living processes, or Vernadsky's biogeochemical strategy for dealing with this, we are focussing upon an effect which itself is subject to chemical study after the fact, but which is produced, to be a fact, by a living process, that in a way which can not be duplicated "spontaneously" ("objectively") by a non-living one. Look for the most significant of the fine distinctions presented by such cases.

Thus, for example, by the standard of relative weight of the material involved, the Earth's atmosphere and water are composed, predominantly, of non-living processes, but their existence as an atmosphere, oceans, lakes, and streams, is predominantly a product of a living process, the biosphere. Similarly, fossil rock formations and soil. The net result is, non-living material produced by living processes, by a principle of life itself. Vernadsky defines such non-living elements of the biosphere as among the *natural products* of the biosphere.

In a parallel case, similarly, the powers of cognition unique to the human individual, act upon the biosphere, to produce effects in the biosphere which could exist as they do, only as products of human cognition. Since all three categories of universal principles are known by their production of physical effects, these effects are each among the *natural products* of the corresponding processes, and each category, non-living, living, and cognitive, is a universal *physical* principle.

The indicated classes of evidence are to the effect, that life is a universal *physical* principle, independent of, but multiply-connected with what are adducibly universal physical principles governing ostensibly non-living processes as such. Vernadsky's biogeochemistry makes that point implicitly. Thus, the universe acted upon the non-living processes, to the effect of producing the preconditions for life. *How did the universe know that it should do this?* Ask this specific question of Johannes Kepler, for example. *How did the universe know that it should produce the preconditions for existence of cognitive life within the development of living processes?* Ask Kepler, again.

Broadly, the implication posed by this evidence, of three, demonstrably distinct classes of universal principle, indicates that their multiple connection must be, a single, multiply-connected manifold, comparable, in the history of philosophy, to the Absolute of Plato, which existed "from the beginning." As Vernadsky suspected, without his having studied Riemann's work in terms of primary sources, the physical universe as a whole is of the Riemannian form associated with the connections among the three distinct types of universal physical principle indicated here.

3. My principled contribution, carrying these conceptions to a higher level than specified by Vernadsky, is two-

fold: a) I defined the form of such manifolds conceptually, from the vantage-point of Riemann's work, which, on the presently known record, Vernadsky (1938) recognized as of interest, but, at last known record, did not actually undertake; b) I defined *the principle of physical-economic anti-entropy,* from which vantage-point the functional character of the noösphere must be defined.

From the considerations summarized up to this point, the notion of anti-entropy must be situated, conceptually, within the framework of the Riemannian overview of those three classes of universal physical principles. The underlying quality of the multiple-connectedness of a universe so defined, is that it is characteristically *anti-entropic.*

The transformations in that entire manifold, brought about through experimentally validated discoveries of universal physical principle, which increase man's power in and over nature, per capita and per square kilometer, are the standard for defining anti-entropy as characteristic of the noösphere. This, stated in the terms of a science of physical economy, supplies the notion for, and, also, proves the existence and definition, and the basis for measurement, of anti-entropy.

4. Each of these three types, when viewed from the standpoint of my indicated, original contribution to this field, is defined as a distinct quality of manifold from the standpoint of those experimental methods appropriate for defining a valid universal physical principle, and yet each successive such manifold, *produces measurable physical effects which can not be generated from within the confines of the relatively lower-order manifold.* As a matter of experimental method, the evidence of this limitation of the relatively lower manifold, as Vernadsky points to that principled method, is what supplies the proof that the relatively higher manifold is a form of existence, absolutely differing in both origin and quality from the relatively lower one.

Again, as I have summarized this above: Vernadsky shows the general nature of this proof, for life, relative to non-living processes, and for the noösphere, relative to the subsumed biosphere. The definition of the explicit role of the cognitive processes in determining the change in relative physical-economic anti-entropy of the noösphere, is uniquely my own contribution, a contribution for which I was, originally, chiefly indebted to my adolescent study and defense of Leibniz's notion of a *monadology* (then, as a defense against Kant's *Critiques*).

This form, in which life and cognition effect qualitative changes in the manifold of an otherwise ostensibly non-living universe, is expressed in the transformation of the functional ordering of relations in the relatively inferior domain, by intervention through action from the relatively higher domain. Thus, *as Vernadsky shows, the principle of life, transforms the characteristics of action within the relevant non-living domain, thus defining the biosphere; whereas, as Vernadsky also shows, cognition's intervention transforms the characteristics of action within the manifold of the biosphere. The characteristic of both transformations, is anti-entropy.* Anti-entropy, not the entropy worshipped by the dupes of such Newton devotees as Clausius and Kelvin, is the expression of the highest determining principle of lawfulness in the universe as a whole.

My contribution, on that specific point, has been, chiefly, to define the physical-economic standard by which anti-entropy in the noösphere is to be defined. It is my work to this effect which has made feasible the kind of method required to conquer a crisis of the type immediately threatening civilization today. Vernadsky points to the crucial, anti-entropic role of cognition as such. I shift the center of the focus to the internal functions of the human will, in willfully ordering the direction of the changes in the biosphere brought about through human cognitive intervention.

Since, in all of these exemplary cases, the form of the action is to impose a physical intention upon the universe, or what Kepler would refer to as the intention of the *Mind* of the universe, *any experimentally demonstrated universal principle, is a physical principle in its effects.* Thus, the universal principles attributable to non-living, living, and cognitive processes as such, are each equally universal *physical* principles.

On this account, from the indicated Riemannian view of the implications of the multiple-connectedness of the three specific classes of universal physical principles, the following issues are begged, and also, implicitly, answered in a provisional way.

Vernadsky's argument, as summarized in the referenced, 1938 location, signifies that the universe is a multiply-connected function of three specific classes of universal principles, each distinct from the other, yet, because they are always efficiently multiply-connected, each and all subsumed by the correspondingly implied, single universal principle. This multiple-connectedness of that single, underlying principle, as I have just summarized the functional implications of that, above, demands that we recognize the universe as the expression of a single principle of universal creation, whose existence, not "Euclidean" calendars, dates an implied "beginning." *The beginning exists for our knowledge of existence of a self-developing universe, solely as certainty of the existence of a universe which is universally bounded by itself: a simultaneity of eternity,* within which sequences are ordered by action, not clock-time. Time is determined by cognitively-defined sequences, not sequences by clock-time.

However, it also prescribes, without any possibility of legitimate disagreement, that if one accepts the notion of that principle, the "beginning" is not to be found in the purely fantastic expanses of sense-certainty's pathetic notion of infinitely extended linear time, but rather, as the allegory of Plato's Cave requires, in the real universe, known explicitly only to cognition. It is only in the physical space-time specific to cognition, rather than bestially naive sense-certainty, that the term "beginning," can be used by sane persons, as it is in the opening of the Gospel of St. John.

When those implications are taken into account, we require a correspondingly appropriate definition of the word *creation*. To the degree that mankind discovers those intentions of the Creator's will which are integral to the universality of creation, man takes unto himself, and to his will, the power to employ those intentions, otherwise knowable as universal physical principles, to change the universe in a manner cohering with the

By recognizing the Platonic implication of the paradoxical curvature of the orbit of the planet Mars, Johannes Kepler located the identity of the planetary orbit in a characteristically incommensurable value corresponding to a universal principle of harmonics.

principle of universal creation. This, in other words, is man guided by, and acting according to those qualities of *reason* which history shows us are specific to the Classical modes of scientific and artistic discovery and composition.

The power to discover the efficient will to act according to reason so defined, lies in the ability of the individual to rise above the prison-shackles of control by immediate pleasure-pain, to see one's mortal existence as an instrument acting within, and for, the furtherance of that intention which reason unveils to us as the intention (i.e., universal principles) of creation as a whole. Thus, the immediate intimation of immortality is typified by the continuing contributions of valid discoveries of principle supplied to humanity by great scientific minds and great composers of Classical art-forms from centuries and longer before our time.

Enter Monadology as Such

What I have just summarized in the foregoing arguments, should be readily recognized as a restatement, in the context of the most general implications of relevant and crucial qualities of modern discoveries since, of the notion of a *monadology* which Leibniz introduced in a number of locations, chiefly among those specifically addressing that named topic. This must seem less surprising to anyone who takes into account, that I was converted to Leibniz's view on this matter during my adolescent wrestling against the arguments of Immanuel Kant's so-called *Critiques,* as, a decade later, against the degenerate expression of Kant's essential argument by Bertrand Russell and such among Russell's satanic acolytes as Professor Norbert Wiener and John von Neumann.

Now, look again at the relationship between Kepler's definition of the intention expressed by planetary orbits, and the emergence of Riemann's apprehension of the intention of Leibniz's notion of the monad. Situate thus, the choice of approach to be taken to the practical employment of the concept of a monadology.

There are two points of reference, both for defining the notion of characteristics, and for presenting the notion of the *monad* in a fresh, modern way. The one is Kepler's notion of the harmonically ordered, characteristic orbit of each planet, as defined by the Solar System as a whole. The second is the notion of sovereignty, as adduced from the characteristic of the cognitive activity of the individual human mind: Kepler's use of *Mind,* in defining the notion of the *intention* governing a planet's orbit.

The notion of a Keplerian orbit, locates the intention of the orbit in the effect of the position it must *intend* to achieve through motion, as opposed to a position determined by a "Euclidean" form, as a predicate of a mathematically determined trajectory. For Kepler, the relative harmonic value of the orbit, as associated with the equal-areas principle, expressed the nature of this *intention.* The harmonic composition of the orbital composition of the Solar system as a whole, is the second degree of approximation of the *intended* objective of the planet.

This *intention,* expressed by a corresponding *characteristic,* defines a *monad.* The types of existing monads, are assorted among four classes: *non-living, living, cognitive,* and *absolute.* By "absolute," we should signify "the universe," as a universal simultaneity of the eternity of *ideas*, in which time exists only in the sense of a sequence of actions of a cognitive form. I intend, such a universe, conceived as a monad.

The same principle of the monad, is characteristic of the method of well-tempered composition of J.S. Bach, the method upon which the development of Classical thorough-composition, and related principles of performance, were developed by Haydn, Mozart, Beethoven, Schubert, Mendelssohn, Schumann, Brahms, et al.[32] The "germ form," the crucial contrapuntal inversion on which the entire composition pivots, is associated in *the expressed intention of the composer,* and of the adequate performers, as the anticipated unfolding of the completed composition is to be heard.

The form of Classical musical thorough-composition, which Haydn, Mozart, Beethoven, et al., adduced from the preceding discoveries and their development by J. S. Bach, has the essential quality of reducing the entire composition to a single idea, conceived within the cognitive processes of the mind, the conductor, and so forth, as a single, as-if-instantaneous *idea:* a monad. It is that idea, implying the subsequent unfolding of the entire composition, which underlies, governs the competent performer's attack upon the first note. The performer who fails to attack the opening interval of the composition in that way, will, therefore, fail to communicate *effectively,* the *idea* of the composition as a whole to the relevant audience. This also applies to dramas such as Shakespeare's *Hamlet,* in which a failed choice of attack on "To be, or not to be," will ensure the failure of the performance of that play from that point through the final, ironical exchange between Fortinbras and Horatio, as the body of Hamlet is carried off-stage.

---

32. In the case of Brahms, the perfected exposition of that principle is presented in his Fourth Symphony, which pivots on the quotation of an inversion from the Adagio Sostenuto of Beethoven's "Hammerklavier" sonata, Op. 106. The performances of this directed by Wilhelm Furtwängler are of special importance, because of the latter's reliance on that notion of "performing between the notes" which is integral to the competent performance of a work of Classical thorough-composition, especially a long work as thorough-composed in quality as that Brahms symphony.

Pause for a moment at this point. From this line of development, Kepler specified the necessary previous existence of a disintegrated planet whose orbit had lain, in a harmonically determined orbit, between the orbits of Mars and Jupiter. About two centuries later, Gauss was to show, that the asteroids were fragments whose orbital characteristics were those attributed to the missing, disintegrated planet by Kepler.[33] The harmonically defined characteristic of the determining orbit of the planet expresses the principle of the Leibnizian monad.

Thus, the planet's orbit, and also the configuration of the Solar system, are incommensurable, but, nonetheless, predetermined trajectories, as the congruence of the orbital characteristic of the missing planet is reflected in the orbital characteristics of the principal asteroids.

We shall return to consider certain functional implications of that, after comparing the apparent sovereignty of the Solar system of planetary orbits, with the sovereignty of the cognitive processes of the individual human mind. Now that we have a general idea of the principles of physical science as such in view, summarize the case for the second type of principles, those typified by both Classical artistic composition, and the study of history and related topics of statecraft from the standpoint of principles and methods of Classical artistic composition. Focus on the matter of the functional relationship of the cognitive processes of the individuals engaged in the discovery and exchange of discoveries of all kinds of universal physical principles, including those of Classical artistic composition.

In the case of Classical irony, such as metaphor or a statement in the form of Analysis Situs, the cognitive action "synthesizing" the solution for that paradox, occurs within the sensorially opaque boundaries of the sovereign cognitive processes of the individual thinker. Nonetheless, the ability to demonstrate the truthfulness of the synthesized hypothetical idea, is verifiable by the standards of *unique experimental demonstration;* and the experience of that synthetic act of cognition can be communi-

---

33. Cf. Jonathan Tennenbaum and Bruce Director, "How Gauss Determined the Orbit of Ceres," *Fidelio,* Summer 1998.

cated, by replication, within the sovereign cognitive processes of another individual.

The effectiveness of that discovery, expressed as applied to practice, shows both the reality of the idea, and the way in which that idea, although invisible to sense-certainty, can be known efficiently, and that knowledge efficiently shared among persons. This is more readily clear for the case of discoveries in experimental physical science, but it is also that quality of Classical artistic composition which distinguishes it, essentially, from the Romantics and such bastard offspring of Romantic licentiousness as modernism and post-modernism.

Furthermore, the ability of the individual to perform such a cognitive action, either as an original discovery, or its replication by another, depends upon the cultivation of those cognitive powers, as in the mode of a Classical humanist education in accumulated such discoveries from previous history.

Compare Classical artistic principles with those of physical science in the following way.

Look at the Leibniz differential calculus from this vantage-point. The differential there is identical, as a character-type, with the distinctive incommensurability of a Keplerian planetary orbit. The differential must be in the mathematical form corresponding to a statement in Analysis Situs, as the role of equal-areas and harmonic characteristic points to the origin of the necessary paradoxical expression for the orbit as a whole. That differential is the characteristic of the trajectory in question.

The quasi-sovereign quality of the Leibniz differential, in opposition to the linearized form of Euler, Cauchy, et al., points in the direction of the concept of the monad. It is to be conceptualized as an expression of the ontological principle, "nothing is permanent but change," rather than an expression in terms of the reductionists' axiomatically "Euclidean" physical space-time. *The individuality of the element is its sovereign quality, not its likeness to a sensory object.* Hence, the notion of its existence in the form of a monad.

The implicitly task-oriented transmission of such conceptions of physical science, and their technological derivatives, within the functioning of society, defines the subject of both

Classical artistic composition, more narrowly, and the Classical study of history and statecraft, more broadly.

The Sovereign Monad

Look again, at Kepler's use of "Mind," in referencing the *intention* expressed by a planetary orbit. Now, first, compare that *Mind* of the planet with the sovereign cognitive powers of the mind of Kepler. Next, from that standpoint, view the *Mind* of the Sun, expressed in terms of the panoply of orbital characteristics of the orbits of the Solar system as a whole. View that *Mind* of the Sun through Kepler's mind.

After that exercise, then regard the function expressed by the intervention of the physical principle of life, into the ordering of the non-living aspects of the universe. Then, view, similarly, the intervention of the cognitive processes into the ordering of the internal processes of the biosphere. After that, then consider these matters in light of the contrary views on thermodynamics, by Clausius, Kelvin, and Grassmann, for example.

At that point, review what has been considered up to this point, by focussing, first, on the subject of the universal physical principles of life and of cognition, and then return to reexamine the matter of universal physical principles of non-living processes. Start with the human mind and its cognitive powers. To measure, we must first know our measuring instrument; we must begin here, because it is here that we have the knowable concept of the existence of a sovereign mind. We must then compare that notion of a sovereign mind, our own, with the intention shown in its relationship to living processes (the biosphere) and to ostensibly non-living processes, such as planetary orbits, too.

Look inside the cognitive processes of your own mind, the mind within whose sovereign confines that act of discovery occurs, through which mankind's power in and over the universe is potentially increased. Focus upon the congruence, as demonstrated experimentally, between Kepler's discovery of the solution for the fallacies of Copernicus's and Tycho Brahe's work, and Gauss's vindication of Kepler's entire system through the crucial experimental case of the asteroid orbits. Contrast the congruence of that discovery of principle, as by Kepler, with the failures of Copernicus, Brahe, et al., to escape from the illusory domain of pseudo-realities, the neurotic domain of naive intuition, which mistakes sense-certainty for the real universe.

Hence, such cases—and there are many others, of course— lead to the specific quality of notion of *becoming* which is associated with Plato's dialogues. It is through the faculty of cognition, rather than sense-certainty, that we really know the universe; the idea of the universe presented to our mind by cognition, is not a universe of things swimming, as if in Brownian motion, within some infinite Euclidean soup, but, rather, a universe known to us only through those transformations which result in *changes of axiomatic quality* in our way of thinking about, and acting upon the universe. It is those *changes,* defined in cognitive terms, which are the most elementary form of existence of *ideas.*

For sense-certainty, on the simplest level, eggs or chickens are popularly regarded as self-evident objects. Such is the opinion concerning eggs and chickens among roost-robbers such as skunks, foxes, and sundry varieties of ferrets. In contrast, among cognitively matured persons, in science, the existence of eggs expresses an intention embedded in the existence of chickens, and in the case of chickens, the intention of eggs. However, that intention of chickens or their eggs, does not exist independently of the functional character of the situation in which such intentions are expressed.

It is in the discovery of such intentions, as Kepler adduced the principle of intention, as his notion of universal gravitation underlying the orbit of Mars, that real knowledge of the universe lies. However, the intention of Mars can not be defined, except within the universal setting (situation) of the Solar system as a whole. These notions of intention, are to be contrasted with the Aristotelean dogma of those philosophical incompetents who tolerated Claudius Ptolemy's hoax for so long; or the credulous sophomores who swallow the popular fairy-tale, that Copernicus discovered the orbit of the Sun by the Earth; or, Sunday Supplement grubs who write, that modern European culture is "Copernican." Kepler's notion of intention, typifies a universal conception of existence, as really occurring in no other form than an intention underlying a *becoming*.

This connection of an intention to the notion of a becoming, is the underlying principle of Leibniz's discovery of an actual differential and integral calculus, a discovery to which he was led by a challenge bequeathed "to future mathematicians" from Kepler. A specific quality of intention, as associated with a specific quality of becoming, represents a *characteristic,* in Leibniz's and Riemann's sense of such a term. This notion of a characteristic, is, in turn, the context within which the notion of a Leibnizian monadology dwells.

This point ought to be clear, merely from the standpoint of the experience of any person who has actually made, or has, perhaps as a student might, reenacted a valid discovery of universal physical principle. I restate it, in summary, now.

The case of a paradox expressed in the form of Analysis Situs, goes to that point. All discoveries occur as the fruit of solutions to paradoxes of an ontological type. The challenge of that paradox provokes an act of conception. It is that act of conception which, if successful, produces the hypothetical form of a solution to such a paradox which is brought into being within an individual sovereign mind. The experimental demonstration of the validity of that hypothesis, defines a universal physical principle.

Thus, the cognitive process which generates a validated hypotheses of that type, is typical of the appropriate mental image of reality. The image of the cognitive process we have experienced in ourselves, in either discovering a valid universal physical principle, or reenacting such an historical discovery, is the only actually existing, rational notion of the real existence of anything. Only to the degree that our conceptions are reached by that cognitive method of generating notions of principle, can anyone say truthfully that, "I know."

A person may say, "I saw," or "I heard," or "I touched," or "I smelled," on the basis of confidence in the reliability of one's ability to distinguish between actuality and illusion in matters of sense-experience. When such a person substitutes the verb "to know," for "I saw," or, "I heard," that person is, in the usual case, speaking untruthfully. Nonetheless, sometimes, as in the case of the experimental validation of a universal physical principle, one can justly say of relevant sense-experiences, "I know."

For example, a person testifying that "I saw," may be rightly questioned, "How do you know that that is what you saw?" The person who defends his observation with the outburst, "What I see is what I know!" is committing a misstatement. We do not know what we see; we require some cognitive form of corroboration, before sense-experience can be transformed into knowledge.

For example, in the case the witness testifies, "I saw that man" (pointing), it is often proper, and may be necessary, to follow that response with a series of queries on the statement with "How do you know. . .?" "How do you know you were not mistaken?" Only in the type of case in which the relevant tests have been actually, or implicitly applied, can a person speak honestly of sense-experience as a matter which "I know."

However, although what I have just written, is a true statement as far as it goes, matters are not quite that simple.

The ability to define reality in a knowledgeable way, free of illusory popular sorts of intuitions, lies in the social relations defined by cognition, rather than in hermetical "Robinson Crusoe" models. It is in the replication of valid discoveries of principle, by one mind in relation to another, that the discoverer becomes *self-conscious of his own cognitive processes,* through their reflection, as the generation of the same idea in the mind of others.

In this reciprocal relationship between two thinkers referencing the same subject of practice, the one recognizes the act of cognition in the other, and anticipates the recognition of the corresponding act of cognition in himself. So, in this reciprocally self-conscious way, the action of cognition is made into an *object* of cognition.

This notion of a *cognitive* form of *self-consciousness,* is the foundation of all competent education in physical science, and the essence of Classical artistic composition and performance.

It is in the ability to share that cognitive discovery of universal principle with others, in a task-oriented way, that real knowledge of the physical universe becomes a subject of conscious intention. It is in the distinguishing of one such idea, from others, of the same cognitive origin, that we are able to distinguish one idea from another one, as a form of existence of ideas, as situated within a social process.

This social aspect of the process of accumulating valid ideas, cognitively, over successive generations, defines what are properly regarded as Classical principles of artistic composition and performance. The validatable principles of Classical artistic composition, also provide the basis for the apprehension of real history and the arts of statecraft. The discovery of the sovereign nation-state, first accomplished during Europe's Fifteenth-Century, Italy-centered Renaissance, is among the most appropriate examples of this relationship between valid methods of Classical artistic composition, as by Leonardo da Vinci and Rafael Sanzio, and statecraft.

For example, a Classical tragedy, such as that of Shakespeare or Schiller, is based on a problem defined by actual or mythical history (such as the Homeric epics) of an historically specific actual setting.[34] Usually, the composition is true-to-life history. The successfully-performed drama on stage provokes the cognitive processes of the audience into recognizing the implicit error, and probable principled solution to that error, in some calamitous situation in history. The application of the critical (cognitive) faculties, to the business of verifying the appropriateness of the dramatic performance, has, then, the function of an experimental test of an hypothesis; if the critical treatment shows the conception generated to be truthful with respect to the principle of actual history so represented, the drama has performed the function of inducing knowledge in the audience, knowledge in the same sense as a validation, in the laboratory, of the claimed discovery of universal physical principle.

Thus, man's mastery of nature, through the progress of physical science, depends upon man's mastery of the develop-

---

34. The case of the work of Schliemann's physical proof of such ostensibly mythical matters as the matter of the *Iliad*'s site of ancient Troy, is of this type.

ment of the social processes within which the unfolding of history and the practice of statecraft are situated. That is the meaning of Classical science, and Classical artistic composition, as expressed, for example, by the 1776 U.S. Declaration of Independence and the 1789 Preamble of the U.S. Federal Constitution.

The quality which separates Classical from Romantic and other vulgar art, is the difference in the quality of emotion which is essential, respectively, to each. In vulgar art, the relevant emotion is, predominantly, sensual effects. In Classical art, it is the cognitive sensation of a "light turning on in the mind." So, in the Passions of J.S. Bach, Christ's Gethsemane decision, is the pivotal feature. In the *St. John Passion,* Bach underscores this by the musical apposition of the hateful cry for Christ's Crucifixion. In the famous Negro Spiritual, "He never said a mumblin' word," it is that "light turning on in the mind" which is the typical referent, in Classical art, for the use of "light," whether in word, or painting. As in Shakespeare's *Othello, There is light, and, then, there is light.*

That "light" of the act of cognitive discovery, or of recognition, is a special quality of passion. That passion is the quality of *movement* in Classical art, and in physical science. This quality of passion, associated with cognitive, rather than deductive-reductionist thinking, is the basis for the emotions described, in thinking about man's physical relationships to the universe, as *motion* and *force* in the universe. In all Classical artistic composition and related thought, this is apprehended as Classical inspiration, and, as the quality of Classical-artistic *action.*[35] These no-

---

35. Here lies the essence of the difference between the Romantic methods, of both composition and performance, of Rameau, Liszt, Berlioz, Wagner, et al., and the Classical methods of composition and performance of Bach, Haydn, Mozart, Beethoven, Schubert, Mendelssohn, Schumann, and Brahms. This is underscored by the way in which that young pupil of the Romantic Czerny, Franz Liszt, went on to attempt, as shown by Liszt's performance transcriptions, even to turn Classical compositions such as Schubert's *Wanderer* Fantasy into Romantic slush. In Classical musical compositions, and their performances, it is the resolution, as of Classical metaphor, of what appear to be contrapuntal dissonances, created by Bachian inversion, which is the distinctive quality of passion in such music.

tions of *inspiration for action,* are the basis for the idea of intention, as Kepler employs precisely that method of Analysis Situs which I have repeatedly referenced here, to focus his own mind's cognitive powers on the matter of intention in the behavior of the orbiting planet and its Solar system.

The "sense-organ," with which the sovereign powers of the individual mind perceive the manifestation of principle in that physical universe within which the individual person exists, is the "organ" of sovereign powers of the individual's cognition. Just as we represent the sense-experience of sight or hearing with the organ by means of which such perceptions are made, we know the manifestations of principle with a different kind of "sense-organ," that of cognition. So, the images of universal physical principle are crafted by the mind according to the requirements of the organ through which such qualities of principle are perceived: the organ of sovereign powers of cognition.

So, for cognition of principle, the notions of "light," "inspiration for action," and "sense of motion," are the qualities expressed by our power to sense the actual universe which has prompted the mere shadows on the dimly-lit cavern wall of sense-perception.

These cognitive experiences have also the quality of willfulness, as contrasted with simple passions of the flesh. It is the sense of the way in which universal physical principle embodies a willful intention, such as that of the orbit of Mars, or the principle of universal gravitation as adduced, originally, by Kepler, which is the essence of scientific thought respecting nature outside man. It is the perception of Classical-artistic forms of discovery and expression of universal principle, which lends the intention and capacity of action given to it by inspiration, which imparts to audiences for that art the will to act in concert for the sake of the good.

So-called abstract, "objective," logical thinking, is the intellectual cosmetician's preparation of the departed for its journey

Furtwängler's "playing between the notes," typifies the method of performance, as opposed to Romantic score-reading for sensual effects, consistent with the Classical world-outlook.

into that mass grave where hoaxster Claudius Ptolemy's astronomy, and many other useless fabrications of the pedant are buried. Without cognitive passion, there is no validatable discovery of universal principle, but only the tomb where Kantians and their like are buried, dwelling in Purgatory, because Hell will not receive the doubly dead.

Like that celebrated calculus-faker, Leibniz-hater Leonhard Euler, and Laplace's protégé and plagiarist Cauchy after him, Clausius, Kelvin, and Grassmann, among relevant others, concocted what became known as three laws of thermodynamics, on the basis of the purely arbitrary, "ivory tower" assumption, that the universe is implicitly the universe of non-living processes as conceived, axiomatically, by the empiricists and their offspring the positivists.

The later, more radical version of the mid-Nineteenth-Century dogma of Clausius, et al., underwent a further moral and intellectual degeneration, into the forms of radical positivism associated with Bertrand Russell and Ernst Mach. Ludwig Boltzmann come to play a leading role in systematizing the dogma of Clausius et al. Russell acolytes Norbert Wiener and John von Neumann, compensated for their expulsion, for incompetence and related offenses, from Hilbert's Göttingen University, by concocting the pseudo-scientific dogmas of "information theory" and "systems analysis," and Boltzmann follower Erwin Schrödinger attempted to degrade the discoveries of Pasteur, Vernadsky, et al., into a dogma not inconsistent with the statistical thermodynamics of Boltzmann.

Thus, today, we have the spectacle of what might be escapees from Jonathan Swift's legendary island of Laputa, promising to create an "artificial intelligence," to replace the human intelligence they have repudiated, and to go to the edge of repudiating life itself, thus to make room on Earth for a proposed proliferation of super-human robots.

With the presently ongoing, epoch-making collapse of the so-called "new economy" based upon such drivel as that of Clausius and his successors, religious adoration of those existentialist Nietzschean supermen called "intelligent robots," will dwindle to the ranks of scattered, Flagellant-like, pathetic bands, as the harsh reality of a need for human intelligence in producing the necessaries of life, will become, once again, predominant.

When we examine the doctrine of Clausius et al., from the vantage-point of considering the axiomatic considerations pervading this present report, that Tower of Babel created by the empiricists and their followers, such as Euler, Laplace, Cauchy, and Clausius, is a self-evident absurdity. These ostensibly human beings assert, as their fundamental, axiomatic assumption, that the universe is created in its entirety, according to a mechanistic sort of implied deductive-reductionist assumption, that "we have yet to discover whether this universe, will or will not, tolerate the existence of life in general, and human life in particular." On recognition of that devastating axiomatic fallacy underlying their entire system of argument, the fallacy of the doctrine of universal entropy should be obvious to all intelligent and reasonably literate adults.

Take the tack opposite to the axiomatic assumptions of those unfortunates. Ask, not whether life is possible, but, rather, what is the nature of the universe, that it brought us into being, and gave us the ability to increase our powers in and over that universe? The argument, expressed as biogeochemistry, by Vernadsky, indicates the direction of the answer to that question which we must ask of ourselves. My own discoveries and related developments in the field of physical economy, enable us today to express what is otherwise implicit in Vernadsky's work, as a basis for shaping policy in and among nations.

The lesser crime of folk such as Euler, Laplace, Cauchy, and Clausius, which is to say, overlooking the evidence of their malicious intentions, is that their focus upon a radical reductionist's deductive scheme for non-living processes, defiantly ignores the Kepler-Leibniz principle of situation (i.e., Analysis Situs). They deny, rather hysterically, the universe within which they themselves exist.

Each orbit of the Solar system within which they exist, has a characteristic, expressed as the notion of an incommensurable number. So, each object of scientific inquiry, is defined by a similar type of characteristic, and thus represents a monad in Leibniz's sense of the term. However, these types of characteristics, although they can be distinguished experimentally, do not have precisely the same value in all situations in which they occur. In practice, the value of their characteristic is adjusted to conform to the *situation/position* in which they lie.

This implies, first, a unique number for the object as such, but, also, a uniquely qualified number locating the existence of that numbered monad within the functional context of its *situation/position*.

Thus, entropy exists as an observed phenomenon within the situation in which it appears. Thus, for Pasteur, Vernadsky, et al., ostensibly inorganic matter behaves differently, as such matter, within a living process as its situation, than in a non-living situation of reference, such as a decaying remain of a living organism, or simply in a situation which is immediately a non-living one. Yet, Vernadsky emphasizes, from the standpoint of biogeochemistry, those natural products of the biosphere which appear as typically non-living material, have an "historic" determination within the development of the biosphere, which is their relevant "historical" situation. Here the folly of Clausius and the dupes who follow him, becomes obvious.

This principle of situation, as I have just referenced it, once again, here, is crucial. The general view to be emphasized, even for laymen generally, is the efficiency with which cognitive processes change the characteristics of the biosphere, and in which living processes (e.g., the biosphere) transform the characteristics of non-living ones, that as Pasteur, Vernadsky, et al., have shown.

3. Physical Economy and Life

To go beyond Vernadsky's mapping of the challenge, to the manner in which mankind may willfully change its ostensible present destiny, we have three interdependent categories to add to Vernadsky's 1938 image of the noösphere.

First, basic economic infrastructure. How must we make the desert bloom? What must we do, beyond the preceding beneficial conditions for human life already provided by the biosphere, to bring the biosphere itself to that higher state of organization required to increase mankind's power to exist in and over the universe? On this point, our argument directly overlaps that of Vernadsky.

Second, the development of those processes of production upon which the maintenance and improvement of human existence at present and improved levels depend.

Third, the constitution of the organization of society, and of the education and general culture of its people, that in ways which make possible the cooperative efforts required to organize society's efforts in ways which are appropriate, for both the needed improvements in basic economic infrastructure, and processes of physical production and distribution of essential goods and services.

The three are suitably combined as a single topic, under the heading of the self-improvement of the reproduction of the demographic characteristics of the human species and its households. The principal measurements are made *per capita* and *per square kilometer* of the normalized cross-section of the biosphere. It is the rate of improvement of those characteristics, which is the focus of measurement of estimated values: i.e., *rate of rate of change* of such values.

I begin by focussing upon the role of basic economic infrastructure as the leading feature of the interface between the noösphere and biosphere. On this point, I include some restatements of what I have stated in locations published earlier.

What Is Basic Economic Infrastructure?

Generically, the term "basic economic infrastructure" should be employed to signify all those improvements in the whole land-area, as land-area, which are required to create the preconditions under which "the desert may bloom." This includes the general development of *transportation, water-management,* and *power systems.* This also includes emphasis on the *development and management of field and forest in ways which increase the rate of conversion of solar radiation into forms of biomass usable in ways which are to the benefit of promoting the maintenance and increase of the productive powers of labor.* Thus, *it includes urban planning and development, in addition to managed fields and managed forests.*

Look at this in the terms Vernadsky defines the relationship between biosphere and noösphere. Now define that relationship in functional terms, first from Vernadsky's standpoint, and, after that, the standpoint of the science of physical economy.

The geological "history" of the Earth, as portrayed from the standpoint of biogeochemistry, indicates that the pattern of apparent evolutionary emergence of species, must focus less on the idea of evolution by species, and more on the way in which the self-development of the biosphere, through accumulation of its natural products (such as atmosphere and oceans), *creates the preconditions on which the emergence of higher types of species depends.* The significance of the emergent species then becomes, primarily, the impact of its existence in changing the characteristics of the biosphere as a whole manifold.

This self-development of the biosphere, as a biosphere-process, came to the point, some unknown quantity of millions of years ago, at which *conditions of the biosphere necessary for the cognitive life-form, man, were sustainable.* Into this image, we must inject the notion of mankind's further transformation of the biosphere, as through what Vernadsky implicitly defines as the *natural products* of noetic (human) life, including cultivated forms of fields and forests, and what we today must recognize as the forerunners of modern basic economic infrastructure.

Suppose, then, that society operates to the effect, that a minority of the total population enjoys the benefits of infrastructural improvements, while the majority does not. Then, the development of the potential productivity of the majority will be crippled. We shall soon return, here, under the heading of the nation-state, to that crucial consideration.

Look at Central Asia today. There are vast areas with abundance of what are called "natural resources," but which are condemned, so far, to be greatly underdeveloped, for lack of the basic economic infrastructure. There, a dense, highly productive population might live. To bring that change about, basic economic infrastructure must be developed to the point that development corridors combining mass transportation, large-scale water-management, and generation and distribution of power, were supplied within development corridors of up to 100 kilometers width. Such a network of emerging corridors would transform much of this sparsely developed region into a rich potential for growth of population and its prosperity.[36]

Moreover, with high-speed (e.g., magnetic levitation) transport of freight across continental Eurasia, from locations such as Rotterdam into Japan, and across the Bering Straits, the efficiency of investment in development of physical production of goods would be greatly increased over the present degree of reliance upon transoceanic freight. Every mile (or, kilometer) of such development corridors more than pays for the cost of building and maintaining such development corridors, a more-than-compensating income experienced in the form of production occurring along each 50 miles or so of the route. This is contrasted with the general lack of production across most of each 50 miles of transoceanic transport. In that sense, because of the increased output and increased productivity it makes possible, a well-developed, and properly explored development corridor, costs the economy much less than a net nothing.

Thus, we must recognize that the superimposition of the noösphere upon the pre-noösphere condition of the biosphere, is not merely something slapped down on top of that biosphere, but, instead, signifies an acceleration of the development within the biosphere as a biosphere, *to the intended effect* of enhancing the preconditions for human development, while also increasing the rate of functional throughput of a biosphere which now includes man and man's activities as part of that biosphere.

I would emphasize the attention of space-scientist Krafft Ehricke to the "industrialization of the Moon," and my extrapolation of that policy, to generating the synthesized natural biosphere-like conditions for a Los Alamos-scale of laboratory-station on Mars. To restate the point: The Solar system developed

---

36. On the European Productive Triangle, see footnote 4. On the Eurasian Land-Bridge, see Jonathan Tennenbaum et al., *The Eurasian Land-Bridge: The 'New Silk Road'—Locomotive for Worldwide Economic Development* (Washington, D.C.: EIR News Service, Inc., January 1997).

Nicholas of Cusa (shown here in a grave monument) defined, in his Concordancia Catholica, *a community of principle among sovereign nation-states; and in his* Docta Ignorantia, *he laid the foundations of modern experimental science.*

Courtesy of Dr. Helmut Gestrich, Cusanus-Gesellschaft

the preconditions for a biosphere's self-development on Earth, in the course of which, the preconditions for human life emerged. In long-term space-exploration, in which men and women stay "in space" for months or longer, we can not rely indefinitely upon so-called "artificial life support." We must utilize the principles of the biosphere, as we learn those lessons from the emergence and maintenance of human life on Earth, to assist us, increasingly, in developing replications of biosphere-like processes "in space."

Therefore, the development of the biosphere was continued, chiefly through what I have described here as basic economic infrastructure, as an integral part of a noösphere which subsumed it. Our continuation of that process of development of the biosphere (under the reign of the noösphere) is a precondition for the emergence of higher levels of human existence. Man, thus, raises the level of development of the biosphere above that achieved by the pre-human biosphere.

Now, thus, the natural products of a biosphere situated within a noösphere, aggregate to a higher level of quality and relative mass than under the "natural" state which might be achieved by the biosphere alone. For example, man-managed forests, if properly managed, are far less prone to devastating forest fires than the forests of an untamed wilderness. For example, the managed distribution and reprocessing of water, makes possible a great increase of the quantity and quality of biomass per square kilometer. For example, looting family farms down to the bone, with Carter-administration-level sub-parity prices paid directly to farmers, turns vast tracts of agricultural and related land-area into Dust Bowls, as occurred in the U.S.A. over the 1920s and early 1930s.

Just as the principle of life intervenes into non-living processes, to change the latter's behavior to the effect we may recognize as the biosphere, so man's cognitive intervention into the development of the biosphere, alters the behavior of the biosphere. In such cases, the subsumed domain's internal laws of behavior of the subject-matter are altered, to the effect Pasteur and others noted in the cases of the fermentation of beer and wine. These changes are measurable, as natural products of life. So, cognition's intervention into the biosphere, redefines biosphere as including those categories of behavior which we recognize as basic economic infrastructure. These changes in the biosphere are measurable ones, and are the preconditions for the maintenance and improvement of human life. They are natural products of the noösphere, and must be so recognized and assessed.

The measurement required, by a science of physical economy, is the *relative rate of increase of the potential population-density of the human population,* taking into account associated improvements in life-expectancy, and improvements in the demographic characteristics of both households and the population in general, their general welfare, as the U.S. Constitution's Preamble specifies that goal to be the inalterable law governing the decisions of our republic.

Production as Such

The standard for measure of productivity is not counted output as such, but, rather, the *relative* rate of increase, stagnation, or decline of the productive powers of labor. This measurement is made in both per-capita and per-square-kilometer terms, and is qualified by the requirement of improvements in the demographic characteristics of family households, and of the population in general. These measurements approximate, and express in that degree, the notion of relative potential population-density. In other words, these are different ways of measuring with fair approximation, the rates of change in the anti-entropy of what Vernadsky defined as the noösphere.

At this point, it is important to forewarn those critics, once more, who might demand a mathematically exact standard of measurement. All important constants in physical science are, by their nature, relative values, and thus ultimately incommensurable. In the topical area of national and world economy, we would warn critics that the value of production, and productivity, considered in the small, varies according to the characteristics of the so-called macro-economic setting in which it is situated. The point of using approximations, is not that our measurements are not sufficiently refined in detail; the point is, that any change in the noösphere in which the economy is situated, alters the functional value to be assigned implicitly to any localized subject-matter.

Take a case from physics in general. There are strong experimental indications, from work conducted by scientists over decades, that what are usually considered universal constants, may not be exactly constant, but may be altered by the impact of radiation from stellar space, and, at least under certain conditions, may be different for materials subsumed within living processes than is to be found among the same species of monad found in non-living processes. Thus, in physical science generally, and in economics more narrowly, we must think of characteristics as being incommensurables in the final analysis, as Kepler did.

The magnitude, the characteristic, we are attempting to measure, at least in a reasonable degree of approximation, is a true characteristic, unique to the orbit or other monad-like existence to which it refers. But, we must never forget, that the universe is not the sum of its parts, but a manifold, which is the context and determinant for the existence of each part. Valid new discoveries will not make a characteristic less characteristic; but the exact number associated with it is never known in the nth degree, and may be subject to some significant modification as the extent of our knowledge of the universe is increased.

In changing the biosphere, as the noösphere's existence does, we are changing the "macroscopic" economic manifold within which each act of production, or other economically significant local action occurs. Thus, all estimates of local economic values of production and related things, are approximations. The distinctions made among local such events may be only approximations, but the estimated relative values have the kind of significance for practical application which the idea of a competent approximation suggests.

The paradigmatic essence of the noösphere, is the act of cognition through which the individual mind generates a valid discovery of universal physical principle. Here lies the essence of the quality of anti-entropy specific to the noösphere, the functional distinction of noösphere from biosphere. *Here lies the key to mankind's unique and specific ability to change the universe.*

The construction of the equivalent of what is called, after Riemann, a *unique* experiment, is not only the indispensable proof of a universal physical principle. It is from the requirements of the design of such an experiment, that what we called *technologies* are spun from scientific discoveries of universal principle. One of the most efficient examples of that, is Wilhelm Weber's unique experimental demonstration of the Ampère angular force principle for electrodynamics. The proof of principle is expressed in the design of the experimental apparatus; conversely, it is from examination of the crucial features of the machine-tooled design of the experimental apparatus, that the feasibility of application of the principle flows.

Thus, in modern economy, especially in connection with what are called "crash" science-driver programs, a close, symbiotic kind of reciprocal relationship should exist among the research scientists, the machine-tool-design functions, and the introduction of the validated technology, through highly skilled development teams, into the processes of product-design and production methods. In such cases, the principal variable in net performance, is the development of a corresponding structure of employment of the total labor-force, such that the "science driver" components and the immediately supporting strata, are an increasing ration of the total employed labor-force.

Thus, a willful up-shift in the composition of categories of occupations and employment in the total labor-force, must be a process of bringing an increasing portion of that labor-force into ever-closer proximity to "pure physical-economic" generation of rapid rates of advances in technology of both production and product design. It would be useful to call that *the sociological principle of anti-entropy in the noösphere.* We shall return to some crucial implications of this same point, but from a different vantage-point, at a slightly later point in this concluding section of my present report.

The development of the accumulation of experimentally validated discoveries of universal physical principles, takes the form of a Riemannian manifold. The addition of new such discoveries, results in the establishment of a new manifold. *It is the implicitly measurable anti-entropy generated by such an unfolding series of manifolds, which is crucial.* The advance of the development of this manifold is the underlying characteristic which drives physical-economic progress as such. However, the relative benefits to an economy depend upon the willingness and ability of the society to utilize the benefit of such discoveries in terms of transformations in employment, product-design, production itself, and also the development of basic economic infrastructure in a manner and degree which these up-shifts in the technological potential require for their effective implementation in production and distribution.

For example, on the matter of infrastructure. Take, first, the case of power. The ability to realize the benefits of valid discoveries of universal principle, and of related technologies, generally requires an increase in not only the energy-output per capita and per square kilometer, but also such qualitative improvements as increased energy-flux density, and coherent organization of the energy-flows in distribution and application.

In the case of water management, the amount of water throughput required, per capita and per square kilometer, increases. This requirement can be satisfied only by aid of increasingly sophisticated methods of desalination and reprocessing of water.

In transport of freight, the ability to balance the relationship between inventories of work in progress, and of final product, requires the kind of revolutionary improvements in transportation which builds freight-classification and related matters of delivery and inventory management into the inherent characteristics of the system. The use of magnetic levitation transport for passengers, is impressive; but should not obscure the fact that the potential benefits in terms of freight handling and related matters, are far more impressive economically than faster transport of passengers.

In the notion of urban infrastructure, it should be easily recognized by persons with even ordinary literacy, that the way in which cities have been transformed during the post-World War II period to date, has been increasingly catastrophic in its projectable medium- to long-term effects. The way in which "suburbanism" was pushed, as with New York's Levittown, or the use of what had been launched, for the nuclear-weapons age, as the national defense highway system, to extract suburbanite ground-rent from former cow-pastures and the like, has been economically, socially, and morally counterproductive, in a very large degree.

Commuters travel further and further. Social life, in the household, and otherwise, deteriorates accordingly. Cities should be built from the subsurface, upward, with principal features of the substructure and other structures intended to remain functional for hundreds of years to come. Given the condition of economic and related rot which has been accumulating inside the U.S.A. and other parts of the world, during, especially, the recent thirty-five-odd years, we are not presently positioned to implement the kind of technological revolution in urban designs to which reason would already point us today. Sometimes, when we have a serious problem, in life, in a nation's economy, we lack the means to make the obvious corrections; but, experience shows, that being aware of the problem, which we might not have the present means to correct entirely, warns us against continuing the undesirable trend, and orients us toward launching the new trends required for the benefit of coming generations, and the national interest, otherwise defined, as a whole.

The Modern Nation-State

The evidence is clear. The greatest rate of improvement of the conditions of life of humanity ever recorded, came as a result of developments within Europe's Fifteenth-Century Renaissance. [see **Figure 9,** p. 248, this volume] Through the intertwined role of France's Jeanne d'Arc, the great ecumenical Council of Florence, King Louis XI's founding of the first modern sovereign nation-state, and a similar revolutionary role played by Richmond (Henry VII) in England, a new kind of political institution was created in Europe at that time. This was the principle, that *no government has the moral authority to govern, except as it is efficiently committed to promoting the general welfare of all of the population and its posterity.* This led to the later Eighteenth-Century founding of the first true modern sovereign nation-state republic, that of the U.S.A., during the interval 1776-1789. I have addressed this matter, in numerous publications and public addresses delivered over a span of decades. It is necessary to summarize some of that material again, here, in order to make a clear point.

All cultures in known history, prior to that Fifteenth-Century revolution in the practice of statecraft, were like the imperial tyrannies spawned in ancient Mesopotamia. They were of a form consistent with what Classical Greek writers knew as the *oligarchical model.* In this general class of types of societies, a relative few, a ruling caste, or oligarchy, aided by a retinue of armed and other lackeys, ruled over the majority of their own and other people, degrading those over whom they ruled to the condition of wild or herded human cattle. The oligarchy variously hunted, herded, bred, and culled those herds, as a farmer takes wild game from the field and forests, and culls his herd of those specimens considered too independent in their impulses, or an excess or otherwise undesirable portion of the total population. Such was ancient Babylon, such was the Sparta designed, like Rome after it, by the Delphi cult of the Pythian Apollo.

This was the condition of mankind under the Roman Empire, both in the West and in Byzantium. This was the condition, as specified by the Code of the Roman Emperor Diocletian, which became the backbone of what passed for law under European feudalism.

Although the idea of the republic was well defined by Plato, and although the fundamental principle of U.S. constitutional law, the so-called "general welfare" clause, was inherent in Christianity, the struggles to bring about a just society, so constituted, were frustrated until Europe's Fifteenth-Century revolution in statecraft, a revolution summed up by two influential writings of that period, by Nicholas of Cusa: his *Concordancia Catholica,* defining a community of principle among sovereign nation-states, and his *De Docta Ignorantia,* the founding work of modern experimental science. It was Cusa and his immediate circles, who prepared the way for, and inspired, voyages such as that of Christopher Columbus, and launched the evangelization carried into such places as the Americas.

During the interval from the period of the Second and Fourth Crusades, and continuing into late during the Seventeenth Century, Venice emerged as the chief enemy of the attempt to develop the modern nation-state. This was the Venice which had emerged from those Crusades as an imperial maritime power, throughout the Mediterranean littoral and Europe generally. In the effort to abort the development of the sovereign nation-state and the new quality of culture it represented, Venice drowned Europe in repeated religious wars over the interval 1511-1648, concluding with the 1618-1648 Thirty Years' War.

Under these conditions of the 1511-1648 interval, and still later, more and more of the republican leaders in Europe looked to the Americas as a place to build up colonies which could be developed into sovereign nation-state republics. There were frustrated, if often heroic efforts to that purpose among the independence movements of Central and South America, but only in the United States was a true such republic established. The 1776 Declaration of Independence and 1789 Preamble of the U.S. Federal Constitution typify this connection to the Fifteenth-Century Renaissance.

Ours was an embattled republic from the beginning. With the July 14, 1789 storming of the Paris Bastille by those who had been or were the agents of London's Lord Shelburne and Jeremy Bentham, France, the U.S.A.'s chief ally of the 1776-1783 War of Independence, fell into the 1789-1794 Jacobin Terror, and, thence, under the reign of Barras and the first modern fascist, Napoleon Bonaparte.[37] With the outcome of the Congress of Vienna, the U.S.A. was isolated and imperilled, from without (from London and the Holy Alliance) and from the American Tories among financier and slaveholder interests within. Then a great protégé of former President John Quincy Adams, President Abraham Lincoln, defeated Britain's Confederacy puppets in the Civil War, and, in concert with Henry C. Carey, launched the great agro-industrial development which established the U.S. economy as the most powerful, and technologically most advanced among nation-states of the world. This established *the American System of political-economy,* of Alexander Hamilton, Mathew Carey, Friedrich List, and Henry C. Carey, as the best form of economic policy existing among the nations of the world.

With the 1901 assassination of President William McKinley, the government of the U.S. fell into hands associated with two unrepentant heirs of the Confederacy, Presidents Theodore Roosevelt, and overt Ku Klux Klan fanatic Woodrow Wilson. Presi-

---

37. The self-defined "new Caesar," Napoleon was the model copied by Mussolini, Hitler, and other fascists of the post-Versailles decades. The model for modern fascism was prescribed by Bonaparte enthusiast, and sometime Metternich agent, Prussia's state philosopher G.W.F. Hegel. Although Karl Savigny was influenced by and sympathetic to Hegel, the most consistent follower of Hegel was the Carl Schmitt on whose Hegelian doctrine of law, and included theory of the state, the enactment of the decree of February 18, 1933, establishing the Nazi dictatorship, was premised.

dent Coolidge was no better. Under the conditions of a great economic crisis and the onrushing threat of a new world war, President Franklin Roosevelt returned the U.S., for a while, to the American intellectual tradition expressed in its Declaration of Independence and the Preamble of its Federal Constitution. Nixon's Southern Strategy campaign of 1966-1968 marked the turn leading into a return to the reign of neo-Confederacy ideologies and practices of Teddy Roosevelt, Woodrow Wilson, and Coolidge, within the top ranks of both leading political parties.

Throughout its history to date, that American intellectual tradition has been inseparable from an ecumenical foreign policy. It was so with Benjamin Franklin. This was expressed by the 1823 Monroe Doctrine crafted by the Franklin-trained John Quincy Adams; it was the heritage of Abraham Lincoln, and the theme of Franklin Roosevelt's "Good Neighbor" policy and President John F. Kennedy's "Alliance for Progress." Nixon's Secretary of State Henry A. Kissinger typifies those who, out of their own mouths, have been consistently on the opposite side.

That summary overview thus supplied, now focus upon those axiomatic features of the sovereign form of modern nation-state which account for its vast superiority over all earlier cultures in promoting the general welfare of mankind.

The functional distinction of the sovereign form of modern nation-state republic, is that it ends the subjugation of the majority of the population to the status of virtual human cattle. It is the shaping of economic and related policies according to that intention, which imposes upon government the responsibilities for: a) protecting the national economic development, as measured in per-capita and per square-kilometer terms; b) the promotion of the development of the basic economic infrastructure of the national territory as a whole; and, c) the promotion of scientific progress and use of the technologies so derived, to promote the advancement of the productive powers of labor of all of the households of which the population is composed.

It was the approximation of such measures, under Louis XI, which resulted in the virtual doubling of the national income of France under the few decades of his reign. The electrifying transformation of England, under Henry VII, is a comparable case. It was these and related policies, derived from the axiomatic features given authority during the Fifteenth-Century Renaissance, which embedded in the impact of those radiated features of the modern sovereign form of nation-state, the impetus for its unprecedented effect of improving qualitatively the demographic conditions of life of populations.

In all of this, the essential point is, the promotion of the development and application of the individual person's cognitive powers, both in terms of science and technology, and in the cultural activities properly classed under the heading of principles of Classical artistic composition.

As is typical of the way in which the United States has been self-destroyed under the influence of existentialist degenerates such as Theodor Adorno and Hannah Arendt, the greatest crime which recent decades have perpetrated upon the families of the U.S.A., is far less the oppression of their bodies, than the degree of success in destroying their souls. By denying the existence of knowable truth, that in favor of mere opinion, and rejecting the Socratic methods by which the individual may discover truth, and by imposing methods of classroom and related education, which emphasize the sensual, as opposed to the cognitive, the mental powers, and morals of the population have been greatly undermined, where they have not been yet destroyed.

It is the eflorescence of Classical education and practice in science and art, which nourishes what becomes both the productive potential of the population, and its inclination to cooperate in bringing related improvements in the material and cultural conditions of life into general practice. The human individual is naturally creative; that distinguishes him, or her, from the beasts. That is the quality of that individual, which, if evoked and encouraged, is the source of upward tracks of revolutionary improvements in the condition of mankind. That, which Plato and the Apostle Paul would identify as the principle of *agapē*, is the power of mankind to change the universe.

Main lines of a worldwide raid network, from the Executive Intelligence Review *Special Report on the Eurasian Land-Bridge. This map, drawn by H.A. Cooper, shows the rail lines involved in full realization of the Land-Bridge concept of development corridors associated with transportation routes.*

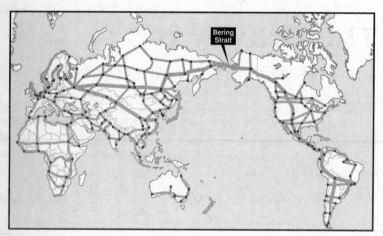

Bering Strait

"There must be a virtual explosion of scientific progress, and technological progress driven by scientific progress, to the effect of increasing the rate of technological gain greatly beyond that which would be possible with the off-the-shelf-plus strategies.

"This means, that the potential volcanoes of large-scale technology export, such as the U.S., Western Europe, Russia, a resuscitated Korea, and Japan, must cooperate with other nations in creating a virtual new category of employment: 'crash-science-driver-program' employment.'"

The Gravity of Economic Intentions

March 10, 2001

This piece first appeared in the March 30, 2001 issue of Executive Intelligence Review *magazine.*

THE PRESENTLY ONGOING crash of the world's present financial system, defines a breaking-point in the century of the preceding, post-McKinley-assassination, cultural and political history of our planet as a whole.[1] The fact, that the present financial system is beyond saving, requires our acceptance of the available new system waiting in the wings. In that new system, economic policy is no longer controlled by the financial system, but is coming under the influence of an axiomatic change, in which financial systems become merely useful, and dutiful appendages of a new quality of a global system of national economies, economies modelled upon the precedent of that American System of political-economy, as Hamilton, List, and Carey defined the notion of national economy.

Either the world accepts that proposed, admittedly radical change, and very soon, or, the likely alternative is the plunge of

_____
1. On the significance of the McKinley assassination, see Lyndon H. LaRouche, Jr., on this subject, in, among other locations, "As Seen and Said by the Salton Sea," *EIR,* Feb. 16, 2001, pp. 29-30.

the planet into a spiral of economic and demographic collapse, what is fairly described as a new dark age. Any effort to defend the present financial system, as opposed to the needed, sudden change, will only make the present world economic situation catastrophically worse than if no such rescue operation had been attempted.

Under the needed new system, which must be adopted suddenly and soon, the emphasis will be on physical economy, as I have defined today's applicable meaning of what Gottfried Leibniz named physical economy. That definition shall be the new point of reference for thinking about all matters of both public policy and private economic practice. Money and financial systems will no longer have any self-evident axiomatic authority, but will be subordinated to perform their necessary functions as the disposable tissues of real economy, physical economy.

Most of the elements of that new and far better world society already exist, waiting to be rescued and nourished to strength, once they begin to arise out from amid the rubble of the hopelessly doomed present financial system.

In all really important developments in history, things are never really what traditional ways of thinking have been able to recognize up to that point. The popular mind clings desperately to its old ways of thinking, up to the proverbial last minute, or even beyond that, and attempts, desperately, even hysterically, to interpret the existence of the crisis-elements of a radically changed, new situation, as a continuation of the doomed old, habitual ways.

Yet, recognized or not, the new reality is lurking, waiting to be called on stage, and will rule a new and happier phase in world history, on condition that the threatened dark age is prevented.

If a successful emergence of the new, from the carcass of the old, is to occur, it will emerge as a new form of a society becoming self-conscious of its distinctive nature, its people smiling wryly at the habits of thinking of the virtually illiterate cultural savages they still were at the time the relevant, most recent existential crisis erupted. Those U.S. citizens old enough to recall the profound change in generally accepted "values," which occurred as the Roosevelt recovery superseded the Coolidge depression, may recognize the type of social change in values I have just identified.

The developments of the most recent weeks, since the abortive U.S. Presidential election events of November 7, 2000, have changed the world. The things I have been saying for decades, are not merely demonstrated to have been true, but the entry of the world's financial crisis into its present terminal phase, during the recent sixty- odd days, has created a new situation, in which a number of those things which I have stated earlier, and which remain true, must be now, once again, restated, this time in light of the present moment's radically changed world situation. The world is now gripped by a fundamental phase-shift, in which, as is usual for such a situation, things which remain true, must be restated in a qualitatively new context, and, therefore, a correspondingly new way.

Some of those things which need be restated so, include the contents of a recently published book, *Now, Are You Ready To Learn Economics?*, which contains some crucially important reports on the background to the current situation, which I presented during the course of the last year.[2] What I have said in those and other locations during the recent months and years, not only remains true, but present events have made it more relevant than ever before. Nonetheless, as you will find in these present pages, last year's concepts must be presented today in a fresh way, as the profoundly more critical immediate situation of the past sixty-odd days demands.

That said, the subject of this report, is a crucial feature of those radical revisions in U.S. financial and economic policies, which are required, not only to overcome the presently accelerat-

---

2. (Washington, D.C.: EIR News Service, Inc., 2000). *EIR* has never been produced to be something thrown away, like yesterday's newsweekly; it has been designed to be kept on file, as a living record of the crucial conceptual developments of the decades, since March 1974, when it was founded. My own featured contributions to those pages, during the recent half-dozen years, are of outstanding relevance to the present situation, on that account.

ing plunge toward a deep world-wide economic depression, but to lay the foundations for the new renaissance of America, in which economics rules over finance, a new type of thinking, which must replace the presently collapsing system. The issue on which I concentrate here, is the unfortunately little understood, but *presently crucial dependency of short-term recovery measures upon an immediate issue of long-term credits for building up basic economic infrastructure and capital-intensive increase of the productive powers of labor.*

Any successful attack upon those problems, whose outcome will determine the future of mankind, must focus clearly upon certain matters of which most economists, journalists, and related policy-influencers are ignorant at this moment. Now, since world events have shown that my long-range forecasts have been consistently correct, and all those of opposing views profoundly misguided, there is a correspondingly increased likelihood, that among those who have previously refused to listen, some will now not only pay more careful attention to what I say on these matters, but actually go through the cognitive processes of knowing what I say, rather than displaying a common gossip's Pavlovian conditioned-reflex reactions to, perhaps, the mere mention of my name.

The citizen must now finally face and accept the fact, that the presently ongoing, general collapse of the present world financial and monetary systems, is the product of more than thirty years of widespread professional and popular acceptance of beliefs which are fundamentally contrary to scientific principle. For example, as a matter of principle, Jean-Baptiste Colbert and Alexander Hamilton were right, and Dr. François Quesnay, Bernard de Mandeville, and Adam Smith, typify those perniciously false, but popularized ideas, whose influence on both high places and popular opinion, has misled the world into the present global catastrophe. In these pages, I concentrate attention on that issue of principles first, and turn, in the concluding portion of this report, to the techniques for those principles' application.

The point which I shall bring into focus, in the conclusion of this report, is that, the central feature of any effective long-term economic-recovery program for today, will be the role which *a series of "crash program" types of science-driver programs, of accelerated scientific discovery and technological change,* must contribute, if the world's population is to escape *a long-term economic catastrophe already built into the current state of combined technological underdevelopment and attrition, of the world at large.*

This poses a profound, and most unsettling intellectual challenge to the present generations of the world's economists and related policy-shapers. The question thus posed is: What *intentions* must be adopted now, to guide the world's day-to-day policy-shaping in those new directions, which will foster achieving the needed growth in the world's productive powers of labor, ten, twenty, thirty years ahead?[3] What choices of medium- to long-term effects must we project, more or less reliably, from the decisions we make today?

The most important choice, is to know those principles. After that, it is most important to know the methods by which our nation will be able to forecast those types of reasonably estimated orders of magnitude of medium-term to long-term improvement in per-capita productivity, which may be the best result of the adopted use of those principles. As a necessary, preliminary step, begin here with a review of the role of the calculus in estimating economic progress.

1. Actually Knowing the Calculus

The mathematical conception of that problem of economic policy which I have just identified, depends upon competent understanding of the actual nature of Gottfried Leibniz's discovery of the differential and integral calculus, not only in contrast to the pseudo-calculus of Isaac Newton, but also the rejection of that linear perversion of the Leibniz calculus itself, which has been passed down to today's typical modern classrooms, from

3. On the subject of "intention," compare Lyndon H. LaRouche, Jr., "The FDR Economic Recovery: Precedent and Practice," Berlin address, March 5, 2001, published in *EIR*, March 16, 2001.

the hateful work of such fanatical empiricists as Leonhard Euler and Augustin Cauchy.

The crucial point at issue, in defining the calculus to such effect, is the quality of *intention,* which the founder of modern mathematical physics, Johannes Kepler, embodied as the centrally underlying universal physical principle of astrophysics.[4] It is that quality of *intention,* which Euler, Cauchy, et al., removed from the calculus, to produce, thus, their mutilated version of it.

The contemporary economist who has not mastered the rudiments of this issue, is not yet qualified to judge what might, or might not be competent economic-recovery policies for today's situation.

The awful truth to bear in mind, is that the Americas and Europe would not have fallen into the present catastrophe, which has been building up over the recent thirty-odd years, had the varieties of doctrines of economics taught in universities not been, chiefly, systemically incompetent ones. Which among them warned of the present crisis, and described its unfolding, consistently, over more than three decades, in precisely the way it has occurred? Which knew what they were doing? Which foresaw the now painfully manifest effects of what they were doing? Let that record of the economy's presently wretched performance be finally heard, speaking for itself.

---

4. It will be made implicitly clear, in the course of this present report, that the effect of the adoption of those "ivory tower" delusions of Aristotle's system which motivated Claudius Ptolemy's hoax, and the impact of both Paolo Sarpi's neo-Ockhamite empiricist dogma and the even more demented practices of the positivists, all have the common effect, of banning the consideration of the causal function of universal physical principles from their systems. Linearization of the Leibniz calculus, as by Euler's dogma, or Cauchy, eliminates the consideration of actual physical cause, *intention,* from the calculations. For example, Galileo made no original discovery, but simply followed the empiricist dogma created by his master, Paolo Sarpi. Thus, the fraud of the modern defense of Galileo from the Inquisition, is that Galileo used the same method as the Aristotelean Ptolemy, to reach a conclusion, as an empiricist, which was arbitrarily opposite to that of Ptolemy's dupes, but based on the same violation of truthfulness as that of the Aristotelean defenders of Ptolemy's hoax.

The explanation of the causes for today's general, systemic failure in the performance of the economists, bankers, and governments generally, must, of necessity, lie in study of those generally accepted beliefs, which were taught in the universities which graduated the relevant professionals. These are the same beliefs also purveyed, as contemporary, credulous popular opinion, by the so-called "Establishment's" customarily lying, mass media. The ideological source of most of the systemic errors, in the teaching of many subjects, is those same sets of axiomatic beliefs, respecting mathematics, which underlie today's commonplace teaching and professional practice in accounting and economics, among many other topics.

The most crippling root-error in the prevalent, contemporary teaching and practice of mathematics, not only among students of economics, but in physical science in general, has been a literally hysterical refusal to acknowledge that basis, in the combined work of Johannes Kepler and Pierre Fermat, most immediately, upon which Gottfried Leibniz's development of the calculus was developed. Had those students taken the opportunity to study the relevant primary sources in the history of modern science, rather than swallowing the generally accepted classroom and textbook gossip, they would have already known the key point I make here.

This lack of this indispensable knowledge, even among many of the most senior physical scientists of today, is chiefly a reflection of pure ideological stubbornness, often veering into hysteria, among the relevant educational institutions and the Babylonian-like peer-review priesthood of the tradecraft's journals. The way in which most university graduates, and others, have been induced to believe the popularly taught errors on this account, is through the cultivation of their fear of that perceived risk to their careers, or simply their reputations among their neighbors and friends, or with the local newspaper editor, if they were overhead saying anything which deviates from what they consider it advantageous to be overheard saying.

Fortunately, the core-problem being addressed at this immediate point in my report, is one within the intellectual reach of any of recent generations of secondary-school students who have been exposed to even a semblance of competent methods of classroom instruction. We focus on that issue of scientific method here, only insofar as that is indispensable for understanding the economic-policy issues immediately at hand. Broader treatment of that scientific question, is left to relevant occasions.

On this account, I encouraged my associate Bruce Director to present an approximately one-hour, video-recorded presentation of the core of Kepler's discovery, as delivered to a recent national conference held in Reston, Virginia.[5] Although this issue had been rather thoroughly addressed, by me and by my collaborators, over earlier decades, to get the same point across to a broader audience, it was pedagogically necessary, given the victimization of recent generations by prevalent, poor standards of contemporary public and higher education, to present the experimental material in the form of animated illustrations, rather than only the otherwise adequate, literary description of the motion to be associated with static images.

A video recording of that approximately one-hour session is being produced. I have proposed that an updated version of that be produced, adding about a quarter-hour, to include a clearer demonstration of that common principle which led to Leibniz's original development of a calculus, and underlay both Kepler's discovery of the principle of universal gravitation, and Fermat's discovery of the concept of a physical principle of "quickest time." I have requested, that an expanded series of such pedagogical exercises be developed and circulated as a much-needed, standard tactic of education in the elementary principles of both physical science and economic policy-shaping.

It is my wish, that the reader should have available a copy of that referenced videotape, either in the form presented at that conference, or the amended version scheduled for later presentation.[6] Here, I limit myself, as much as is tolerable, to summarizing those selected, crucial issues of immediate relevance to the subject

---

5. Presidents' Day Conference of the Schiller Institute and International Caucus of Labor Committees (ICLC), Reston, Virginia, Feb. 17-18, 2001.

6. Call 1-888-EIR-3258 (toll-free) for ordering information.

of economics. To situate the discussion, I summarize the immediately relevant historical background as follows.

Kepler and the Orbit of Mars

The scientific knowledge, that the Earth orbits the Sun, was already well established knowledge within Plato's Academy, prior to the ideologically motivated hoax crafted by the Roman Empire's Claudius Ptolemy. Blind faith in the so-called Ptolemaic system, persisted even in modern European civilization, as recently as the Seventeenth Century, willfully misrepresenting Earth as a fixed point in the universe. This Ptolemaic doctrine was a purely ideological concoction, introduced to bring the teaching of astronomy into conformity with Aristotle. The characteristic feature of that hoax by Ptolemy, is the assumption that science must be limited to abstract deductive concoctions, such as formal mathematical schemes, with no effort to discover the physical causes for action in the universe.[7] That same error has been continued, in an even more vicious version, and pervasively, by the modern empiricists and logical positivists.

In modern times, the evidence that the Earth moves with respect to the Sun, had been shown by the Fifteenth-Century founder of modern experimental science, Cardinal Nicholas of Cusa.[8] It was a follower of the work of Cusa and Leonardo da Vinci, Johannes Kepler, who settled the issues scientifically, with his original discovery of a principle of universal gravitation, as detailed in his *New Astronomy*,[9] and also the general law for configuration of the Solar System, in his *The Harmony of the*

---

7. Modern empiricism, such as that of Galileo, Hobbes, and Newton, is Ockham follower Paolo Sarpi's vulgarization of Aristotelean method; logical positivism, is simply empiricism vulgarized in the extreme. Notably, the exact same "ivory tower" foolishness of the Aristoteleans and empiricists, underlies the argument of the followers of Thomas Hobbes, John Locke, François Quesnay (*laissez-faire*), the pro-satanic Bernard de Mandeville, and Adam Smith, in social theory and economics.

8. E.g., *De Docta Ignorantia*.

9. Johannes Kepler, *New Astronomy* (1609), William Donahue, trans. (Cambridge: Cambridge University Press, 1992).

World.[10] Kepler's crucial accomplishment in this matter, was his empirical demonstration of the incompetence of the statistical method employed for mapping observations of the orbits, by Ptolemy, Copernicus, and Tycho Brahe.

The proof of Copernicus' and Brahe's error, subsumed Kepler's discovery of both a universal principle of gravitation, and also, the related harmonic composition of the Solar system's planetary orbits. The relevance of this to a physical science of economics, is that which I have underlined in a previous publication.[11] As I stressed in that earlier publication, as in my Berlin Address of March 5, the common feature of the physical sciences of astronomy and economics, is the principle of *intention*.

Kepler's solution for defining an elliptical, or approximately elliptical, orbital pathway of Mars (and other planets), was, in first approximation, his adducing the controlling feature determining the combined position and change of velocity of such a non-uniform curvature, according to equality of the area of the angle swept from the relevant focus of the ellipse. That ratio implies the integral value of the orbit as a whole. By adducing the musical-harmonic values of the orbit so defined, and comparing those values for the principal planets considered, Kepler also defined the planetary system, including the specification of a required former planet occupying a harmonic position later shown to correspond to the mass of planetary fragments known, since the work of Gauss, as the asteroid belt.

Thus, in first approximation, the combination of the equal-areas principle respecting each planet, and the harmonic characteristics among those orbits, defined a controlling intention of both the planet individually, and the relative pathways of each orbit within the system as a whole. This combination of conditions which the planetary orbit must satisfy, to reach the next position in a pathway of non-uniform curvature, represented the

---

10. *The Harmony of the World,* E.J. Eiton, A.M. Duncan, and J.V. Field, trans. (Philadelphia: The American Philosophical Society, 1997).

11. Lyndon H. LaRouche, Jr., "A Philosophy for Victory: Can We Change the Universe?" see above, p. 99.

intention which controls such an orbit, as a regular mathematical trajectory could not, prior to Kepler's work.

Such controlling intentions are also called *universal physical principles*. The planet acts as if it were governed by a conscious intention to satisfy those conditions; that intention is otherwise to be recognized as an efficient principle, which acts constantly upon the entire domain in which the action is occurring. That is the simplest of the truthful definitions of a universal physical principle.

From these considerations, Kepler adduced his discovery of such a principle, known as *universal gravitation,* including what are mistakenly identified by empiricists as "Kepler's three laws."[12] Kepler's relative success on these accounts, implied the need to supersede what were then generally taught ideas about mathematics, by a new kind of mathematics, one suited for dealing with those physical processes which, like the Solar system, could only be described mathematically as pathways of action with non-uniform curvature. Kepler's relegation of the task of addressing that problem to "future mathematicians," prompted the discovery and initial development of the calculus by Gottfried Leibniz.

This Leibniz calculus employed the concept of the smallest interval of action, as *not* reducible to a straight-line pathway between dots, but a trajectory of categorically non-uniform curvature.[13] It is that view of the calculus, as situated within the

---

12. The attempt to reduce Kepler's discovery of universal gravitation, as by the followers of Newton, to the so-called "Three Laws," must be recognized for what it is. In order to detour around the crucial issue posed by non-uniform orbital curvatures, the attempt was made to represent the notion of a universal physical principle as an empirically manifest *intention*. To that latter purpose, the effect of intention was described, by a true believer in the reductionist schemes of Aristotle and Galileo's master Paolo Sarpi. It is that fraudulent description which is responsible for the three-body paradox of Newton et al.

13. Thus, explicitly contrary to the argument against the monadology by Leonhard Euler, and contrary to the vulgarization of the Leibniz calculus by Augustin Cauchy.

190 LYNDON H. LAROUCHE, JR.

context of the Leibniz monadology, which was lost to most modern classrooms, lost through the intervention of empiricists working in the vein of Euler, Lagrange, Cauchy, Clausius, Grassmann, et al.[14] It is the quality of *intention,* as Kepler defines the notion, which distinguishes Leibniz's related notions of a principle of least action and a monadology, from the reductionist fantasies of an Aristotle, or the empiricists and positivists.

The significance of the Leibniz calculus were better appreciated, when we consider how much the progress of modern experimental science owes to the application of intense rigor to the treatment of what are *relatively tiny, but also globally significant, measurably characteristic differences in long-range effects.* This is the *universally characteristic* feature of the work leading to the founding of modern astrophysics, and the discovery of universal gravitation by Kepler. This, as I shall emphasize in this report, is the key to forecasting the long-range effects of current economic policy.

This focus of experimental method, on seemingly tiny, but persistent margins of deviation from the predictions of some pre-existing standard theory, is the history of the development of the notion of the relativity of physical time, from the discovery of a principle of "quickest time," by Fermat, through the development of this notion through the combined work of Huyghens, Leibniz, and Bernoulli. Similarly, we have the case of the proof of the folly of Isaac Newton's doctrine on light, as Arago's experimental apparatus proved the case for Fresnel's argument.

In partial, first approximation, Kepler's measured trajectory of the Mars orbit, defines the intention of that planet's motion, by the notion that equal areas are swept, in equal time, by the radius of one of the two foci of the ellipse. In Leibniz's hands, that expressed intention of the orbit assumes the form of the non-linear differential of the Leibniz calculus, the form of *non-uniform curvature.* To locate the orbits among the planets, one must refine the differential, in accord with the tuning of the orbital harmonics. Thus, the case of Kepler's determination of

---

14. LaRouche, op. cit.

the existence of a missing orbit of a planet, later discovered to be the asteroid belt, which must have formerly existed, is crucial experimental physical proof of the validity of both the Kepler conception as a whole, and also the implications which Leibniz adduced for mathematics from Kepler's challenge to "future mathematicians."

In the same vein, the successive contributions to the mathematics of a multiply-connected manifold, by Carl Gauss and Bernhard Riemann, provide us today the needed framework of conceptual reference to deal with the evidence showing that life is itself a universal physical principle, existing independently of principles adduced from only non-living processes. Finally, in this same vein, my own original work, in the science of physical economy, enables us today to subsume the notion of a noösphere, as that was defined by Vladimir Vernadsky, within a generalized macroeconomic conception.[15]

These immediately preceding observations bring us to defining the physical significance of a notion of *intention,* as Kepler employs that for his principal discoveries in astrophysics (and also other cases), and as I emphasize the same notion, as key for long-range forecasting, in the science of physical economy.

The significance of very small margins of difference, is shown most dramatically, by the argument of Vernadsky for the biosphere. The development of the atmosphere, oceans, and so on, by the action of life, over billions of years, corresponds to a major change in the non-living planet, through the cumulative, marginally small, momentary action of life as a universal physical principle. To make clear the significance of the term "universal physical principle," as the empirical evidence of biogeochemistry attests, we must recognize that life, as a category of universal physical principle, is characterized by its expression of an inten-

15. It was from the standpoint of this view of living processes, that I developed my original discoveries in the science of physical economy, during the course of work of the 1948-1952 interval. The explicit adoption of Vernadsky's conception of the noösphere, occurred first in my letter of March 1973, leading to the subsequent founding of the Fusion Energy Foundation. See LaRouche, op. cit.

Fermat's Principle Of Least Time

When a ray of light passes from air into water, the light ray is bent. In the illustration, AB is the light ray in air, BC, the new direction of the ray after it enters the water. When the ray passes from a less dense to a more dense medium, it always bends towards the normal (perpendicular) to the surface, but the angle depends upon the density of the medium it is entering.

In 1661, a French philosopher and mathematician, Pierre de Fermat, proved that the light bends at such an angle that it always traverses the path from A to C in the least time. This is Fermat's celebrated *Principle of Least Time,* which he hypothesized to be a universal law of nature ("Nature always acts by the shortest course").

The following consideration might aid in understanding it. Suppose a lifeguard, standing at A, must rescue a drowning swimmer at C. What is his fastest path? As he can run faster than he can swim, to run directly to the water at D, and swim to C would maximize the time spent in the water; it would thus be the slowest path. However, to run all the way to E, and then plunge into the water, while giving him the shortest path through water, would not minimize his time. The path of least time, is to run to an intermediate point B, and then swim a slightly diagonal course to C. To calculate where the precise point B lies, which will minimize his time, might require a course in optics followed by some calculations, which we hope the lifeguard does not pause to carry out.

tion which we recognize as making the difference between living and non-living forms of organization.

The actions of human cognition, over millions of years, resulting in the emergence of major changes in the biosphere, include the development of the biosphere to a degree not possible without the cumulative, momentarily tiny, but nonetheless efficient effects of cognitive action. The principle of cognition, like the categorical principle of life, similarly, expresses an intention,

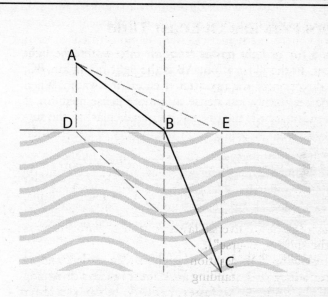

Now, consider the light beam, aimed at the point A. When it enters into the water, it will bend at precisely the correct angle, such that, when it reaches C, its total path from A to C will have been completed in the least time. How could the light ray "know" to do that? If Fermat's principle is correct, it is *as if he were attributing a will* to the light ray. So, argued the opponents of Fermat, including the prominent Cartesian, Clerselier, who concluded on this basis that Fermat's Principle must be wrong. But it is not! In this way Fermat's Principle elegantly illustrates the concept of *intent* in nature.—*Laurence Hecht*

an intention which is otherwise identified by a strict use of the term *reason*.

In each of the three key instances referenced, Kepler's discovery of universal gravitation, and Vernadsky's definitions of the biosphere and of the noösphere, we have often a relatively very small margin of deviation from what would otherwise be defined as mathematically uniform curvature. This difference is identified by Kepler as corresponding to a margin of *intention*,

intention in the sense of action directed by a cognitive mind. In the practice of physical science, experimental physical science as distinct from mere mathematics, such demonstrated cases of *intention* always identify the proof on which the discovery of some universal physical principle depends. The term *intention*, so employed in the sense of Kepler's argument, is equivalent to all proper use of the term *universal physical principle*.

With Bernhard Riemann's 1854 habilitation dissertation, all arbitrary definitions, axioms, and postulates of a formal mathematics, such as customary classroom teaching of Euclidean geometry, are banned from science.[16] They are replaced only by experimentally validated universal physical principles. Each such principle, expressed as an efficient intention, corresponds to a "dimension" of a Riemannian multiply-connected manifold.

In Vernadsky's noösphere, as in the Platonic universe known to the experimental work of Kepler, there are three multiply-connected categories of universal physical principle: a) non-living; b) living (biosphere); and, c) cognitive (noëtic). All three, taken together, are multiply-connected, in Riemann's usage of that notion; all three are equally existent "from the beginning" of the universe so defined.[17] The three, combined as a Riemannian-style multiply-connected manifold, represent a noösphere. My contribution to this configuration, is defining the composition of the sub-manifold of universal cognitive principles. That latter sub-manifold constitutes a category of universal physical principles, so defined experimentally because its efficient existence is expressed as physical effects which are *intentionally* products of its action. The noösphere subsumed by cognitive action, is the experimental domain corresponding, as subject, to the science of physical economy.

To complete the outline of the point made, concerning scientific method, thus far, I must restate the argument, respecting this use of *intention*, made in an earlier location.

When we today, following Kepler, use the term *intention*

---

16. LaRouche, op. cit.
17. This is not to argue that human consciousness existed as if "from the beginning," but only that the principle expressed for us as cognition, did.

as a synonym for the concept of the Leibniz calculus, we are using *intention* as synonymous with *Mind*. Does a planet, then, have a "mind"? Or, is "Mind" a metaphor for what Kepler reads as a controlling intention embedded into the planetary orbit by the Creator of the universe? Why should that metaphor be considered as necessary?

In Kepler's work, *Mind* and *intention* are qualities which the cognitive powers of the human mind are able to recognize, as what we may rightly term *universal physical principles*. Man recognizes that distinct quality of Mind, and that corresponding *intention,* as underlying certain distinctive qualities of trajectories. The scientist employs such use of the terms *Mind, intention*, and *universal physical principles,* as of the same set of metaphorical notions, because *the cognitive power of the human is able to recognize the Mind and intention expressed by a Keplerian orbit, as the intention of a universal Being of a nature It shares with the individual human cognitive personality*. That image, of the Creator as made in the cognitive image of man, is the mirror-reflection, for the scientist, of man as developed by the universe, uniquely, in the image of the Creator, that according to the *intention* of that Creator.

This use of *metaphor* in physical science so-called, is not literary decoration, not optional usage. As I have made the elaborated argument in sundry locations published earlier, any physical principle occurs only in a form which is *not directly representable* in terms of sense-perception.

To represent a principle, using languages which are commonly employed for reporting sense-perceptual types of imageries, we are obliged to resort to ironical juxtapositions of terms, phrases, and clauses, in a language otherwise used for pedestrian sorts of communications. This objective is accomplished in the only way possible, by forcing the mind to recognize a paradoxical expression, which is not explicable in simply sense-perceptual terms. These paradoxical expressions are identified in scholarly usage, as forms of *irony,* of which the most perfect type is *metaphor*.

In physical science, as usually considered to be distinct from Classical forms of artistic composition, these paradoxes occur in exactly the type of form confronted by Kepler in the matter of the non-uniformity of the curvature of the Mars orbit, and by Fermat in the instance of "quickest time" in refraction of light. The hypothetical intuition of a solution for such a paradox, if that hypothesis is validated experimentally, becomes an addition to the repertoire of known universal physical principles. This discovery of principle then exists as an *efficient idea*. This idea, is not reducible to a form in sense-perception, but rather exists as the unseen object which causes what Plato describes, allegorically, as the perceptible shadows cast on the irregular surface of the wall of a dimly firelit cave.[18]

The recognition of such an experimentally rooted paradox, is an act of cognition, of *Mind*. The paradox, if experimentally validated, corresponds to an efficient *intention*, whose efficiency as a principle exists externally to any object of sense-perception, but whose efficiency as a principle, as an intention, is experimentally demonstrable. Such notions, such as experimentally validated universal physical principles, are *ideas* in the strictest sense of the term; they exist as objects of thought only within the domain of cognition, but they are rooted in the paradoxes of sense-perception, and are demonstrated to be efficiently existing principles of physical action by their experimentally demonstrable, crucial quality of effects upon the domain of sense-perception.

That connection, once shown, is a subject in its own right; but, one qualification must be made here, and at this point in my account.

As typified by the discoveries which Kepler elaborates in his *New Astronomy* and *Harmony of the World,* and as Riemann's 1854 habilitation dissertation implicitly defines this notion, the discovery of an experimentally validatable universal physical principle, corresponds to a paradox within the pre-established representation of the universe.[19] Relative to a formal mathematical physics, this paradox is always expressed in terms of what Leibniz named *Analysis Situs,* or paradoxical geometries

---

18. Plato, *The Republic,* Book VI.
19. LaRouche, op. cit.

of position.[20] The first-approximation determination of the Mars orbit, in terms of intention expressed as equal areas in equal time, by Kepler, typifies this, and, as Fermat's experimental case for a principle of quickest time, also expresses this.

In such matters, the use of *Mind* and *intention* in respect to physical principles, thus signifies the question: "To whose Mind are we referring?"

In the general case, of the universe as merely observed by man, "Who?" is the Creator. In the case of man's efficient intervention into the order of the universe, "Who?" signifies man acting, by nature, as a creature made in the image of the Creator, who, like the Creator, and subject to the limitations the Creator has imposed, acts to impose the intervention of the qualities of Mind and intention into the consequences of mankind's willful interventions.

It is there, and nowhere else, that the subject of a science of economics is situated.

2. Long-Term Investment

There are two currently popular delusions, respecting economies, without which the presently onrushing form of global financial collapse would not have occurred. The name for one of these delusions is "money," as in "monetarism." The name for the other is "the market." Once the student is liberated from that pair of delusions, the true nature of an economy can begin to be brought into focus.

The rational notion of paper money, found its origins as a constitutional idea, early in the history of the English colonies of North America. This idea was first practiced as a successful use of the issue of paper money by the pre-1688 Commonwealth of Massachusetts. That success was referenced in a crucial proposal by Cotton Mather, and echoed afresh by a follower of Mather, Benjamin Franklin.[21] Nonetheless, although the issue

---

20. Ibid.
21. H. Graham Lowry, *How The Nation Was Won: America's Untold Story* (Washington, D.C.: Executive Intelligence Review, 1988).

and circulation of paper money, as an expression of public credit, by a government, can be a very beneficial practice, paper money itself remains forever "only paper," as the leaders of the Massachusetts Bay Colony made very clear in issuing such currency. Money is sometimes worth less even than the paper on which it is printed, as we ought to be reminded by events such as Germany's 1923 hyperinflation, and both the 1929-1932 and today's collapsing financial markets.

The happier leaders within the Massachusetts Bay Colony already recognized, during the Seventeenth Century, that we must make a categorical distinction between the issue of money by a nation's government, and the use of the form of money circulated from foreign agencies, such as that of the Seventeenth Century's Stuart monarchy of the Massachusetts colonists' time. That difference lies, essentially, in the fact, that our nation is sovereign (or, should be) in the case of a domestic issue of paper currency, and not in the case of our use of a foreign currency. Otherwise, that said, paper money remains "only paper"; neither it, nor so-called "shareholder value," has any intrinsic economic value. Any contrary opinion about money or shareholder value, is to be recognized as a delusion, and, under the circumstances of the world's present financial crisis, a very dangerous delusion, often even, perhaps, a morally criminal, as much as a painful one.[22]

To understand any economic process, an elementary distinction must be made between the two principal sets of relations which define a real economy, which is to say a *physical economy*, as distinct from a mere money-economy. On the one side, we have mankind's physical relationship to nature, as this is measurable in physical terms, per capita and per square kilometer of "macro-economic" area. In the other aspect of physical economy, there are the sets of social relations within society, which affect, and largely govern the willful evolution of society's practiced relationship to nature, per capita and per square kilometer. In relationship to a purely physical economy, money, paper or

---

22. Typical of such delusions is the argument that there exists a category of "honest money," as an alternative to paper money.

otherwise, comes into play, as a sometimes useful, as a necessary *political fiction,* in the physical organizing of the social relations within the economy. Paper money, issued as public credit, by a sovereign (or, worse, anyone else), remains always a mere political fiction.[23]

To understand all of those crucial issues of policy-making posed by the present global financial collapse, the most efficient approach is to look at Vernadsky's view of the physical universe as I look at the work of Vernadsky.[24]

The first step toward understanding how a real economy works, therefore, is to sort out those connections. All taken together, any economy is essentially a physical economy, and is an expression of a complex of *intentions,* as I have just previously described the use of the term "intentions" in the preceding pages.

On the matter of what might be called a "theory of money," we must, as I shall indicate, derive the function to be assigned to money in a rational way. That is to say, that, in a sane society, it is the physical economy which defines the meaning and value of money; this is in opposition to those foolish people who attempt to derive economic processes as a secretion from one of those "ivory tower" concoctions called "monetary theory."

However, before coming to the matter of the real economy, we must dispense with the second of the two distracting delusions which I referenced above, the delusion called "the market." I shall summarize the relevant argument by, first, quoting once again, as on some earlier occasions, a relevant passage from Adam Smith's 1759 *Theory of the Moral Sentiments,* and then use that citation as the pivot on which to make, once again, my general observation on the heathen doctrine of "little green men under the floorboards," which is the essence of the *laissez-faire*

---

23. A monetarist is like the man who took only the shadow cast by his bride on his honeymoon, while leaving the bride herself, for the rest of eternity, gathering dust at the altar.

24. This also means, to look at the distinction between living and non-living processes as Kepler did, and as Kepler relied on the work of Plato before him. We must include the view of man, as distinct from other living creatures, as Vernadsky did, a view which is implicitly pervasive throughout Kepler's work, as in such locations as Plato's *Timaeus.*

argument commonly used by such ideologues as François Quesnay, Bernard de Mandeville, Adam Smith, and Jeremy Bentham.[25]

That adversary of civilized life, Adam Smith, wrote:

"The administration of the great system of the universe . . . the care of the universal happiness of all sensible and rational beings, is the business of God and not of man. To man is allotted a much humbler department, but one much more suitable to the weakness of his powers, and to the narrowness of his comprehension; the care of his own happiness, of that of his family, his friends, his country . . . But though we are . . . endowed with a very strong desire of those ends, it has been intrusted to the slow and uncertain determinations of our reason to find out the proper means of bringing them about. *Nature has directed us to the greater part of these by original and immediate instincts. Hunger, thirst, the passion which unites the two sexes, the love of pleasure, and the dread of pain, prompt us to apply those means for their own sakes, and without any consideration of their tendency to those beneficent ends which the great Director of nature intended to produce by them.*" (italics added)

Decades prior to Smith's writing those lines, the "mephistopholean" Mandeville had already insisted that evil must not be banned, since, according to his argument, it is by allowing both good and evil to have free play in man's affairs, that good will be ultimately brought about. Mandeville's Faustian sophistry is the model imitated by those, such as his devotees of the Mont Pelerin Society, who condemn, invidiously, as "corrupt," adver-

---

25. As cited in Lyndon H. LaRouche, Jr. and David P. Goldman, *The Ugly Truth about Milton Friedman* (New York: New Benjamin Franklin House, 1980), p. 107. Mandeville sets forth his pro-satanic doctrine in his *The Fable of the Bees* (1714); the late Friedrich von Hayek designated Mandeville as the virtual "patron anti-saint" of von Hayek's Mont Pelerin Society; Adam Smith was a lackey of Britain's Lord Shelburne from 1763 on; the British Foreign Office's Bentham, another Shelburne lackey, is the putative founder of the utilitarian current in economics.

saries of the "free market" principle, such as governments or persons who oppose legalizing the trade in so-called "recreational" drugs.[26]

Pro-feudalist Quesnay argued that the profit of the aristocrat's estate, was brought into being as a predicate of the aristocrat's mere hereditary title to the estate (e.g., "shareholder value"), on which the role of the serfs was defined, by Quesnay, as essentially that of human cattle.[27] The doctrine of English and British empiricism, introduced to the English-speaking world by Venice's Mephisto-like Paolo Sarpi, defines social processes, including economic processes, as like percussive interactions among Hobbesian particles floating in Euclidean space-time; empiricism defines history, including economy, as a kind of statistical result of those amassed kinematic interactions.

Hence we have in today's U.S., the frankly corrupt doctrine of the "free market" upheld by the Mont Pelerin Society, the American Enterprise Institute, and like-spirited followers of Britain's nastiest nanny, Margaret Thatcher. It is truly a lunatic doctrine, as also a modern parody of the medieval *Bogomil* cult of "the chosen ones."

On the one side, the economists of that curious persuasion

---

26. This has been the argument in favor of legalization of the cocaine and heroin traffic by such devotees of the Mont Pelerin cult as Professor Milton Friedman. See LaRouche and Goldman, op. cit., pp. 305-322.

27. To situate the role of the strange Dr. Quesnay in the history of political-economy, it is essential to locate the opposition to the policies of France's nation-builders, Cardinal Mazarin and Jean-Baptiste Colbert, by the alliance of the feudalist *Fronde* with that pagan monster Louis XIV. This alliance overlapped the Europe-wide network of salons, operating under the direction of Venice's Abbé Antonio Conti. From the relatively momentary period of a few years, that the possibility existed, that Gottfried Leibniz might become the future Prime Minister for the British monarchy, Conti played the leading role, until his 1749 death, in organizing both the Newton myth, and the anti-Colbert and anti-Leibniz campaign throughout Europe. The position of the disgusting mere tinkler Rameau, and the use of the Rameau myth against Johann Sebastian Bach, were, like the creation of the figure of Voltaire and the role of Quesnay, expressions of the early Eighteenth-Century campaigns coordinated by Conti from the Paris of the pagan Sun-King Louis XIV, and of the minority of Louis XV.

insist, that mankind must not interfere with the magical statistical processes of the so-called "free market." At the same time, those brainwashed doctrinaires insist, that that perfectly anarchical market, like a crooked gambling table, is mysteriously rigged, as if by an invisible hand, to ensure that the prices will ultimately be "right," and that privileged people will be rewarded by the influence of some magical taint of bias, a bias in favor of the "chosen ones," built into that crooked gambling-table which that market is in fact.[28]

Neither Mandeville, Smith, nor Bentham, ever claimed to have rational knowledge of why this allegedly perfectly democratic statistical process assured such a statistically consistent, corrupt result. As Smith spoke for himself, blind faith in the "free market" principle, *"prompt[s] us to apply those means for their own sakes, and without any consideration of their tendency to those beneficent ends which the great Director of nature intended to produce by them."* Although they admit they have no knowledge of what the efficient principle is, or how it operates, they insist that it would be morally wrong of anyone, to attempt to interfere with the unfathomable logic of that wonderful underworld domain where such little green men, often disguised as investment bankers, dwell and reign.

If society legalizes crime, it adds criminal proceeds to its official gross national product accounts; if it counts the proceeds of crime as part of the nation's wealth, it thus legalizes crime. If the state intervenes to legalize the international traffic in recreational drugs, the state becomes a drug-pusher, as Secretary of State and H.G. Wells devotee Madeleine Albright's reign did; if it accounts the income of prostitution as part of the taxable gross national product, the President becomes a pimp. In short, leave it up to whatever little green men, whoever or whatever they

---

28. The type referenced here as "the chosen ones" suggests the cases of two U.S. Presidents Bush, neither of which showed any talent for actually earning money by their own independent skills, but had wealth bestowed upon them by the relevant little green men under the floorboards. See Anton Chaitkin and Webster Tarpley, *George Bush: The Unauthorized Biography* (Washington, D.C.: Executive Intelligence Review, 1992).

might be, controlling the universe from under the floorboards of the universal gambling hall. Smith's economics is not science, it is a religion of heathen crap-shooters, probably a tradition of the Babylonian or kindred origins which economist J.M. Keynes attributed to the content of the chest of collected scientific papers of Sir Isaac Newton.[29]

The most insane variety of that English-speaking empiricist tradition, are those monetarist models concocted in the spirit of John Law, in his time, or, in ours, such as John von Neumann's and Oskar Morgenstern's radically positivist concoction, the *Theory of Games & Economic Behavior*.[30] Von Neumann, like "information theory" hoaxster Norbert Wiener, was a former acolyte of Bertrand Russell, whose work reflects the wildly ivory-tower rantings of Russell's *Principia Mathematica*.[31]

At their least bad, all of those beliefs associated with today's fashionable varieties of monetarist teaching, are derived from the same "ivory tower" fantasizing which Kepler pointed out as the root of the fallacies of the astronomical systems of Ptolemy, Copernicus, and Brahe. Each fantasist of that collection, begins, as von Neumann and Morgenstern did, with a made-up, arbitrary set of assumptions: the logical positivist's equivalent of a set of arbitrarily chosen definitions, axioms, and postulates. That set of assumptions, like some game just made up by mischievous children, then defines what they are willing to take into account as the acknowledged variety of social facts which they select as belonging to their scheme, their whimsically chosen, childish "rules of the game." That scheme becomes, for them, as for Claudius Ptolemy and his modern dupes, the substitute for a "universe," as represented by the specific mathematical fantasy which they construct.

29. John Maynard Keynes, "Newton the Man," in *Essays in Biography* (New York: The Norton Library, 1951).

30. John von Neumann and Oskar Morgenstern, *Theory of Games and Economic Behavior,* 3rd ed. (Princeton: Princeton University Press, 1953).

31. Alfred N. Whitehead and Bertrand Russell, *Principia Mathematica* (Cambridge: Cambridge University Press, 1994, reprint of 1927 edition).

Other evidence, for which no place is provided in the set of definitions, axioms, and postulates of their system, they ignore, as irrelevant to their system. No physical principles, as I have defined physical principles above, are allowed to intervene in their analysis. On this account, they imitate exactly the willful fraud against physical science perpetrated by Claudius Ptolemy and his modern devotees. The devotees of those constructs then insist upon explaining everything they choose to notice in a real economy, according to the ivory-tower model they have constructed.

We shall define a completely different, much happier notion of a market, at a later point in this report.

Biosphere and Noösphere

The principle of production is, that, *through the realization of scientific and technological progress, the average member of the human species, is able to improve the longevity and other demographic characteristics of his or her society's entire population, and to increase its per-capita useful output within a diminishing amount of required, average land-area per capita.* The performance of an economy, is to be measured as the increased production of people, people who are of increased per-capita power to exist and reign, that within what Vernadsky identifies as the noösphere.

The increase of the physical-economic potential associated with the individual can be defined in two distinct, functional ways. Most simply, it implies the individual's potential *for society* within the bounds of the specific state of development of the society/economy within which the individual is functionally situated. However, we have other significant cases, in which we must assess what the individual would have as the more or less immediate potential to become, were he, with his existing personal capabilities, situated in, for example, a less underdeveloped society/economy. To similar effect, we must sometimes emphasize what a present labor-force, or some part of it, has the potential to become merely by virtue of being situated in more favorable sorts of relevant conditions; as for example, the increased potential for society represented by a trained engineer transferred from crude manual labor, to an occupation consistent with his, or her potential.

Such an increase of power, is to be considered as analogous to a trajectory, in the sense that a specific planetary orbit is *a trajectory of constant, if not uniform change,* a trajectory defined by intention. That signifies a quality of trajectory which is distinguished from what is still, today, an ordinary classroom-mathematical type of trajectory, in that it expresses an *intention,* rather than a mechanically predetermined outcome, such as the latter might be implied by the application of conventional methods of today's financial accounting.

We are not defining the individual as, thus, fixed in quality, or of fixed absolute needs. In the language of Heraclitus and Plato, the trajectory of development of the individual in society, and of the society per individual, is *the trajectory of becoming:* of bringing both the individual and the society continually to a higher state, per capita and per average unit of relevant area.

In first approximation, this distinction connotes Kepler's use of the terms *Mind* and *intention.* It signifies, thus, the validation of *a universal physical principle,* as I have defined the correspondence of intention and universal physical principle, in the preceding section of this report. In the case of economy, such intentions include all the connotations associated with the general category of regular non-living and living processes; but, in addition to that, there is also a qualitative change included in the connotation. Man's intentions are *cognitively willful,* in a sense that the *quality of intention* associated with either non-living processes, or lower forms of life, is not.

Thus, physical economy represents a category of universal physical principle, but a principle of a different specific quality than either non-living or living processes otherwise defined.

We come now, to the point where we must state and address the crucial paradox upon whose solution all long-range economic forecasting depends. This paradox presents us, at this stage of the report, with an interim result, which I shall now summarize, and address more adequately at a later point in the report as a whole.

At first, perhaps, the argument which I shall introduce in a paragraph a short space below, will not be an easy one for many readers, at their first reading of it. It is paradoxical, but it is essential that it be made; otherwise some essential facts are overlooked. As all important statements of principle, this must be stated in the form of *Analysis Situs,* and must, therefore, assume the quality of metaphor. It is necessary to pose the issue in such a paradoxical way, that the solution to the paradox can be provoked, and then discovered. The secret of knowledge is never to turn one's back on a well-formulated paradox; to turn away from such a paradox, is to turn away from the possibility of gaining what Socrates' principles would recognize as being actually knowledge.

Besides, you should not balk at being challenged to make a serious mental effort. Making discoveries is *fun!* It is fun in the sense connoted by our mind's hearing Archimedes' shout of "Eureka!" People labor greatly to make discoveries of principle, because, as it was for Archimedes, it is great fun to do so. Such fun is a way of life, a way of practicing being alive. It is the quality of playfulness of the great scientific discoverer, the greatest Classical composers and performers. One does it, because it is good to do it.

Having fun, in the sense of Archimedes' cry of "Eureka!" expresses the joy of doing good, and it therefore is the essence of morality. It is the quality of *agapē* of Plato's Socrates, and of the anti-pharisaical (anti-"single issue") Apostle Paul's I Corinthians 13.

Science and great Classical artistic compositions are not entertainments; they are a way of life; all progress in the human condition depends upon individual personalities which have such fun in doing good for mankind. *Fun,* as I have implicitly defined a special meaning for that term here, is that special quality of playfulness which sets the happy human child, and the greatest scientist, a Mozart or a Beethoven, apart from, and above the happy playfulness of the boy's companion, that puppy. Thus, I rarely say "Bless you!" to my friends; I deliver a much happier injunction, "Have *fun!*" Or, I enjoin them, "Be careful; don't behave yourself. (Don't be another miserable Kantian!) Have *fun!*" Or, in the terms of Friedrich Schiller, reach upward, from the tragic to the *sublime.*[32]

The result of making such a necessary distinction as I have made here so far, between a universe which includes mankind, and another, which, at least conjecturally, might not, is to imply that the universe in which the universal physical principle known as economy exists, is of the general form of a Riemannian manifold. That universe incorporates three categories of universal physical principle: non-living, living, and cognitive. These specific categories of principles, are multiply-connected, in Riemann's sense. The characteristic of the manifold, is the universal physical principle of physical economy. Such is the nature of the universe in which *the sheer fun* of human cognition is the dominant consideration, the end-result toward which all multiply-connected features are rightly aimed.

Therefore, now, let us have some *fun!* Start a run of such fun, by noting, that, from this point on, you will be considering a physical economy in its role as a *macroeconomic noösphere.* In other words, we are defining the noösphere as "under the management of" a macroeconomy defined in the language, and by the methods of physical economy. That means, that we are restating everything Vernadsky has stated for the noösphere and its subsumed biosphere, but, this time, restated, and amplified in the language of my approach to the science of physical economy.

From this standpoint, the functional relationship of the noösphere to the biosphere, is expressed chiefly as what macroeconomics views as *basic economic infrastructure.* This means, chiefly, *the development of the land-area of a national physical economy as an indivisible unit of action, that over a relatively long-term period of not less than approximately a quarter-cen-*

32. Friedrich Schiller, "On the Sublime," op. cit. The sublime is the point of difference between Plato and the Classical Greek tragedians, as Plato's Socratic dialogues epitomize that distinction. In modern Classical drama, the notion of the sublime is typified by both Schiller's Joan of Arc and the real-life Jeanne d'Arc whose essential historical reality is captured by Schiller. She died horribly, but not tragically; she spent her life for a mission of great outcome for European civilization as a whole. So, the truly sublime Christ, no tragic figure, died for the benefit of all mankind.

tury, or even much longer. This apparently paradoxical principle of national-income accounting, is crucial; therefore, I elaborate the point I have just made.[33]

The most general of the inherent fallacies of today's conventional financial accounting and national-income accounting practice, is of the same type as those who, unlike Kepler, tried to explain astronomical processes in terms of simple mathematical connections among observed point-positions of celestial objects. Just as Kepler recognized the importance of adducing the moment-to-moment principle governing an orbit, from the study of the paradoxes posed by the orbit as a whole, so we must judge the significance of localized, relatively short-term economic developments from the vantage-point of both the whole process within which those developments are situated, and over a time-span sufficiently long to expose the long-term major effects of what seem small, even insignificant variations within a small portion of the short-term developments.

Generally, the minimum interval of time, during which the relationship between short-term aberrations and their large-scale long-term effects, becomes empirically clear, is in the order of not less than a quarter-century, approximately the span of development of a newborn child into a fully defined-as-functional adult individual. How, then, can we know results of today's actions, a quarter-century or more hence? How do we know the orbit of the planetary body on which we discover ourselves travelling at this immediate moment?

Since infrastructural development, and long-term capital improvements, or the lack of either or both, define the net outcome of an entire generation of an economy's unfolding, we must never attempt to define the policies properly governing so-called microeconomical functions, except in an axiomatically well-defined macroeconomical setting.

Why the U.S. Is Bankrupt

Take as an example, the trillions of U.S.- dollars-equivalent of unremedied attrition of basic economic infrastructure since the

---

33. This is the paragraph of which I forewarned you a bit earlier.

FIGURE 1

The South Korea Won Collapses Under Speculative Attack

Nixon Administration. See similar trends in continental Western Europe, and the worse state of affairs similarly induced within the United Kingdom, as in the brutish looting and ruin of the economies of New Zealand and Australia. Under existing, post-1965-1972 trends in policies, that damage to those economies could never be reversed, but, in fact, would become ever worse, and inevitably so.

There have been several ways, which, combined in effects, have contributed to the ability of governments and others, to concoct fraudulently optimistic reports on overall national economic performance of these nations' economies.

One way has been to conceal the increased degree of looting of nations outside the U.S.A., Western continental Europe, and the so-called "developed" nations of the British Commonwealth, by collusion among the world's London financial center, the IMF and World Bank, in organizing runs on national currencies [**Figure 1**], and against specific commodities. By aid of these measures, national currencies were, repeatedly, arbitrarily depressed, and the foreign indebtedness, including debt to the IMF added, as a way of deflationary looting of South and Central

America, Africa, and so on, under the so-called "floating-ex-change-rate" monetary system. This latter was called the "liberal system," because it enabled predator nations to loot victimized nations and continents so liberally. The prosperity of the U.S. and the British monarchy's reign, and also Western Europe, such as it has been, has depended increasingly on this specific method for post-1971 looting of the nations of South and Central America, Africa, the former Comecon bloc, Southeast Asia, and so on, under the so-called "floating-exchange-rate system."

Another way of perpetrating the fraudulent appearance of net profitability of the predator nations' economies, was to understate the rate of inflation in those economies. One of the most naked of such frauds perpetrated by the U.S. government, was a practice which I denounced in a national TV network broadcast, early in 1984: the hoax called the Quality Adjustment factor [**Figure 2**][34]. That hoax continues to be perpetrated, to the present time.

Another accounting swindle to kindred effect, was simply ignoring the material loss to the national economy from depreciation and depletion of basic economic infrastructure [**Figures 3 and 4**]. By failing to take the current cost of replenishment of this margin of depreciation and depletion into account, in national income and product accounting, the irreversible loss to the future of the economy, caused by abandoning essential infrastructure, was fraudulently suppressed for sake of presenting a success-story, where ruin was actually in progress.

NAFTA and "globalization" generally, have looted most of the world in a two-fold way. The production of more and more of the commodities used in so-called industrialized economies, was "outsourced" to cheap-labor markets abroad [**Figures 5, 6, and 7**]. The included results, were the accelerated collapse of the earned real income of the U.S., for example, the vanishing of essential production capacities and productive skills from the thus-depleted, importing former agro-industrial powers, and the devastating collapse in the real income-rates of the lower 80% of U.S. family households, for example.

---

34. The broadcast was aired on ABC-TV on Feb. 4, 1984, during my campaign for the Presidency.

FIGURE 2

Increase of Actual New Car Price Compared to BLS Computation of CPI for New Cars

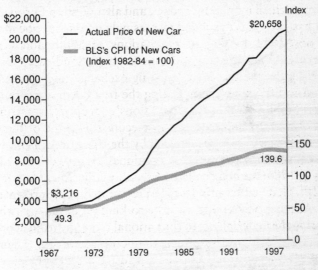

Sources: Department of Commerce's Bureau of Economic Analysis; Department of Labor's Bureau of Labor Statistics; *EIR*.

Typical of one of the relevant greatest accounting swindles of them all, was the 1995-2001 hoax called "Y2K." Under the pretext, that a computer-accounting disaster threatened the world economy on Dec. 31, 1999, a vast financial bubble was generated in the area of what was called, variously, "information technology," or the "Third Wave" [**Figure 8**]. While some part of the computer and related technologies involved are intrinsically potentially useful, especially for administrative functions, the "new economy" bundle was, predominantly, a vast swindle, with about the same benefit to national income as might be reflected in IRS estimates, that by legalizing prostitution, legalized supermarket sales of heroin and cocaine, and legalization of all forms of crime generally, the national income might be increased.

Virtually all of those factors on which net rates of sustained

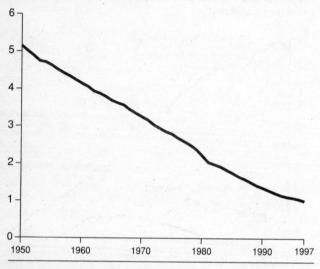

FIGURE 3

U.S. Railroad Mileage

(Miles per 1,000 Households)

Sources: Association of American Railroads; U.S. Department of
Commerce, Bureau of Census, *Population Surveys,* various years.

real physical-economic growth depend, were buried under an
avalanche of bubbling swindles of one variety or another.

Thus, we have come to the point today, that the outstanding
financial debt of the world at large, could never be paid by a world
economy attempting to meet those presently required, cancerously
multiplying demands for payments. The reason we have entered
the worst, greatest financial collapse in all human existence, now,
is that the reported economic growth of the world's economy, especially of Europe, the British Commonwealth, and the U.S.A., of
the past thirty years, has been one gigantic swindle. The cupboard
is bare, because it has been emptied, not by ordinary burglars,
but by the lunatic, Thatcher-like greed of the London-centered
shareholder-proprietors themselves.

By the standard I have specified above, and taking related
facts into account, the so-called developed sector of Western

FIGURE 4

Hospital Beds per 1,000 U.S. Population Overall, and in Community Hospitals

(Beds per 1,000 People)

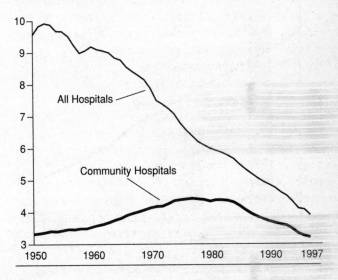

Europe, the Americas, and the British Commonwealth, has not actually earned a net profit, as national economies, since the tragic trends set into motion over the 1964-1972 period, by that pestilence typified by Wilson in Britain and Nixon and his "Southern Strategy" in the U.S.A. All reports of net growth in national incomes of these nations over the period since, have been a gigantic accounting fraud. It was my recognition of, and understanding of that *systemic* fraud and its nature, which was essential to my becoming the most successful long-range economic forecaster known to the public in the world at large today.

Basic Economic Infrastructure

From the standpoint of Vernadsky's outline, this development of basic economic infrastructure is expressed in two clearly distinguishable ways. In some actions, mankind's action simply

FIGURE 5
Mexico: Comparative Growth Rates
(Annual Averages)

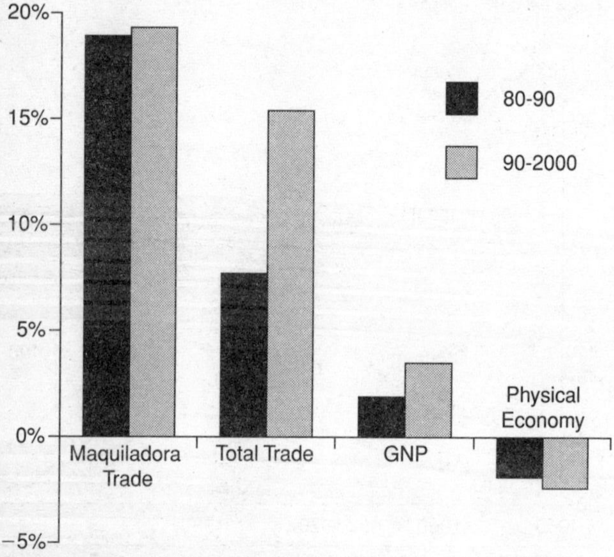

Sources: Banco de México, INEGI, *EIR*.

improves the development of the biosphere as man finds it, as through the transformation of arid regions into biologically rich farmlands.

In the second class of actions, man improves the variety of content of the biosphere, qualitatively, by adding to it new kinds of what Vernadsky calls "natural objects,"[35] adding to the repertoire of natural objects already produced by forms of life inferior to mankind. Such "natural objects" introduced to the biosphere

---

35. "Natural products" is employed here in the sense of Vernadsky's argument. As cited in Lyndon H. LaRouche, Jr., "A Philosophy for Victory: Can We Change the Universe?" (see above, p. 99), see Vladimir I. Vernadsky, "On the Fundamental Material-Energetic Difference Between Living and Non-Living Natural Bodies in the Biosphere" (1938), Jonathan Tennenbaum and Rachel Douglas, trans. (see below, p. 275).

FIGURE 6

Mexico: Maquiladora Wages and Employment

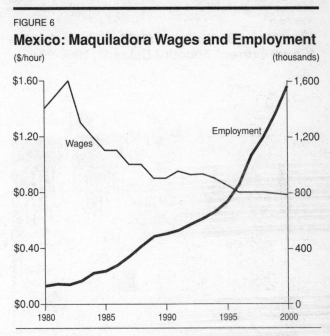

Sources: Banco de México, INEGI, CTM; *Twin Plant News*; AFL-CIO.

as products of cognition, include transportation and power systems. Water management systems represent the combined effect of human promotion of the kind of natural objects already produced by the biosphere as such, combined with added elements which are natural objects of a type unique to the products of cognition. Urban development is chiefly an example of natural objects of cognition.

The development of educational systems, like the role of principles of Classical artistic composition, is a part of the essential infrastructure of the biosphere; but that is a matter to be taken up in the more suitable setting of review, conducted in the immediately following section of this report, of physical economy as a social process, rather than as simply the measurable relations as defined, in effect, per capita and per square kilometer.

For reasons which I shall clarify at a suitable later point in this report, it is necessary to make a certain functional distinction

216   LYNDON H. LAROUCHE, JR.

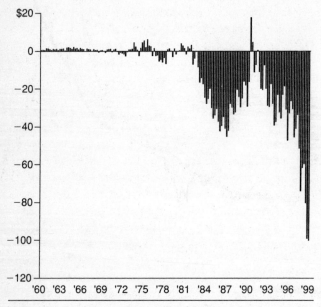

FIGURE 7

The United States Is Living Off the Rest of the World: Current Account Balance, 1960-99

(Billions $)

Source: U.S. Department of Commerce.

between what is usefully designated as basic economic infrastructure, and other qualities of specifically economic activities.

Broadly, the distinction is, that basic economic infrastructure's development and maintenance, reflects a society's conscious sense of its government's unique responsibility for the economic and related potential embodied in the improvement of *the land-area as a whole,* and *the population considered immediately in its entirety.* Thus, these represent the accountability of the government for the promotion of the interest of the cause of the general welfare, as represented, inclusively, by the entirety of the land-area, per se, and the entirety of the population, per se. Thus, basic economic infrastructure is distinguished from

FIGURE 8

Nasdaq Composite Index, 1997-2000

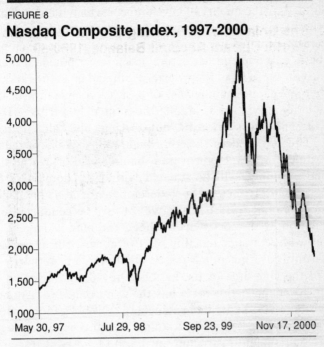

Source: Nasdaq.

that which, under the American System, usually falls within the province of private entrepreneurship, such as agriculture and manufacturing industry. There is, as I shall show in due course, a deeper distinction, but what I have just stated will suffice as a working observation at this juncture.

Usually, areas other than basic economic infrastructure, are associated with the application of man-made discoveries of universal physical principles and their derived technologies, to the design of products and productive processes. This is usually associated with an entrepreneurship of one or a number of persons, acting within the bounds of general law for the society as a whole, but on their own initiative.

In general, functionally, the existence of the latter entrepreneurships is situated on the basis provided by the development of the society's basic economic infrastructure. Their potential is delimited by the quality of environment which the development of the basic economic infrastructure represents. In general, an enterprise situated in an area with relatively poor development of basic economic infrastructure, has a lower potential than the same enterprise would represent, if situated in an area of higher development and maintenance of basic economic infrastructure. The latter is typified as among the ultimately terrible errors in the recent decades' resort to "outsourcing" and "globalization."

Thus, in modern society, roughly 40 to 60% of the total investment in development and maintenance of a healthy national economy, will be situated within the domain of basic economic infrastructure. Such development and maintenance of basic economic infrastructure will always be conducted under regulation by the society as a whole, and may be largely, even entirely an economic function of government. This is necessary, since only government has responsibility for, and authority over all of the land-area of the nation. Only the government of a truly sovereign nation-state has the competence to assume responsibility for the assured payment of debt-obligations incurred on the kinds of long-term accounts which the development of basic economic infrastructure incurs.[36]

However, since the development and maintenance of basic economic infrastructure depends largely upon its own consumption of the products of production, both directly and indirectly, the investment in the development and maintenance of basic economic infrastructure, is a principal stimulant for the growth and maintenance of the level of output and productivity of the population and its production as a whole.

---

36. On this account, the development of the principle of Chapter 11 bankruptcy, during the 1930s, remains indispensable policy for any area of long-term commitment to the development and maintenance of basic economic infrastructure, such as a public-health system for a nation, a region of a nation, a region of the planet, or the world as a whole. The claims of debtors' creditors, in such bankruptcy proceedings, must be subordinated to the public interest, that according to the U.S. Constitutional principle of the general welfare. Thus, government meets its responsibilities for honorable treatment of debt incurred in an honorable way to an honorable purpose. This obviously conflicts with any claims presented on the account of a predatory form of "shareholder interest."

In the general form of the functional relationship between the noösphere and biosphere, we are presented with two kinds of expression of qualitative change which the macroeconomic development of the physical economy introduces into the development of the biosphere and noösphere alike. One kind of qualitative change is associated with extension of scale of development, without the additional introduction of new kinds of "natural products" of the noösphere; the other, with the introduction of new qualities of "natural products" of the noösphere.

For example, the simple extension of large-scale water management, extended development of agriculture, and of managed forests, increases the amount and effective energy-flux-density throughput of "biomass" over large areas, with associated qualitative effects on the weather systems within entire regions. Such transformations complement, but are distinct from the transformations caused by introduction of new kinds of natural products of the noösphere to the biosphere. Thus, we must distinguish between qualitative effects of increase of scale and intensity of use of existing programs and technologies, and the qualitative effects of introducing new kinds of technologies, or even new, virtually man-made physical principles of practice.

In the longer run, it is the role of the introduction of new kinds of "natural products" of cognition (discoveries of universal physical principle and their technological derivatives) to become an integral part of the functioning of basic economic infrastructure, which is determining. Despite that, the qualitative improvement in the characteristics of land-area, as biosphere, and as infrastructure, through extended application of already existing principles, is extremely significant.

Functions of Physical Economy

So far, as a matter of emphasis, I have confined the development of my argument to the first aspect of scientific and technological progress: our species' increase of its power over nature, as measured per capita and per square kilometer. I have referenced the cultural factors, but have not integrated their role. For the remainder of this section, I shall continue to maintain that emphasis. That limitation should be taken for granted by the reader, until we come to the following section of the report.

The essential feature of the process by which mankind increases its species' power to exist, in and over the universe, is the discovery and application of additional, validated discoveries of universal physical principle. In the experimental validation of such a discovered principle, the design of that experiment includes willful features which express the new principle being tested. Those features of a successful such experiment, then become, in turn, the model for applying the validated principle to man's willful control over nature. The class of derivatives of successful such proof-of-principle experiments, is called *technologies*.

These technologies appear in various guises. They appear in a somewhat different form in their application to different kinds of materials. They also appear in the testing and measurement of the functional relationships among varying combinations of materials and technologies.

For example, the fact that a technology works in its direct application to one choice of material, does not mean that it will work in the same way in another. Nor, can we assume that a technology will work to the same effect when a change is made in the combinations of technologies employed for a common function, or when a different material is substituted.

All these and related challenges require the ministrations of a class of specialists expert in the matter of designing the apparatus appropriate to, and conducting, proof-of-principle experiments. The attempt to substitute computerized "benchmarking" for such traditional engineering abilities, invites catastrophes. *The universe is not linear.*

With those and related kinds of considerations taken into account, the immediate relationship of human action to the universe, is a function of the accumulation of valid new discoveries of universal physical principle. This includes the categories of universal physical principles specific to living processes, and also to cognitive ones. For the moment, the argument is made only for the case of non-living and living processes, not cognitive relations among persons. With that restriction, man's power in and over the universe, per capita and per square kilometer, is bounded by the accumulation of valid discoveries of universal physical principles.

This signifies, that man's per-capita power in and over the universe, as the universe is defined in terms of mankind's per-capita relationship to it, is to be seen as a function of the accumulation of valid discoveries of universal physical principle. It is the application of that accumulation, in whole, or in part, which delimits man's potential power in the universe.

In that sense, the universe, as defined in terms of mankind's relationship to it, is Riemannian. By Riemannian, I mean, in first approximation, the then-revolutionary implications for mathematical physics, of Riemann's 1854 habilitation dissertation.[37] Each validated *intention,* otherwise known as a *universal physical principle,* functions as a "dimension" of a physical geometry from which all so-called Euclidean and related sets of arbitrary definitions, axioms, and postulates have been excluded.

Such a geometry of "n" such dimensions, differs from a kindred geometry of "n+1" dimensions, by an experimentally defined change in "curvature" in passing from one to the other. In physical economy, this is expressed as a change in the characteristic curvature of an economic action occurring within the system as a whole.

So, to illustrate that point in the relatively simplest terms, the introduction of large-scale application of electrical motive-power for individual machinery, replacing reliance on belt-driven-shaft systems used for entire factories, represented a qualitative change in the characteristics of the actions performed by the relevant operatives of machinery, even when the skills and techniques of the operatives were not changed in other respects.

In first approximation, a Riemannian geometry premised upon that habilitation dissertation, would be presumed to include only one class of universal physical principles. In the case at hand, the noösphere as a physical geometry, we have three

---

37. Bernhard Riemann, *Über die Hypothesen, welche der Geometrie zu Grunde liegen, Bernhard Riemanns gesammelte mathematische Werke,* H. Weber, ed. (New York: Dover Publications reprint, 1953).

distinct, but multiply- connected classes of principles: non-living, life, cognition. There is no inherent objection to treating this case as a Riemannian geometry in the conventional sense of Riemann's own intentions.

To the degree such a Riemannian geometry is embodied efficiently in the macroeconomic noösphere in which the members of a society exist and act, a change from a geometry of designation "n" to one of designation "n+1," signifies an increase of the net power of the average action taken by the individual existing and acting within the framework of a noösphere of that latter designation. In other words, an increase in the relative anti-entropy of the system, and also of the action of virtually every person within that society.

Some brief practical illustration of this principled conception is in order at this moment.

When we increase the availability of usable water, of sources of power of increased energy-flux density, of more rapid, more efficient transport of people and goods, we improve the available performance of each person in that society, even if no other change in their behavior is introduced. If we improve both sanitation and health-care, thus reducing the economic losses attributable to illness, impairments, and death, we increase the productivity of that society as a whole.

If, on the other hand, society's zeal to reduce the cost of goods to the lowest possible price, prompts it to cut back on both public expenditure for basic economic infrastructure, and also to eliminate regulation of this area to the effect of ensuring its development, then the average productivity of the labor-force will collapse, as a result of the lack of meeting the costs to be included in prices of all goods, and of developing and maintaining basic economic infrastructure.

3. Physical Economy as a Social Process

In the opening section of this report, on the subject of the Leibniz discovery of the calculus, I distinguished the notion of processes governed by a universal physical principle, as expressed in the form of *intention,* from that false, mechanical notion of "causality" associated with the work of empiricists such as Isaac Newton and his followers. The latter, mechanical notion, is the false, "Newtonian" notion of "causality" which is still widely accepted in the secondary and university mathematics classroom, today.

As I have also stressed there, in physical systems, we are confronted with two general classifications of *intention*. In the one case, we have the ordinary intention expressed in the non-mechanical determination of a result by a universal physical principle, such as that expressed by a Solar orbit, or the consistent difference which may be manifest, between what are otherwise ostensibly identical chemical processes, when one is associated with a living process, and the other not. In the other case, we have the notion of *willful intention*, in the case of an original cognitive discovery, or its reenactment by a second person. It is the social implications of the second type of case, to which this report turns your attention now.

Empiricists, such as empiricist Galileo's mathematics pupil Thomas Hobbes, degraded society into a collection of so-to-speak kinematically interacting individual objects, like the particles of a gas theory. They assumed a set of fixed, built-in definitions, axioms, and postulates, as underlying the possible behavior of these particles. This is the system of John Locke, satanic Bernard de Mandeville, David Hume, Adam Smith, and utilitarians such as the British Foreign Office's Jeremy Bentham. That is the underlying basis for their definition of what they term "human nature." Empiricist-turned-Aristotelean Immanuel Kant, insisted upon the same underlying notion. The modern logical positivists have carried that notion to extremes, beyond even that of which the depraved old Hobbes might be accused.[38]

---

38. Kant makes clear, most emphatically so in his *Critique of Judgment*, that the empiricist principle, which he defends from a quasi-Aristotelean standpoint, is a principle of pure irrationalism. He makes the point most explicitly in respect to aesthetics, in which he shows himself a pure romanticist, in the literally pagan-Roman sense of *vox populi*. The same is true of G.W.F. Hegel's fascistic (i.e., Napoleonic) theory of the state as revolution, as echoed by Carl Schmitt during the Twentieth Century. Similarly, the empiricist, positivist, and existentialist doctrines of "free

Put the point in the following terms. If, as I have shown repeatedly, the distinction between the human being and the beasts, is the power to discover a valid universal physical principle, what is the corresponding, natural expression of human relations? If such a discovery typifies the human individual's characteristic potential, what are "human relations"?

It is the communication of those ideas corresponding to valid universal physical principles, from one mind to another, which enables the human species to behave as a human species, rather than a mere interacting collection of particle-like human individualities. It is the accumulation of the transmission of such discoveries of principle, over successive generations, which distinguishes the human species, as a species, from the beasts which Hobbes and his admirers aspired to become. Thus, how does this communication of such notions of principle occur? How, therefore, does mankind develop as mankind?

The pivotal question, so posed, is: How does the transmission of the idea of the actual discovery of a valid universal principle occur? I have covered this in so many previously published locations,[39] that I need only summarize the response, once again, here.

The discovery of an *idea*, a Platonic form of idea, as the discovery of any valid universal physical principle typifies this, can not be communicated from one person to another in the medium of sense-perception as such, but only by replicating the act of discovery and validation. This is precisely what does occur in any system of education consistent with Classical humanist principles, such as those of Germany's exemplary, former Humboldt reforms.

The distinction of the human being from mere animals, such as the higher apes, is the ability of the human will to discover the quality of intention which I have associated here with what

---

trade" and "globalization" today, are based upon the pure irrationalism which is axiomatic in the arguments of Hobbes, Locke, Mandeville, Quesnay, Hume, Adam Smith, Bentham, et al. before Kant.

39. LaRouche, op. cit.

Kepler called *Mind* or *intention*. By adopting that intention, such as a valid universal physical principle, as our own intention, we are able to exert that idea as an efficient act of the individual human will, as a universal physical principle, upon the universe. The ability to discover, or recognize such a quality of *idea,* depends upon our creating that idea within our own cognitive processes. Typical is such transmission of such Platonic forms of ideas from Plato's dialogues to the present-day reader, approximately 2,500 years later. It is sufficient that today's reader relive the drama of the Plato dialogues, thus to find himself, or herself, a living participant today in the dialogue as it occurred then.

To identify the method of such transmission, I describe the process once again, summarily, now.

Ideas come into existence as ontological paradoxes. That is to say, more precisely, ideas come into existence in response to what the conscious mind is able to represent to itself in the form of such a paradox. A well-stated such paradox, is represented in the form known as *Analysis Situs,* or, in Classical artistic composition, as *metaphor.* Given the equivalent of a standard theory, if the experience of an actual event or condition, requires that experience be stated by standard theory in ways which are either simply outside, or represent an impossible inconsistency within that standard theory, the juxtaposition of two or more mutually contradictory statements, each consistent with standard theory for describing events, represents an ontological paradox within the terms of that standard theory.

The paradox of the Mars orbit, as adduced and presented by Kepler, is an example of the way in which a statement in the form of *Analysis Situs* arises within the framework of reference proffered by a prevalent standard theory. If a validated *hypothesis* is discovered, which creates a new standard theory eliminating the ontological paradox, we have the discovery of a new valid universal physical principle.

Thus, we have the three-step method by which valid universal physical principles are made known, and communicated so from one person to another. First, there is the valid statement of an ontological paradox. Second, there is the formation of an *hypothesis,* as a proposed solution for that paradox, in the mind of the individual. Third, there is the demonstration which validates the hypothesis as a universal physical principle.

Although no such idea can be perceived by sense-perception, the first and third steps so indicated, are rooted in sense-perception. The paradox is demonstrated to be a paradox by the standards of evidence applicable to sense-perception. The validation of the hypothesis is similarly experienced. By aid of those two reference-points, two persons can recognize that they have experienced the same formation of an hypothesis. That validated hypothesis is a Platonic *idea. All valid notions of universal physical principle, of all types, are Platonic ideas,* and, like the ideas of functions within the domain of atomic and nuclear microphysics, could not exist in any different form.

Thus, to enable a student (for example) today, to know what principle Kepler discovered, that student must replicate Kepler's experience in such ways as re-experiencing each step of Kepler's experience, as reported by him in *New Astronomy* and related relevant locations. This method, which is the direct opposite of today's customary textbook education or other transmission of mere "information," is the Socratic method, or, what is otherwise known as a Classical humanist mode of education.

In such ways, persons long dead transmit ideas to us from the past, as if they were alive and speaking directly to us today. Similarly, ideas are transmitted in a cognitive mode among contemporaries, sometimes over great distances. So, we speak to the future.

However, we must go a step further at this juncture. We do not know ideas of that sort in isolation from one another. Knowledge is not only the accumulation of individual such ideas; knowledge is a process of integrating an ongoing accumulation of such ideas, into the kind of world-outlook which Riemann's habilitation dissertation implies.

Ideas are produced by the influence of previously extant ideas, in enabling us to define and resolve newly considered paradoxes of an ontological quality. By this process of integrating assimilated, discovered, and re-discovered ideas of universal physical principle, we develop a quality of mind which may be regarded as "hypothesizing in general," as a way of thinking about the universe.[40] So, the process of discovering individual new universal physical principles, and integrating such discoveries of principle with our knowledge of principle in general, becomes a self-developing philosophical world-outlook.

Although two persons who have shared the same experience of an idea, may recognize the commonality of their cognitive experience of the idea's generation, that does not suffice to enable them to recognize that idea as *a distinct idea*. Ideas become distinct for the conscious mind as they are integrated in a process whose implied goal is an unfolding process of hypothesizing-in-general, a process of the form implied by Riemann's habilitation dissertation. It is only as the mind locates each idea within a domain of ideas, and locates their relationship to one another, that the act of cognitive discovery of an individual universal physical principle assumes the quality of a *distinct idea*.

It should be emphasized, as a point of clarification, that most universal principles of physical science are known to us today by the name of the putative discoverer. The student who has relived the original discoverer's experience, has thus reenacted the cognitive generation of the relevant hypothesis, as if that student had been the original discoverer. The student may, thus, reenact the experimental validation of that hypothesis, and thus rightly claim to know, rather than have merely *learned* (like a trained parrot, or a mere dupe of contemporary "information theory") the principle involved.

These features of a moment of Classical humanist education in acquiring knowledge of scientific principles, become generalized through the student's repeating the same kind of reenactment for other discoveries. The social relations among that panoply of discoverers, and the student's personal relationship to them and their work, through cognition (e.g., Classical humanist methods of education), define a multiply-connected manifold of distinct ideas in the cultivated mind of the well-educated graduate.

The essential fallacy of the Hobbesian view of society as a

40. I.e., in Plato, higher hypothesis.

collection of "interacting particles," should be obvious from the standpoint I have just summarized.

Since the progress of the human condition is the distinction of the existence of the human species, the natural relations within society are cognitive relations of the type just illustrated, in the foregoing discussion of transmission of those cognitive qualities of ideas, which correspond to elements of an integrated plenum of valid universal physical principles. It is such ideas, which are transmitted as a living form of idea over even thousands of intervening years, which express the characteristic of the natural form of human relations. It is this quality of relationship, not that of kinematically interacting Hobbesian particles, which defines the reality which the term *society* ought to connote.

Modern Suburban Savages

The difficulty which the foregoing remarks pose for most people today, should not be considered evidence that what I have just described suffers a fault of abstruseness. Rather, the resistance to my argument reflects the fact, that the existing forms of practice in today's prevalent culture, work to the effect of aborting the natural cognitive powers of the human individual in today's society. To state that point more vividly, but without exaggeration, we should reference the more typical U.S. suburbanite from the upper 20% of the nation's family-income brackets. If not physically, then emotionally and cognitively, an increasing fraction of this stratum today is virtually "brain-damaged," hopefully, not beyond remedy.

Generically, the problem is an old one in type. The causes fall under two headings.

First, there is the need for a certain natural fostering of the cognitive and emotional development of the new individual, through the successive phases of infancy, childhood, adolescence, and young adulthood. This represents a period of approximately a quarter-century, from birth, to a mid-twenties level of potential young-adult maturity. An inadequate, or misdirected approach to the development of the young person during those successive phases, such as an abandonment of principles of Classical humanist education, may cause crippling damage to that personality, presenting us the infantile child or adolescent, the childish, or even dangerously, emotionally infantile adolescent or adult, and so on.

Second, there is the factor of the willful damage to the cognitive powers of the maturing individual, imposed by certain oligarchies, and families, as a way of dumbing-down those more numerous members of society, who are intended, by current policy of practice, to be herded, by the methods of George Orwell's "Big Brother," into the status of virtual human cattle. (E.g., "Let us not educate young people above the level of the employment with which we destine them to be occupied." "Let us not educate them to imagine themselves above the social status to which we intend to degrade them. Promise them everything, but fill them with gin—or marijuana, or cocaine, or nonstop, dumbed-down forms of popular entertainment.")

The folly of mankind in general, is chiefly the result of a combination of those two methods, of negligence or willful malice, for aborting the redeemable goodness which exists as innate potential within each newborn individual person.

The orchestration of public opinion, as by the Webbs and others of the British Fabian Society, and by the American Fabian Walter Lippmann's prescription, typify the mechanisms which have been employed in the effort to degrade the U.S.'s so-called "middle class" and others, into a condition which, in effect, degrades them politically, intellectually, into the social status of virtual human cattle. This tactic of "dumbing-down" the mass of the human herd, as by aid of today's popular mass-culture, is sometimes praised, by malicious ideologues, as a popular virtue of "other-directedness." One should remember those human cattle, called the citizens of Rome, marching into their seats within the arena, where they, the paragons of *vox populi,* the mass of Roman predators,[41] would drool with pleasure at the sight of lions killing and eating Christians.

---

41. As I have emphasized, repeatedly, in earlier locations, the Latin term *popular* has the intentional connotation of "the predators," the class of Roman subjects whose chief function was to conquer, loot, or even

That, essentially, was the social doctrine of Francis Bacon, Hobbes, John Locke, Bernard de Mandeville, François Quesnay, David Hume, Adam Smith, Jeremy Bentham, et al. That was the aesthetics of Kant, the doctrine of law of Hegel's confederate Savigny, the principle of the Nazi Nuremberg rally, of the recent motion-picture spectacular *Gladiator*, and the Romantic doctrine of law of the Twentieth-Century neo-Hegelian fanatic Carl Schmitt.

The functional significance of what I have just underlined, is shown by comparing a Classical-humanist school room, in which the pupils relive the cognitive experience of original discoveries of valid principle, with the type of classroom in which students rehearse the expression of those opinions which they are instructed to regard as authoritative opinion. In the latter case, the brutish sort of teacher or parent, will warn the student, "When you have graduated from college, then you should think for yourself; in the meantime, in this classroom, you will learn to think and speak as I tell you." Or, a surly parent menacing his child, "When you grow up, you can think for yourself; in the meantime, you will believe what I tell you to believe!" Not surprisingly, the usual victim of such rearing reaches the age of twenty-five, or so, having successfully lost the greater part of his, or her innate potential to actually think cognitively, creatively.[42]

Thus, wherever the principle of Classical humanist educa-

_____

exterminate other cultures, especially superior ones such as Hellenistic culture. The first modern fascist, the Consul and Emperor Napoleon Bonaparte, typifies the conscious use of the pagan Roman tradition in law and other institutions to create the kind of Caesarian society of the predators, which Napoleon established as the model to be imitated by Napoleon III, Mussolini, Hitler, et al.

42. Psychiatrist Dr. Lawrence S. Kubie studied what he termed "the neurotic distortion of the creative process," and applied that study to the specific case of the pattern of cognitive sterility erupting in formerly gifted students at a point proximate to gaining a terminal degree. Hence, the often ironical implications of the academic term, "terminal degree." Lawrence S. Kubie, "The Fostering of Scientific Creativity," *Daedalus,* Spring 1962.

tion does not prevail, the student is conditioned to react in ways which conform to generally accepted classroom, or similar standards of social prejudice and teaching.

The case of that fraudulent description of Kepler's discoveries, associated with the admirers of Newton, is typical. Anyone who had actually worked through the documentation of those discoveries, step by step, could not be taken in. Why, then, are so many otherwise more or less distinguished scientists taken in by that Newton hoax? Simply, because it is the generally accepted classroom mathematical outlook, toward which they make fearful obeisance, for the sake of their careers and reputations among their peers. That typifies the way in which the brainwashing works.

That perversion of the all too typical contemporary classroom, is repeated, in most family households, in places of employment, and in the domain of general expression of what passes for opinion. The majority of today's under-fifty-five university graduates, typify the suburbanite fads of substituting perceived authoritative opinion, for thinking. The tyranny of popular opinion, as the lemming-like financial suicide of so many who have plunged into the market, typifies this syndrome.

This problem has been aggravated by the sympathy afforded to such degenerates as the late Theodor Adorno and Hannah Arendt. This exemplary pair of existentialist, anticivilization fanatics, have been used to popularize their cult of hatred against persons they target as representing "the authoritarian personality."[43] Arendt, for example, premised much of her claim to academic achievement, on her mimicking of both her Nazi friend, Jean-Paul Sartre's Martin Heidegger, and Karl Jaspers, in promoting what was presented explicitly as a pro-Kant denial of the existence of truth. The result is equivalent to the kind of "Big Brother" syndrome of mass lunacy portrayed by George Orwell's 1984. Those who follow such creatures as Adorno and Arendt in their abhorrence of truth, will therefore

---

43. T.W. Adorno et al., *The Authoritarian Personality* (New York: Harper, 1950).

function in their relations toward other persons as do all true existentialists, as Friedrich Nietzsche did, like hungry rats in a crowded cage.

In the healthy development of the young individual, it is the fostering of the development of the cognitive potential of the infant, child, and adolescent, at every level, which is of paramount importance to family, schools, and society in general. The premium is on development of the child's and adolescent's capacity to discover truthfulness, to develop a sense of truthfulness as an inward source of personal identity and authority in society.

The root from which depraved existentialists such as Adorno, Heidegger, Arendt, Sartre, Frantz Fanon, et al., acquired their tradition, was, most immediately the legacy of pagan Rome, or, what is known in modern European history and culture as *Romanticism*. The denial of truth, in favor of caprices of public opinion, as the mob in the Colosseum typifies this, is characteristic of what is known to history as the oligarchical model, the model adopted by European feudalism, promoted by imperial Venice, and continued by the British monarchy to the present day.

The ugly fact about pre-modern forms of society, is that they were, at least predominantly, oligarchical models, in which the relative few, as a ruling caste or oligarchy, treated the majority of humanity as simply wild prey to be hunted, or as virtual human cattle. This is the predominant cultural feature of all known society prior to Europe's Fifteenth-Century Renaissance, even societies which contributed from within them, some of the most precious contributions humanity today enjoys from earlier times. Do not look for noble savages and their cultures in so-called primitive societies; none are evident, except in the childish fantasies of the credulous. The characteristic faults, moral and otherwise, of present-day, globally extended European culture, are the rotten fruit bequeathed to modern culture by ancient and medieval cultures, all of which were predominantly, viciously examples of the oligarchical model.

The moral and intellectual decadence, on these accounts, of recent generations of young American victims of these trends, must take into account the moral effects of pattern-shifts in the quality of both employment, and of education for employment, especially during the recent thirty-five years.

During the immediate post-war period, there erupted a tendency for disdain for "blue collar" careers, which was expressed in the coordinated emergence of post-war suburbia and of related fads described, during the 1950s, as "White Collar" and "The Organization Man." Even in the relatively healthy side of this trend, there was a shift away from the identity of the scientist, to that of the engineer, and a related moral degeneration in the quality of engineering training, expressed by hostility to Classical artistic and related studies and concerns.

These and related trends in the national culture transmitted to the post-war generations, represented a shift away from earlier emphasis on the "rugged individual," whose sense of identity in acquiring knowledge and doing work, was one's own "inner-directed" development as a citizen, implicitly equal in moral sense of social status, even to those who held greater relative authority in political and economic life, and so on. The shifts into what I have emphasized as the new-suburbia trends in decadence of the post-war generation's experience, represented a political and moral down-shift in the sense of the personal identity, from that of often poorly paid, but proud citizen, to the person whose crippled, "other-directed" sense of identity, is that of the menial lackey, even lackeys, such as our present-day Talleyrands and Fouchés, who may have recently risen, if only temporarily, to levels of incomes in the order of millions of dollars.

"Who you are," became less significant, and what your relative status as a lackey might be, took over the world-outlook of the younger generations, more and more, especially during the recent thirty-five years.

The Cost of Mediocrity

All viable human cultures are characterized by growing populations. Only catastrophes, either natural or man-made, produce any different result. Whenever the collapse of life-expectancies or population-growth is caused by the society itself, rather than external interventions, the determining factor is a triumph of a type of mediocrity akin to that which has been spreading, like a cancer, in Europe and the Americas during the recent thirty-odd years.

The typical cause for all the catastrophes which a culture has brought upon itself, is the mass phenomenon known to Europe, since the literature of ancient Greece, as *the oligarchical model*. The recent thirty-five years' increasingly widespread and virulent cultural degeneration of the U.S.A. and European populations, typifies the way in which a culture may drag itself to the brink of even threatened extinction. The referenced example of what has happened to the U.S. suburbanite "Baby Boomer" stratum and its offspring, contains some of the most relevant evidence to this effect.

What we know of principles underlying such patterns, is learned chiefly from study of the evidence of the emergence of historical societies in the aftermath of the last great, cyclical melting of the glaciation of great portions of the Northern Hemisphere, a glaciation now approaching, in its customary timely way, once again, unless our development of science enables us to prevent that calamitous effect. What we know that is relevant to the matter before us here, respecting the emergence of mankind from the post-glacial period to date, is fairly summarized as follows.

The highest levels of development of those cultures known to us, present us with calendars and other products of relatively great transoceanic maritime cultures which developed during the millennia preceding the melting of the last great glaciation of the Northern Hemisphere. The characteristics of the relevant, most developed such calendars, are those which contain crucially significant characteristics of transoceanic maritime cultures. We know that the emergence of post-glaciation civilization, and of the cultures which produced it, were concentrated either in coastal areas, or through penetration inland along the course of principal large river-systems.

Typical is the transoceanic culture which dominated much of the development of the Mediterranean littoral, including its great influence on Egypt, and, the relatively inferior culture which developed in Mesopotamia, through the colonization of southern Mesopotamia by the maritime culture of that Dravidian-speaking set of colonizers, the "black-headed people" who founded Sumer.

As the case of the Egypt of the period of the building of the great pyramids attests, some of these cultures attained a high level of technological achievement, and yet they fell, repeatedly, into what appear to have been cyclical collapses into relative barbarism and collapse of population-levels, even on "dark age" scales.

This pattern is echoed in richer detail of its records in more recent historical periods of ancient and medieval societies. Most relevant is the fact, the net effect of both Latin Rome's and Byzantium's culture, was a pattern of catastrophic decline in the level of Mediterranean culture, relative to the higher level of culture represented by Classical Greece and its influence on Hellenistic society prior to the crushing of the Greek states of southern Italy.

The general pattern of decay of Latin Rome and Byzantium alike, was reversed by the coincidence of the Abassid Caliphate in the East and Charlemagne in the West, and by the expression of the Augustinian tradition in the great cathedral-builders associated with Chartres, or the developments under Barbarossa, Frederick II, and Alfonso Sabio; but, the legacy of Rome, Byzantium, and the rising imperial maritime power of Venice, imposed recurring disasters, even dark ages, for the culture of medieval Europe and the adjoining Mediterranean littoral.

Even after the founding of the modern sovereign form of nation-state, during the course of the Fifteenth-Century Renaissance, the contest between, on the one side, the oligarchical model, typified today by the British monarchy and its influence over Anglo-American power, and, on the opposing side, the tradition of the American Revolution's model of sovereign nation-state republic, has been the characteristic struggle between the relics of the oligarchical and republican models throughout the recent five centuries.

All of the great tribulations of modern globally extended

European civilization, are to be attributed chiefly to the role of the oligarchical model, and the impact of this degeneration within Europe upon other regions of the planet.

Throughout all of the known prehistory and history just referenced above, the crucially determining feature of society's existence, has been the impact of the persistence of the oligarchical model. By "oligarchical model," we should understand, an arrangement, under which a relatively small portion of mankind, called an oligarchy or a caste, rules over a majority of mankind which is degraded to the condition of wild and hunted, or herded, bred, and culled, always as virtual human cattle. The ruling oligarchy exerts its power through the instruments of associated armed and other lackeys.

Only playful children would track deer, or herd cattle, out of zeal for enjoying conversation with either. Cattle who are more intelligent, saner than their peers, are said by those holding a shareholder interest in cattle, to be too smart for their own good.

Typical of the point, are those provision of the Roman imperial Code of Diocletian, which is fairly described in modern terms as a malthusian population doctrine. Thus, just as the collapse of Latin Rome was chiefly the fruit of slavery's effect on the population, and its fertility as a whole, so Byzantium, which had survived for a time because of the superiority of its demographic characteristics and Greek culture, died for the same reasons of self-depopulation built into such customs as the Code of Diocletian.

In both examples, the combination of population policies like those of modern malthusians, and the dumbing-down of the majority retained as virtual human cattle, as has been shown by U.S. mass-cultural innovations of the recent thirty-five years, resulted in a lowering of the *potential* demographic and physical economic levels of the population per capita and per square kilometer.

Similarly, it was the anti-nation-state, globalization, and usury policies of the Venetian maritime power and its Norman allies which, over a period from shortly after the Fourth Crusade to a hundred years later, plunged Europe into the great economic, cultural, and demographic decline, culminating in the New Dark Age of the Fourteenth Century.

The significance of the panoramic view I have just described, becomes clearer, when we take into account some of the great known contributions to knowledge and technology supplied from within some of the cultures otherwise self-doomed to collapse. That irony points up the fact, that even a culture which produces greatness from within part of itself, may be also self-doomed, that because of its suppression of the cognitive potentials and sense of political identity of the mass of its population. Thus, the recent two generations' trends in U.S. policies of public and higher education, typify the contributing causes for both the present global economic collapse in progress and the recently ongoing moral, and intellectual degeneration of the population and its leading political parties and mass media.

The effect of the oligarchical model, in all its manifestations, including the post-World War II "suburbanization" of the U.S. culture, to which I have referred above, is to dehumanize the great majority of the population, actions which suppress the cognitive development of the population at large, and, thus, depress the ability of the economy to continue to meet the requirements of maintaining that culture.

In the typical case of past cultures, there is a repression of that cognitive cultural development upon which the maintenance of the potential relative population-density of the culture depends. Thus, even though some parts of the culture's intelligentsia may make fundamental contributions to the perpetuation and improvement of available knowledge, the lack of participation in the acquisition and practice of knowledge by a "zero-growth" form of social culture, brings the continued existence of that culture into conflict with its own self-imposed ecological boundaries.

Thus, to maintain a submissive majority of the population, the cognitive development of that majority must be forcefully suppressed, as the Code of Diocletian specifies relevant measures to this effect, and as feudalism continued that Code's practice in such forms as the systems of serfdom and guilds. It was under such leading policies of Byzantium, Venice, and "globalizing" tendencies within feudalism generally, that the natural impulses toward the emergence of modern nation-states were suppressed, as this is typified by the brutish wars against the Holy Roman Empire's Frederick II and the efforts to eradicate the legacy of Alfonso Sabio in Spain, and the brutish conduct of Richard II, the brutish campaign of the Normans against France's martyred Jeanne d'Arc, and, later, the typically Norman evil of Richard III, in England.

The great net advances in the conditions of life of the human population on this planet, effected within modern European civilization, over the course of the interval circa 1400-1901, have been the result of the impulse supplied by the introduction of the modern sovereign form of nation-state, under France's Louis XI and his follower England's Henry VII. The principled source of this improvement is the introduction of a revolutionary new conception of statecraft, called the principle of the general welfare. Every evil experienced by, or caused by globally extended modern European civilization since, has been caused by the opponents of that constitutional principle.

Notably, the direct forerunners of that great Fifteenth-Century revolution, which is called the Renaissance, were the great educators, such as Abélard of Paris, Dante Alighieri, the Augustinian teaching order, certain Franciscans working to similar effects, the work of Dante's great follower Petrarch, and the exemplary great teaching order known as the Brothers of the Common Life. The characteristic of that great work, as Cardinal Nicholas of Cusa typifies the extension of this into the form of the Fifteenth-Century Renaissance, was the adolescent pupils' reliving the cognitive experience reflected, chiefly, in the great Classical Greek legacy, from which all of the great achievements of European civilization as such have fallen to mankind since. The role of Cusa in founding modern experimental physical science, with his *De Docta Ignorantia,* and the role of his self-designated followers, such as Luca Pacioli, Leonardo da Vinci, England's William Gilbert, and Kepler, typifies the historical process.

Admittedly, since that time of the great Fifteenth-Century

Renaissance, globally extended modern European civilization, has been a battlefield between those forces of the modern sovereign nation-state, and its general-welfare principle, and the oligarchical model most significantly typified, over these centuries, first, by imperial maritime power of financier-oligarchical Venice, and later the transfer of that role of Venice to the global, financier-oligarchical maritime power of Venice's chosen heirs, successively the oligarchs of Portugal, Spain, the Netherlands, and London.

However, that division within modern European civilization only defines the issue of principle the more clearly. The issue is the conflict between the principle of the sovereign nation-state, the principle of the general welfare, and, its opponent, the infinitely murderous, financier-oligarchical, imperial interest expressed by the Anglo-American financier tyranny of today.

Thus, in the history of the U.S.A., all of the important political struggles, including the internal struggle against the slave-system, have been a reflection of this conflict between the principle of the sovereign nation-state and the London-centered international financier oligarchy. The central expression of the issue of principle, has been that established by the Fifteenth-Century revolutionary change in political institutions, the establishment of *a sovereign nation-state whose fundamental law is that the moral authority of government is conditional upon its efficient promotion of the general welfare of all of the people and their posterity.*

The issue of Classical education, as education bears upon political and economic practice, is the central expression of the principle of the general welfare. Do we educate our young as cognitive beings, or do we develop them as virtually human cattle? Do we develop, or suppress the development of the cognitive potential within them, which sets human beings apart from lower forms of life?

The perpetual consequence of the kinds of policies of education, culture, and economic practice, of the U.S. during the recent thirty-five years' trend, has been to degrade the cultivation and expression of the cognitive potential of our young, to a state corresponding to a self-doomed culture of virtual human cattle. Such has been the cost of the rampant mediocrity expressed in the economic and financial trends leading into the present systemic crisis of the system as a whole.

The pattern of the recent thirty-five years, since approximately the time of Richard Nixon's 1966 launching of his neo-Confederacy "Southern Strategy" campaign for President, has been the systematic destruction of the productive, educational, and infrastructural basis for a healthy society. Not only have the conditions of life of those in the lower 80% of family-income brackets been looted; the means for providing such employment, income, and standards of the general welfare, have been ripped up, by measures typified by the Nixon Administration's 1971-1973 campaign to nullify the Hill-Burton health-care law, and replace it with the predatory HMO policy.

Friedrich von Hayek's followers have thus achieved, in correspondingly great degree, the true, never really secret ambition of that co-founder of the Mont Pelerin Society, the return of globally extended European civilization, from civilization to serfdom. The fact that so many fools exist, in addition to Senator Phil Gramm, who admire Britain's Margaret Thatcher, who have embraced Mont Pelerin's neo-feudalist philosophy, is to be considered as one of the costs of the widespread mediocrity. Only mediocre, or very cruel minds could be taken in by von Hayek's perverse use of the term "freedom."

Thus, the U.S. among other modern nation-states of European civilization, has condemned itself to the same kind of oligarchical cycles which are typified by the rise and inevitable doom of the relatively powerful empires of the past. We are being destroyed, by ourselves, because we have allowed our children to adopt the intention that we be destroyed. That intention, is the cultural world-outlook which has prevailed in the U.S., increasingly, during the recent thirty-five years. That intention is most clearly expressed by the way in which we educate, entertain, and employ the future and present members of the labor-force and the members of their households.

The Cost of Classical Culture

I have thus indicated the negative features of the process. I conclude this section of the report with a summary of the positive factors to be considered.

Physical economy, as I have addressed that here thus far, is essentially the development of the power of the individual human mind to act in ways which increase mankind's power to exist in the universe. This power is found in the interdependency among chiefly several leading, contributing elements. I list each of those on which attention is concentrated here.

First, there is the quality on which I have already focussed here, the role of the cognitive powers of mind, in generating and communicating validated universal principles as solutions for otherwise insoluble ontological paradoxes of man's relationship to the "physical universe" so-called. So far, in this report, I have emphasized the discovery of those universal physical principles which bear on the per-capita relations of man to the physical universe.

Second, there is the first aspect of the social side of this power of the individual in the universe, the communication of not simply single valid principles, but a manifold of multiply-connected such principles, as Riemann's cited dissertation describes such a manifold: the ability of the individual to impart to and invoke in other persons a specific sense of knowledge of distinct ideas.

Third, there is the class of universal principles which pertains to the processes of cognitive interactions among groups of members of society, and within society generally. In this case, we are studying social processes in the same general way we apply cognitive powers to discovering and conquering the ontological paradoxes encountered in our experience of the universe in which mankind exists. A competent study of economics, as from the standpoint of the science of physical economy, illustrates the existence of the same structure of multiply-connected principles, in the domain of social processes, as in man's conception of non-living and living processes.

Fourthly, there is the role of cognitive forms of motivation, as expressed by the sense of cognitive "fun" to which I have referred earlier. This is a quality of passion, as it spills over from the playfulness of the original discovery in science, a cognitive playfulness which is associated most closely with great works of Classical modes of artistic compositions, as in both plastic and non-plastic art-forms. It is this latter quality of passion which motivates us to dedicate ourselves, sometimes with overriding compulsion, to effects as much as a generation or more in the future. It is, therefore, this aspect of the matter which is of special concern to us in the subsuming topic, long-range policy-planning, of this present report.

Although this latter quality of motivation is as characteristic of so-called physical scientific discovery as of great experiences in Classical art, it is in the greatest compositions and performances of Classical art that the significance of the passion is most immediately evident to explicitly social qualities of individual experience. The most relevant illustration of this point, is the Classical stage, as typified for our present purposes by the comparison of the great Classical Greek tragedies with the modern cases of Shakespeare and Friedrich Schiller. What is notable on that account, is the fact that the subject of that drama is politics, as situated historically. This latter connection serves us here, to emphasize both the importance of Classical art for fostering a rational basis for shaping the historical world-outlook of the mind of the statesman and citizen. Thus, as Classical tragedy illustrates most plainly, statecraft, and history, are situated under the reign of principles of Classical forms of artistic composition.

In several locations, within the present report as a whole, and in published writings earlier, I have emphasized the importance of the negative side of Classical drama, as typified by tragedy, and the positive complement to tragedy, which Schiller defined as the *sublime*. There is a point to be made on that account, at this immediate juncture.

Classical tragedy performs the indispensable function for society, of confronting society with its own propensity for bringing disaster upon itself. Through the great works of the Classical stage, tragedy shows us how entire cultures, acting under the influence of their leading institutions, such as a leading political figure, bring the entire society to an avoidable ruin, like the avoidable ruin under discussion in this present report. The positive side of tragedy, is that in a great performance of a well-composed work, the audience becomes aware of the fact that a willful alternative to doom existed in the case presented; the audience senses, thus, that if such a folly were to be encountered in some coming situation, that insight into the alternative to folly would provide society an escape from the type of calamity enacted on stage.

In the sublime alternative to tragedy as such, as in the case of France's Jeanne d'Arc, the cruel fate of the principal figure is not a subject of failure, but a triumph over evil. Without Jeanne's courageous commitment, to the end, France and the modern nation-state would not have come into actual existence, as it did because she had lived and acted as she had done.

This matter of the sublime, is no mere artistic elegance; it is an issue which confronts every sane person. We know that we each were born, and shall die, sooner or later. Thus, it would be a tragedy indeed, if ours were such a society of fools as to think that individual self-interest lies in the kinds of hedonistic considerations listed by Adam Smith, as he argues for this in the passage I cited from his *The Theory of the Moral Sentiments*. Since we know that we all die, our interest in life is what we take out of it: For what should we spend that coin we call individual life, knowing that the meaning of our having existed will be nothing but what our living has given to the future? The rule of the wise person, is: *You have but one mortal life, spend it well; what you purchase will be the meaning of your existence for future mankind, throughout all eternity*. Only a person who lives so, is not intrinsically corrupt.

There lies the sublime, as the case of Jeanne d'Arc illustrates the point, both the Jeanne of history, and the Jeanne d'Arc as Schiller presents her on the stage. That is the passion which motivates all great Classical compositions, such as that of Johann

Sebastian Bach and his anti-Romanticist followers, such as Mozart, Beethoven, Schubert, Mendelssohn, Schumann, and Brahms. It is so, as Brahms sets I Corinthians 13 to song. The passion so prompted, is that which Plato, and also the Apostle Paul, define as *agapē*.

This was the subject of an important essay, written by a great Massachusetts figure who was also a mentor of young Benjamin Franklin, Cotton Mather. Mather's injunction of the motive "to do good," expresses that passion which motivates the incorruptible ("inner-directed") part of the scientific discoverer, the great artist, and the great statesman.

Economics as Classical Art

One of the greatest frauds commonly practiced today is *the myth of objectivity*. The myth is, that the hallmark of honesty is disinterest in the issue under consideration, and that lack of passion bespeaks a disinterested assessment of the impassioned issue at hand. "Sorry to kill you, fella. Nothing personal; just doing my job," might the judge have said, when he condemned an entire section of the population to an increased morbidity rate, purely out of dispassionate regard for "shareholder interest." The only truly disinterested man is the "hanging" judge who, in matters of truth and justice, expresses the quality of disinterest otherwise shown by the female praying mantis, eating the head of the mate who is copulating with her.

It is the unfortunate consequences of an action, including actions of negligence, which deserved the passion which might have averted the calamity. Sometimes, it is indispensable not to avoid naming names; sometimes, on important issues, such as the career of Adolf Hitler, it is urgent to be very, very personal. In some cases, such as the genocide actually being willfully practiced throughout most of Africa, by known Anglo-American interests, such as those associated with London's Lynda Chalker, and formerly condoned by Secretary of State Madeleine Albright, the lack of passion is, in itself, an unspeakable crime.

Enough of tragedy; return to the sublime.

Take as an example, President Franklin Roosevelt's injunction respecting the awfulness of the situation produced by former President Coolidge's creation, the 1929-1933 Great Depression. So, today, it must be said: *We have nothing to fear as much as fear itself.*

The remedies exist, but they each and all depend upon predicating present action on confidence in a longer-term perspective. The use of the power of the sovereign nation-state to create national credit, is the indispensable means for organizing a process of general recovery from a catastrophe such as that of 1929-33, or the worse situation erupting today. This course of action depends upon mobilizing a passion in support of feasible programs which will not be self-sustaining in less than the medium to long term. On the basis of confidence in the prospect that such programs will become self-sustaining in their effects, government issues regulated credit to tide the nation and its people over, during the process of building up to a self-sustaining economic recovery.

The mustering of a combination of public and private credit for such medium- to long-term undertakings, requires the corresponding arousal of a passion for the future in a large part of the population, at least. A people will put up with much for quite some time, if three conditions are met. First, that the relative sacrifice is necessary; second, that the goal is credible; and, third, that we shall manage to get along decently, with gradual but significant improvement, in the meantime. Precisely that is required for the situation confronting the U.S. and its people, among others, today.

The great danger today, comes from the corrosive cultural influence of what is sometimes called "the Now generation." This is the silly generation which tolerated the obscene delusion, that universities should not compel students to study the works of "dead white European males." The characteristics of the victims of such a mis-education, are that they are hostile to cognitive activity, and have no passion for the realities of either the past or the future. They are not future-oriented. In that sense and degree, they have no future, and the society which adopts their opinion will have no future, either.

This point is best illustrated by contrasting the quality of passion evoked by the qualified performance of a great tragedy, such as that of Shakespeare or Schiller, and the emotional response of the current rash of entertainments which substitute mere succession of sensual effects for a process of development. Even the pedestrian sorts of popular detective-story fiction from the 1930s through 1950s, contrast sharply with the gore-splattered-against-the-windshield sorts of TV crime-story productions today. To describe a film such as *Gladiator* as having some "redeeming" quality of plot, insults the imagination of anyone operating above the zombie-like level of a Nintendo-game addict.

It is only through those forms of communication which are best typified by Classical artistic composition, and study of statecraft and history in the same mode, that we muster the ability of a population and its leaders to respond with passion to the cause of bringing the future into being.

It is the great projects of nation-building and space exploration, which will motivate today's imperilled populations into reaching to the future as a way of rising from the otherwise insufferable conditions which grip the present.

4. The Sovereign Nation-State Economy

For anyone who is not ignorant of that revolutionary improvement in the demographic characteristics of human existence which was brought about through the Fifteenth-Century European creation of the modern nation-state, European civilization over the course of the recent six centuries has brought forth a degree of improvement in the human condition without precedent in all human existence before that time [**Figure 9**]. The causes for this success are encapsulated in the creation of a revolutionary form of state, one without actual precedent in any part of all human existence beforehand: the sovereign form of nation-state brought into being in the context defined by the great ecumenical Council of Florence, a Council whose leading organizers included the founder of modern experimental physical science, the later Cardinal, Nicholas of Cusa.[44]

---

44. For another view of the uniqueness of the Fifteenth-Century founding of the modern sovereign nation-state, see Friedrich-August von

The revolution which produced this new institution, the sovereign nation-state, is the point of origin of all modern economy.

What Cusa proposed in his *Concordantia Catholica,* echoing significantly the *De Monarchia* of Dante Alighieri,[45] can be fairly summarized by stating, that what he proposed was not a sovereign nation-state as such, but rather a system of sovereign nation-states, a system of the kind referenced later by then-U.S. Secretary of State John Quincy Adams, as a "community of principle." Cusa's grasp of the significance of the same notion of *intention* later echoed by his follower, Kepler, is of crucial significance for understanding the practical considerations of principle involved.

From the standpoint of the considerations identified in this report thus far, the notion of promoting the general welfare, subsumes the notions of maintaining and improving an existing level of *anti-entropic potential* for the present and future population as a whole, and also the corresponding development of the basic economic infrastructure of the society. This includes, prominently, the level of education and related development of the young and others in households. This requires the allocation of physical sources and protected conditions of individual and family life, for that population and the area of its habitation and other uses. These responsibilities imply real costs (as distinct from merely nominal, or money costs).

This means, in turn, setting the equivalent of wages and prices, per capita and per square kilometer, for the existence and functions which must be sustained in the interest of the general welfare. In effect, it becomes the responsibility of the government, under the principle of promotion of the general

---

der Heydte, *Der Moderne Kleinkrieg als wehrpolitisches und militärisches Phänomen,* 1972 (also published in English translation under the title *Modern Irregular Warfare in Defense Policy and as a Military Phenomenon* [New York: New Benjamin Franklin House, 1986]). For Cusa on science, the reference is, again, to his *De Docta Ignorantia.*

45. Nicholas of Cusa, *The Catholic Concordance,* Paul E. Sigmund, trans. (Cambridge: Cambridge University Press, 1991).

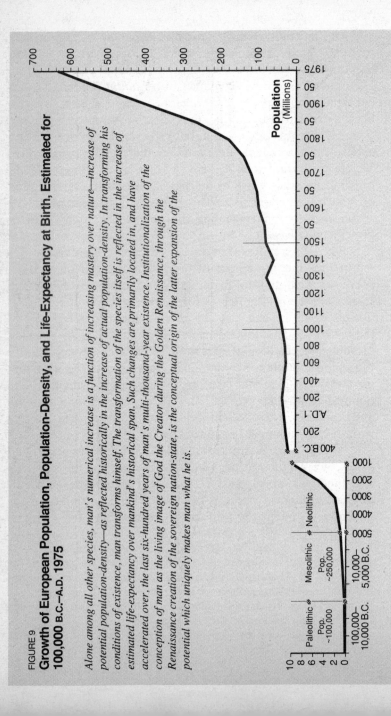

FIGURE 9
Growth of European Population, Population-Density, and Life-Expectancy at Birth, Estimated for 100,000 B.C.–A.D. 1975

Alone among all other species, man's numerical increase is a function of increasing mastery over nature—increase of potential population-density—as reflected historically in the increase of actual population-density. In transforming his conditions of existence, man transforms himself. The transformation of the species itself is reflected in the increase of estimated life-expectancy over mankind's historical span. Such changes are primarily located in, and have accelerated over, the last six-hundred years of man's multi-thousand-year existence. Institutionalization of the conception of man as the living image of God the Creator during the Golden Renaissance, through the Renaissance creation of the sovereign nation-state, is the conceptual origin of the latter expansion of the potential which uniquely makes man what he is.

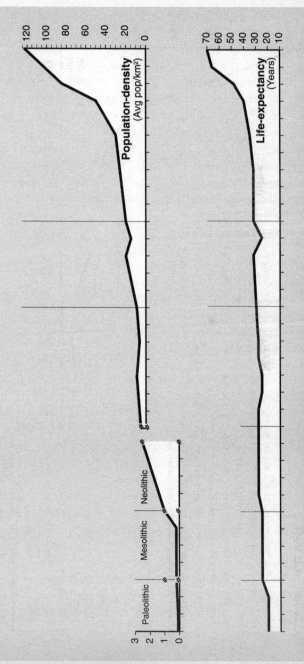

All charts are based on standard estimates compiled by existing schools of demography. None claim any more precision than the indicative; however, the scaling flattens out what might otherwise be locally, or even temporally, significant variation, reducing all thereby to the set of changes which is significant, independant of the quality of estimates and scaling of the graphs. Sources: For population and population-density, Colin McEvedy and Richard Jones, *Atlas of World Population History*; for life-expectancy, various studies in historical demography.

Note breaks and changes in scales.

welfare, to foster protectionist regulation of costs and prices, and also to stipulate allocations for basic economic infrastructure, and some other things.

Under such arrangements, what is called the "market" is bounded by the way in which protection affects, chiefly, prices, costs, and certain priorities in allocation for basic economic infrastructure. The institution of these measures of protectionism, motivated by the principle of the general welfare, was the birth of modern economy. The complexities of European economy since that time, can not be understood, without reference to the indicated interdependency between the notions of protectionism and the promotion of the general welfare.

The First Nation-State

Elements of this complexity are to be seen under France's King Louis XI. The case of Louis XI, as the beneficiary of Jeanne d'Arc, serves us a double purpose here. We cite that case again, now, to make clear both a lesson from the panorama of history, and to make history clearer by means of a corresponding example from Classical artistic composition.

History is not a fiction practiced on the stage of a *tabula rasa*. This rule is clear in the process leading into Louis XI's coronation, and the circumstances under which he ruled thereafter. The case of Jeanne d'Arc, the intersection of her case with the reemergence of the Papacy during the decades immediately following her martyrdom, and the convergence of both her role and that of the outcome of the Council of Florence, are key to understanding how Louis XI came to power as he did. The mixed defeats and continued achievements of the circles of Cardinal Nicholas of Cusa, following that Council, were reflected in the increasing difficulties Louis XI and France suffered in the later part of his reign.

The history of Europe from the time of Venice's Fourth Crusade, near the beginning of the Thirteenth Century, until the accession of England's Henry VII, was a nightmare, caused chiefly by the alliance of the imperial maritime power of Venice with the Norman interests largely controlling England and France, a legacy which continued to plague Europe into the time of the *Fronde's* alliance with France's Louis XIV.

The great New Dark Age which erupted during the middle of the Fourteenth Century, had begun with the wars against the Holy Roman Empire's Frederick II and his successors, during the middle decades of the Thirteenth Century, a war which had been continued through the so-called "Hundred Years' War" and, in England, the "Wars of the Roses." Meanwhile, the fall of Constantinople had, for that time, ruined the ecumenical agreement reached during the Council of Florence, thus enabling Venice and its allies among the old Norman interests to reassert the authority lost during the earlier parts of the Fifteenth Century, leading thus into Venice's fomenting and orchestration of those religious wars of the 1511-1648 interval which threatened to eradicate the accomplishments of the Florence Council and Renaissance.

In this context, Jeanne d'Arc played a crucial role, leading toward the liberation of France and the revival of the Catholic Church from the ruinous political strife of the Fourteenth and early Fifteenth Centuries. For that, her French and English Norman foes, the latter allied with a current anti-Pope, feared and hated her.

Although Friedrich Schiller uses a piece of fiction in dealing, on stage, with the issue used, in history, as a pretext for retrying and burning her, in transposing the events from the vast panorama of France to the pin-hole of the Classical stage, Schiller never deviates from the historical issue posed by the richly documented historical record of her case. On this account, Jeanne not only makes history, but serves as a vehicle for Schiller's efforts to lift drama from the relatively more primitive art of tragedy, to the higher Classical form of the sublime. As Bach's *St. John* and *St. Matthew Passions* use the New Testament to present Jesus Christ's mortal life and actions as the epitome of the sublime, so Jeanne walked in the pathway of Christ, losing her life, not through a tragic flaw, but for a sublime higher purpose, as Plato, earlier, had used the case of Socrates to assert the principle of the sublime, in contrast to the standpoint of the Classical Greek tragedians.

Thus, do real history and Classical artistic composition converge as one. Moreover, it was in the same setting of Jeanne's combat and martyrdom, that Cusa composed his *Concordantia Catholica*.

The principle of the general welfare, as a principle of natural law, is the specification that no government has the moral authority to rule, except as it promotes efficiently the general welfare of the living and their posterity. The principle is more or less clear, from what we have considered in the preceding pages. However, that leaves a not-unimportant issue unresolved: *Who shall decide what promotes the general welfare? How shall that decision be judged? Who shall judge?*

The general answer to those questions, is fairly stated as *reason.* That means reason as defined by cognitive determination of truthfulness, in the Socratic sense of truthfulness, as all matters of universal principle must be defined in no other way. Who shall then judge whether or not, by reason, a government does, or does not meet the Gettysburg standard of *government of the people, by the people, and for the people? How shall the people know that they are being governed properly according to that principle?*

This points to a twofold issue posed by Dante Alighieri, the issue of Classical art. Since cognition occurs through the ironical use of language, the determination of the suitability of government must be made in terms of the language of the governed; however, that is not possible, if the language itself is not developed to the level of capacity for communication which such cognitive responsibilities imply. What shall then replace Latin as the language of government? Admittedly, within medieval Latin, the influence of Classical Greek had uplifted the use of Latin to a certain degree of literacy and related sophistication; but the problem of the use of language for government persisted. Thus, the pioneering by Dante and Petrarch founded the possibility of establishing the nation-state, as the reading of Dante's *Commedia* in the public places in Florence, showed the pathway to elevating Italian into the condition needed for government according to reason.

Thus, for these and related reasons, it is clear that a nation must not be so small, a virtual micro-state, that it is not capable of a reasonable degree of sovereignty; but, we can not simply lump populations together, without a concurrence in the shared use of a literate form of language, a form of language conditioned to serve as a medium for cognitive communication.

The net result, is a system of nation-states, each immediately, and sovereignly responsible for its own general welfare, but, not indifferent to the general welfare among nations. So, there must be a standard of natural law, by which consenting nations agree to order their mutual relations in ways consistent with the promotion of the general welfare of each and all.

The Quality of the Citizen

The great affliction which threatens the best efforts of any modern statesman, is the persisting tendency of the great majority of the population to accept a self-policed status as a virtual herd of human cattle, rather than true citizens. Thus, in the recent U.S. Presidential election, the majority of those who voted, voted in the fashion of slaves begging for favors at the back-door of the master's mansion. They proposed to support a candidate, not because he was actually worthy of the office, but because they deluded themselves they might glean a favor or two from the one that they might not gain from the other. What was good for the nation, for their posterity, was, generally speaking, not their concern. They were like the slaves who said, "Master! We aren't asking for freedom; all we ask is that you pay us off with a few shekels' worth of reparations." All for one measly, miserable bowl of pottage.

That state of mind of the generality of the U.S. adult population, is in itself a far step down from the temper of the same strata of the population thirty-five years earlier. The curve of the declining share of U.S. national income represented by the lower 80% of the nation's family households [**Figure 10**], since

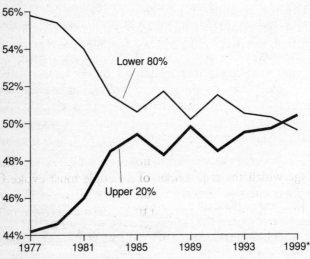

FIGURE 10

America's Richest 20% Now Make More than the Other 80%

(percent)

* Projected
Sources: Congressional Budget Office; *EIR*.

President Carter's inauguration, shows the way in which the majority of the U.S. population has become accustomed to its economic and political degradation under the trend set by the Nixon "Southern Strategy" campaign of 1966-1968.

This decadence in the generality of the citizenry, is reflected in the moral degeneration of the educational system, in the degraded characteristics of what the population tolerates as popular entertainments.

The citizens of the U.S. have, in fact, the constitutional authority to free themselves from this oppression. They have reached the point they have temporarily lost the desire to do so. Better to be a fed pig in a pen, even if the butcher is not far off, than a beaten child in the master's house.

The responsibility of leadership, as long as society slides again, and again, into the habits of human cattle-likeness, is to awaken the people to their essential humanity. To arouse from the swinishness of Adam Smith's filthy doctrine, and to adopt a sense of mission which makes their life meaningful in the eyes of the Creator, meaningful in their own eyes.

The only method by which such attempts at leadership have succeeded, in the past 2,500-odd years of European civilization, is the method of Plato, the method which theologians sometimes term "spiritual exercises," as the referenced discoveries of Kepler typify such arousals of that in the individual which is made in the image of the Creator.

It is not with do's and don'ts, that the individual soul is saved. It is with a sense of mission, the mission of being, and acting as a creature made in the image of the Creator. That is the image which the true leader of a people must evoke from within those citizens he seeks to uplift to rediscover their own true nature. That is the image of a true citizen of a true republic, which this republic of ours was founded to become.

5. Quarter-Century Cycles as a Standard of Accounting

As I wrote here of this paradox, in an earlier section of this report, in economics, the future lies in the present, and the success of the present is to be seen only in the mirror of its future. In practice, the future of immediate reference for the present, is a generation ahead, a period of approximately twenty-five years' lapse of time, from today's newborn to the matured young adult of about twenty-five years.

For example, one to two generations, is the lapse of time which, in saner times, used to be required for a medium-income-level family household to acquire the ownership or equivalent of a suitable residence. Important infrastructure represents an investment in the same general magnitude.

Indeed, when we build a home, or equivalent housing, we should design and build it to last without disastrous costs of maintenance, for fifty to a hundred years or more: glorified tar-paper shacks with pasted-on Hollywood exteriors, at $400,000 and up, are not really the answer to the housing need, especially when a large ration of such speculative, low-grade, cheap-labor-built construction, has been dumped onto a market defined largely by the lately hired "new economy" recruits presently being dumped in droves. As might be recognized already, this aspect of the "Y2K"-keynoted, 1995-2000 "new economy" bubble, has not been particularly kind to the banks which have been involved in conducting credit into these not merely highly speculative, but even dubious markets. The way in which a new household formation brings forth a matured next generation, is thus a fair approximation of the span within which the making of the future must define the present.

Large-scale infrastructure, such as public utilities, educational institutions, should be designed with adaptation to new developments in mind, but the basic platform on which those new developments will be superimposed, should last for a quarter-century at least, and, with reasonable ratios of maintenance, better fifty to a hundred years.

Thus, for example, the idea of a wage can not be defined competently as the income paid to an individual. We must think in terms of household income, and of the conditions of household life needed to ensure the healthy production of the required quality of the next generation of the labor-force and its associated households. We must therefore think in terms of the conditions of life within the framework of that household, and associated extended families, and of the conditions of the community of which the household is a part. We must think of the organization of the living day in the household, including the hours in commuting daily, and of personal life associated with the household, as this bears upon such prominently included considerations as the rearing, and education of children and adolescents.

We must be alert to those errors in child-rearing and circumstances of childhood and adolescent life today, which tend to produce an impairment of the functional development of the individual who is presumably on the way toward adult maturity.

These and many considerations confronting us when we think approximately a generation ahead, usually involve cost, in some sense of cost to society. These costs must be paid, in one way or another. How shall we be able to pay?

For one thing, we must set certain priorities. Keep the unnecessary overhead down, for example. Generally, after all the relatively obvious measures of economy are taken into account, there remains a substantial deficit in what might be projected as available future income against morally unavoidable future physical costs. We must always think, first of all, in physical terms, rather than financial ones. Whence the additional margin of income?

In general, the answer to the question so posed, is scientific and technological progress. The question becomes: What programs of accelerated investment in scientific and technological progress will foster the rates of increase of the physical productive powers of labor needed to balance the implied budget of the economy overall?

The dull-witted sort of accountant, perhaps a fellow-traveller of Senator Phil Gramm, will answer "slash expenditures; we can not afford more investment in research and development at this time." The problem of the linear mentality, to which I have made frequent reference here already, has thus cropped up once again.

The solution to the problem is human in nature. The human being, if properly educated and inspired, is an ultimately inexhaustible source of creativity, as discovery of valid universal physical principles typifies this creativity. This creativity, so expressed, is characteristically anti-entropic. That is, the more we are able to spend for that anti-entropy, the greater the rate of growth of the real net national income.

The shaft of the spear of anti-entropic progress, is education combined with the fostering of Classical culture. However, to get the shaft through the target efficiently, we must put a sharp point on the spear. The best choice of point is what is called an economically broadly based "crash science-driver program," as typified by the pre-1966 phase of President Kennedy's manned Moon landing program.

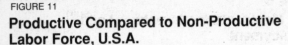
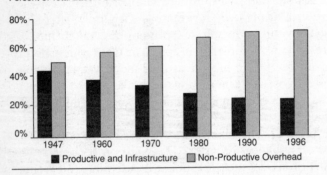

FIGURE 11

Productive Compared to Non-Productive Labor Force, U.S.A.

Percent of Total Labor Force

■ Productive and Infrastructure   ■ Non-Productive Overhead

I explain a few crucial points respecting such a much-needed "crash science-driver program" for the world today.

Reconstruction

Turn your attention to the categories of employment of the U.S. labor-force over the interval 1946-1965, prior to the injection of the pro-malthusian phase-shift of 1966-1967, into the U.S. Federal budget. Trace the decline of those categories of employment which had been associated with technologically-driven increases in development of basic economic infrastructure and physical production of physical goods, prior to 1966. Contrast this with the shift in composition of categories of total employment over the interval 1971-1987, and, again, the shift over the interval 1989-2000. [See **Figures 11 and 12.**]

Now consider reducing the percentiles of employment in services, by category, to the levels of 1946-1965. Then, intend to shift the percentile cut from employment to the effect of restoring the percentiles of composition of employment to levels consistent with 1946-1965 trends in composition of employment of the total labor-force. This means, in effect, the shift of composition of employment of the total labor-force, back to the more productive composition of the earlier, pre-1966 interval.

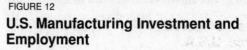

FIGURE 12

U.S. Manufacturing Investment and Employment

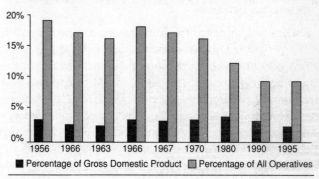

■ Percentage of Gross Domestic Product ■ Percentage of All Operatives

Since we are presently headed for massive unemployment, the kind of shift of composition of employment indicated will be best accomplished simply by absorbing new employed into expanded employment in categories corresponding to the more physically productive component of employment. This means, of course, government programs, in the spirit of FDR's recovery effort, which steer credit into the categories of employment which are more desirable, because of their impact on the desired increase of the physical productivity of the labor-force as a whole.

This means, of course, much higher rates of Federal and other taxation on those relatively upper-bracket personal and business incomes which are not recycled as investments in the physically productive sectors of the economy. This would be aided by reversing Kemp-Roth and related follies, to increase radically the financial capital-gains tax-rate, but with a compensating investment-tax-credit program along lines not dissimilar from President Kennedy's program.

The idea that increasing the ratio and amount of tax-free financial gains would promote productive investment, was a fairy-tale in the first place. The way to manage the job, is to reward those who employ their gains for the increase of physical productivity of the economy, and tax those relying upon speculative appreciations at the relatively highest rates. We must learn the lesson of thirty-odd years of liberal folly, recognize the mistakes of deregulation and the like, and restore what had worked before the ruinous effects of Nixon's and Carter's elections as President.

The leading edge for the initial mass of raw growth such a recovery program will set into motion, will be infrastructure. Here, my outline earlier of the implications of the infrastructural interface between mutual development of noösphere and biosphere, should predominate in policy-shaping. The increase of water throughput, energy throughput, and higher energy-flux densities, per capita and per square kilometer, chiefly through public utilities, will provide the initial leading stimulus for economic recovery in both infrastructure and those entrepreneurial activities affected by expansion of infrastructure.

This emphasis upon infrastructure, should build the platform for a two-fold approach to upgrading the productive powers of labor in the so-called private sector generally. In short, the two approaches are, respectively, bottom-up and top-down. Bottom-up, means the traditional approach of the 1939-1965 interval: upgrading the quality of employment of so-called "blue-collar" and other productive employment, with emphasis upon technology-intensive, capital-intensive modes for bringing this effect about. Top-down, means a "crash science-driver program" approach, in which the mere development of scientific discovery is treated as the highest-priority quality of product produced by the economy as a whole.

To situate the top-down aspect of the program, look at the global prospects for a U.S. long-term economic recovery.

U.S.-Eurasia Cooperation: Science as a Product

Among the crucial economic situations in the world at large, is the collapse of the export margins of the German economy, the economy on whose support the entirety of Western continental Europe depends for its economic vitality. The natural export market for Western continental Europe as a whole, is chiefly Eurasia. The pivot for any such cooperation between Western continental Europe and Asia, is Russia. Relations among Russia, China, and India, are the keystone upon which broader coopera- tion in Asia depends more or less absolutely. It is through West- ern continental European cooperation throughout Eurasia, in cooperation with Russia, that a general and durable economic recovery of Eurasia as a whole becomes feasible. In a rational state of affairs, the government of the U.S.A. would eagerly cooperate with its partners in Western continental Europe in such a Eurasia undertaking.

This is not to deprecate the importance of Africa or of Central and South America, or of Australia and New Zealand, either. Rather, unless the Eurasian land-mass pivot is viable, the world lacks the net resources to provide much-needed rescue for Central and South America, or Africa.

There are two economic fulcra in this Eurasia project. One is the underdeveloped landmass of Central and North Asia. The other, is the fact, that without massive infusion of technology into nations such as China and India, beyond the internal re- sources of those nations themselves, the amount of technology which could be infused into those two most populous nations would not be sufficient to overcome the burden of the deep impoverishment of the less developed portions of the populations and areas of those nations, in particular.

The solution for these and related challenges internal to Eurasia, is a long-term reorientation of the economies of the traditional technology-exporting nations of the world, toward the technology-hungry appetites of East, Southeast, and South Asia. Essentially, this means applying the lessons actually and implicitly learned from the 1946-1965 cooperation between the U.S.A. and Western continental Europe, to the expanded hori- zons of Eurasia as a whole.

It would be a great mistake to imagine that such a program could succeed on the basis of off-the-shelf technologies from present U.S. and European enterprises. The degree of technologi- cal leverage represented by such inventories, is not sufficient to accomplish the implied mission in a timely degree. There must be a virtual explosion of scientific progress, and technological progress driven by scientific progress, to the effect of increasing the rate of technological gain greatly beyond that which would be possible with off-the-shelf-plus strategies.

This means, that the potential volcanoes of large-scale technology export, such as the U.S., Western Europe, Russia, a resuscitated Korea, and Japan, must cooperate with other nations in creating a virtual new category of employment: "crash science-driver program" employment.

Realistically, such a program must come chiefly from national governments, mobilizing such a new industry on the basis of lessons from projects such as the Manhattan Project and the post-war space programs. This means a heavily overloaded, ostensibly "over-staffed" initiative, not one conducted according to today's accountants' notions of efficiency. This means, heavy engagement of universities, with build-up of their science departments and research projects, with much emphasis on pre-benchmarking notions of engineering design for advanced experimental work.

It means the inclusion of such programs as the Sänger project's scramjet program, for lower-energy-cost access to geostationary Earth-orbit, and every other plausible avenue of task-oriented space-exploration work. It also means, a crash-program approach to the noösphere-biosphere concepts of Vernadsky et al., with much emphasis on the kinds of biophysics implied by that work, as opposed to the dubious claims for molecular biology's cure for practically anything.

The intended by-products of such a broadly defined "Vernadsky Project," should include new assistance to crop programs, aimed to secure the world's food supply, in both quantity and quality. It should include broader-based study of infectious and other diseases, and the possible remedies. It should emphasize helping the biosphere to transform wastelands into viable crop-lands and areas of habitation. It should include the build-up of useful, managed forests, as part of the build-up of the biosphere. It should foster improved approaches to developing long-term residential areas, public facility areas, and commercial and industrial areas, in ways which a deeper understanding of noösphere and biosphere suggest.

The most crucial thing in all of this, and related work, is

to instill in the population an informed sense of mission, looking toward what must become a quarter-century ahead, and still further. Then, as Franklin Roosevelt said, we shall have nothing so much to fear from this new great world-wide depression, as fear itself.

Vladimir Ivanovich Vernadsky (1863-1945). He developed the concept of the biosphere, and the related conception of the ways in which human creativity has transformed the biosphere into the noösphere.

"With the emergence of Man and human society, the biosphere has entered a new stage, which Vernadsky called the noösphere, in which human creative reason becomes increasingly the dominant, guiding influence in the further expansion and development of the biosphere—including its eventual extension beyond the Earth, into the solar system and beyond."

Introduction: Why Dead Minds Can't Know the Noösphere

by Jonathan Tennenbaum

This article by Vladimir Vernadsky with its introduction first appeared in the Winter 2000-2001 issue of 21st Century Science & Technology.

FROM ANCIENT TIMES until today, those who have sought to comprehend the organization of our universe, have generally distinguished among three main *classes* or *domains* of phenomena: First, phenomena occurring in inert or *nonliving* matter, outside of the action of living organisms. Second, *living processes,* that is, the domain of biology. And third, processes connected with the cognitive activity of the *human mind*.[1]

Yet, with the triumph of reductionist thinking in natural

---

1. These three domains seem so utterly different in character, that they have often been treated as disjoint "worlds unto themselves." Into the Eighteenth and early Nineteenth Centuries, for example, it was commonly believed by the so-called vitalists and others, that the difference between living and "dead" matter was caused by the presence, in living organisms, of some special "living energy," "living force" or other physical entity unique to living matter. There were strong doubts, for example, whether the organic chemical substances, generated by living organisms, could even in principle be synthesized in the laboratory, outside living tissue. Meanwhile, for centuries, philosophers occupied themselves with the question, how the *soul* could act upon the *body*—given that mind or soul, and the ideas and thoughts generated by them, appear to be entities of a completely different nature than material bodies.

science, and above all with the vast development of molecular biology since the middle of the Twentieth Century, the borderline between the living and nonliving has become more and more fuzzy, or even nonexistent, in the minds of scientists.[2]

The Error of Reductionism

The failure to recognize this third alternative—despite Vernadsky's work, and despite the fact, that the essential point involved was familiar long before to Leibniz and even to Plato—reveals an *elementary methodological error,* pervading both modern molecular biology and the attempted approaches of Schrödinger, Prigogine, and others to the physics of living processes.

The nature of the error was clearly identified, more than 500 years ago, by the great Renaissance thinker Nicholas of Cusa, in his critique of Archimedes' work on the *squaring of the circle:* In attempting to approximate a circle by a series of inscribed regular polygons of increasing number of sides, we *appear* to come closer and closer to the circle, but we can never actually *reach* the circle. Even if the number of sides of the polygon were hypothetically to become *infinite,* it would still not resolve to complete *identity* with the circle, because the circle constitutes a higher *species* of geometrical existence. The circle embodies a *higher principle,* namely, that of continuous *rotational action,* which is entirely absent from the linear domain of the polygons. Although the polygons can be constructed from the circle—and in that sense the circle subsumes, as a "higher species," the "lower species" of the polygons—, there is no way to arrive at the circle from the polygons.

Nevertheless, geometers and others expended untold efforts, down through the centuries, in fruitless attempts to *square the circle,* making the same type of mistake as those who, from

---

2. I do not even mention the field of "artificial life," Siamese twin to the equally absurd pseudo-science of "artificial intelligence." The current popularity of both raises the question: Have computers really become intelligent, or have people just become stupid?

the time of Pythagoras on, refused to accept the existence of *incommensurable magnitudes* in geometry. The same error emerged later, in the resistance to Leibniz's notion of the infinitesimal calculus, and in the bitter opposition by Kronecker and others to Georg Cantor's introduction of the transfinite numbers.

The attempt of molecular biologists to treat living organisms as "molecular machines" exemplifies the problem perfectly.

There is no doubt that the vast and intricate arrays of biochemical reactions and related processes, identified by modern molecular-biological methods, *do* actually take place in living cells. It *appears* also to be the case, that changes in a living cell, can always be *correlated* in some way with changes in the configurations and motion of molecules. There is thus little doubt, that molecular biology can *approximate* the workings of living processes—perhaps even up to the point of "asymptotic convergence"—in terms of ever more extensive mappings of the purported "molecular machinery" of cells. The latter corresponds, in a methodological sense, to Nicholas of Cusa's polygons with increasing numbers of sides.

Now comes the difficulty: None of the molecular-biological approximations, taken by itself, can account for the functional characteristics of living matter in the biosphere, as demonstrated by Vernadsky. We never get, so to speak, to the "living part," that is, to the unique characteristic of *action,* which distinguishes living from nonliving processes. That higher characteristic, bears an analogous relation to the domain of "molecular machinery," as rotational action bears to the straight-line action embodied in Nicholas of Cusa's polygons.

To go beyond this, at first glance, purely *negative* observation concerning the limits of reductionist methods, let us go back to the three-fold division of the universe and have a look at the specific contribution of Vernadsky and of his successor in this matter, Lyndon H. LaRouche, Jr.

Living Matter in the Biosphere

A scientific understanding of the three-fold division of the universe begins, when we abandon the naive tendency to interpret the basis for the distinctions between the three domains, in terms of the supposedly inherent properties of *objects per se*— for example, living and nonliving objects. What we are really dealing with, as Leibniz emphasized, is distinct *classes of physical principles,* all acting upon the universe at the *same time,* and which stand in a well-defined hierarchical relationship to each other. That hierarchical relationship is the immediate focus of Vernadsky's life work.

Consider the characteristic *activity* of living matter on the Earth, as exemplified by the case of plants. Living plants grow and maintain themselves by virtue of their ability to absorb water, minerals, and other inorganic materials from the soil, and gaseous molecules from the atmosphere, and to work up this nonliving material into living tissue. Thereby, nonliving matter has been transformed into living matter!

Looking at this on the microscopic level, the question poses itself: What is the nature of the *physical change* which occurs during this transformation? How does an atom of *nitrogen,* for example, which is now part of the plant's living tissue, *differ* from its earlier existence in the mineral fertilizer the farmer put into the ground?

Present-day molecular biologists would characterize the change as merely one of a different chemical *bonding* of the nitrogen atom in the living tissue—for example, in a protein or other organic molecule—as compared to the inorganic compound it was part of in the fertilizer. They might hasten to add, that same organic bonding could also be realized in a laboratory just as well, outside of living tissue. Hence, in their view, there is no change on the atomic or molecular level which could be shown to be *unique* to living processes *only.*

Some modern biophysicists, however, would rightly disagree with the simple-minded chemists' conclusions. They will point out, for example, that the physical state of an atom depends upon much more than simple chemical bonding; the behavior of atoms and molecules in living tissue is modified by a common quantum-electromagnetic field, which imposes a coupling of processes occurring at distant locations within living tissue. Exactly that feature, is a matter of ongoing, experimental investigation.

Responding in this way, however, both the chemist and the biophysicist would have failed to point out the *most elementary feature* of the process at issue, namely: the *active role* played by the living organism itself, in *imposing,* so to speak, a *higher state of organization* upon that nonliving matter. In this way, the organism acts as the *physical cause* of *a continuous and highly directed transformation of its environment.*

It was Vladimir Vernadsky, who most clearly recognized and demonstrated the nature of that biogenic transformation, by shifting the focus of the investigation from the level of isolated individual organisms, to the aggregate of *all* living matter existing on the Earth at one time, and by studying the *impact* of living matter upon its environment (the biosphere) over the *longest time scale* which is available to precise observation: geological time. Thus, in place of the perilously abstract question "What is life?," Vernadsky substituted a concrete geological question— one concerning the specific role of living matter in the geological history of the Earth.

Vernadsky's main conclusions, based on the analysis of an enormous body of empirical data, can be summarized as follows:

(1) In the course of evolution, the aggregate "free energy" of the living matter in the biosphere—its ability to do work on the environment—has been constantly increasing.

(2) As a result of that increase in free energy, living matter has become the *most powerful geological force* in the biosphere—even though the total mass of the living organisms themselves, remains a nearly *infinitesimal fraction* of the total, growing mass of matter directly and indirectly affected by their activity within the biosphere.

(3) In the course of evolution, living matter has constantly expanded the "envelope" of the Earth that is populated by living organisms—that is, the biosphere—extending it upward into the atmosphere, into the depths of the oceans, and ever deeper into the Earth's crust.

(4) The capacity for this specific sort of *evolutionary development,* leading to a continual increase in the free energy of living processes in the biosphere, is *unique* to living organisms and is not found in the nonliving domain.

Analysis Situs

But Vernadsky adds a crucial additional conception:

With the emergence of Man and human society, the bio-sphere has entered a new stage, which Vernadsky called the *Noösphere,* in which *human creative reason* becomes increasingly the dominant, guiding influence in the further expansion and development of the biosphere—including its eventual extension beyond the Earth, into the solar system and beyond.

As regards the question of the Noösphere and the role of human reason, Vernadsky's work remained incomplete. In this respect the direct continuation and completion of what Vernadsky had begun, lies in the work of the American economist and statesman Lyndon LaRouche.[3] Among other things, LaRouche showed:

(1) The absolute distinction between Man and all other forms of life in the biosphere, is empirically demonstrated by the fact, that the human species has been able, through deliberate changes and improvements in the mode of individual and social activity vis-à-vis the biosphere, to increase its overall population-potential by more than a *thousand-fold* in the course of prehistoric and historical development. No other living species has demonstrated that ability.

(2) The *cause* of that thousand-fold increase, in the course of history, in the size and quality of the human population that can maintain itself on the Earth, is located solely in the *creative powers of individual human reason* to discover, assimilate, and apply *new scientific principles* and analogous discoveries of principle in art and statecraft, with the effect of improving Man's power to command the forces of Nature (technology).

(3) The action of individual creative reason, upon which the capacity of the human species to effect successive increases in its population potential is based, has a specific and completely *unique* form. It lies in the ability to deliberately seek

---

3. See, for example, Lyndon H. LaRouche, Jr. "In Defense of Strategy," *21st Century,* Summer 2000, p. 18, and "Where Do We Attach the Head?" *21st Century Sciene & Technology,* Fall 2000, p. 47.

and discover errors or imperfections in the commonly accepted assumptions underlying the practice of a society, and to correct or supplement those assumptions, through the discovery and validation of a new universal principle, shown to govern the universe—and which was either contradicted, or at least not accounted for, by the previously existing assumptions or axioms of thought.

(4) Acts of original *creative discovery* and acts of *creative learning and problem-solving*—of the sort needed to adequately assimilate and apply such discoveries (in the form of new technologies) in the successful practice of society—are generated *solely* within the "sovereign" mental processes of *individual human beings*. Thus, the process of increase of the population potential of the human species, occurs as a successive integration of specific creative mental acts by individuals, which have the net effect of transforming the overall practice of society. This *unique historical relationship of the individual to the whole* is found *only* in human society, and *only* in connection with human reason; it is entirely lacking in both the other two, lower domains of the universe.

A Paradox Resolved

What Vernadsky had accomplished for the relationship of *living* to *nonliving processes* in the biosphere, LaRouche has done for the uniqueness of *human reason* relative to *living processes in general*. Thereby, LaRouche brought the questions, *What is human reason?* and *What is the absolute distinction between Man and all other living species?* into the domain of rigorous *empirical-scientific demonstration* and *measurement*—as opposed to what had commonly been regarded as the merely "subjective" realms of religious belief and philosophical speculation.

Combining LaRouche with Vernadsky, we obtain a most lucid and powerful overview of the three-fold division of the universe.

What we are dealing with, is the differentiation among three, interconnected *classes* or groups of *physical principles* constituting human knowledge of the universe. For convenience, let us designate them as follows:

A equals physical principles pertaining to nonliving processes generally; *B* equals physical principles pertaining to the unique characteristics of action of living processes, relative to nonliving processes; *C* equals physical principles pertaining to the unique characteristics of human reason.

Note the following paradoxical, but crucial point: Physical principles, insofar as they are valid principles of human knowledge, must be *universal;* they must, at least implicitly, apply to the universe *as a whole.* The unity and coherence of the universe (and of human knowledge) would thus seem to demand, that (for example) the principles governing nonliving matter (class *A*) must also apply in some way to living processes; and conversely the principles of living processes (class *B*) must also apply to nonliving processes; and similarly for class *C*. But doesn't this contradict the *absolute, fundamental distinction* between living and nonliving processes, and between living processes and human reason, demonstrated by Vernadsky and LaRouche, and which was the whole point of our discussion so far?

Recalling Vernadsky's demonstration of the *dominion* of living processes over nonliving matter in the biosphere, and LaRouche's related proof for human reason, shows the way out of the paradox.

The principles of living processes are principles for the *action* by which living matter "conquers" and transforms nonliving matter, as the increasingly dominant geological force in the biosphere. Similarly, Man's demonstrated power to deliberately increase his per capita power to command the forces of Nature, through the exercise of human Reason, points to the implicit *universality* of the principles underlying human Reason. Insofar as the universe "obeys" human Reason,[4] even nonliving matter

---

4. Here I do not mean to imply that Man per se, in an unqualified sense, represents a higher principle commanding the universe. It is *only* insofar as Man obeys *Reason,* that Man can continually increase his power over the forces of Nature. The unique potential of Man, relative to other

is implicitly subject to the principles of human Reason, albeit in a different way than the human mind itself. Conversely, living matter, including the brain tissue which is an indispensable substrate for human mental activity, is composed of the same atoms and molecules as nonliving matter; and living matter appears subject to the principles of class *A*, while not being completely determined by them.

What we are therefore dealing with, is a *multiply connected universe* in the sense of Bernhard Riemann: The principles of classes *A*, *B*, *C* are all acting on one and the same universe, simultaneously and (implicitly) at every location. But at the same time, the three classes of principles stand in a definite *hierarchical* relationship $A < B < C$ to each other, in terms of *physical power* or what Cantor called *Mächtigkeit*, and as evidenced by the growing dominion of living over nonliving matter, and of reason over the living and nonliving domains within the biosphere. Being of different *Mächtigkeit*, the classes *A*, *B*, *C* are strictly differentiated from one another; and yet, an overall harmony exists between them, insofar as they jointly define a self-developing, anti-entropic universe.

This sort of relationship of classes of physical principles, which is well-defined and yet cannot be expressed in logical-deductive terms, is the subject of what Leibniz called *Analysis Situs*. Vernadsky's work is a brilliant application of that method, to the empirical domain of the naturalist.

Implications for Biophysics

The following article by Vernadsky exemplifies exactly this use of *Analysis Situs* as a *method of discovery*. How does the difference between living and nonliving matter, so clearly manifested on the level of the biosphere over geological time-scales, correlate with the physics of living and nonliving processes at *microscopic* scales of space and time? Although the chemical

---

living species, lies in his *capacity* for Reason. Whether or not that capacity will be nurtured and developed in each individual, or rather, willfully destroyed, is the central political issue facing the world today.

structure of living tissue is totally different from that in matter of inorganic origin, the basic laws of physics and chemistry *appear* to apply to both. No special physical entities, like the "living force" or "living substance" many vitalists believed must exist in living organisms, have ever been found.

Focussing on this paradox, Vernadsky puts forward a bold hypothesis: The peculiar organization of living organisms is a function of a *"different geometrical state of space-time,"* existing inside those organisms, and *different* from the space-time of nonliving processes! Vernadsky suggests, that the space-time of living organisms might be a special type of *Riemannian geometry*. He calls on mathematicians, physicists, and biologists to collaborate on this problem, which, he foresees, could lead to a revolution not only in biology, but in physical science as a whole.

Judging from his discussion of the problem, Vernadsky himself did not have a completely adequate comprehension of Riemann's original geometrical conception. The latter went beyond the idea of a single, fixed geometry (in the sense of the customary non-Euclidean geometry, for example), to embrace the notion of an expanding, *multiply connected manifold* of physical principles or "dimensionalities"[5] as the mathematical *image* of a *self-developing universe*. Put another way, we must redefine the relationship *A:B,* from the standpoint of the higher relationships expressed by human reason.

Supplementing Vernadsky's argument on the space-time of living processes on this crucial point, we obtain the outlines of an entire program of experimental research. Recent work on "biophoton" interactions of living organisms[6] and related areas of biophysics, is obviously directly relevant to the issue raised by Vernadsky. Placing such work in the broader context indicated here, should help to bring forth its revolutionary implications.

---

5. See Note 3.

6. See "Russian Scientists Replicate 'Impossible' Mitogenetic Radiation," *21st Century Science & Technology,* Winter 2000-2001.

On the Fundamental Material-Energetic Distinction Between Living and Nonliving Natural Bodies of the Biosphere

by Vladimir Ivanovich Vernadsky

This first complete English translation of a 1938 article by the innovative Russian biogeochemist, who saw the human mind as the highest development of natural processes.

Editor's Note

This article was translated from the Russian by Jonathan Tennenbaum and Rachel Douglas. An abridged translation into English, by Vernadsky's son, George, appeared in the June 1944 Transactions of the Connecticut Academy of Arts and Sciences.

Two systems for the transliteration of Russian into English are used here: The bibliographical references in the notes are given in the Library of Congress system. In the text, the transliteration is modified to better approximate Russian pronunciation.

Translator's notes are included in brackets. The numbered footnotes are V.I. Vernadsky's. His parenthetical references to "Sections" refer to the numbered sections of the article.

Foreword

Three years have passed before the author has been able to return to *Problems of Biogeochemistry*.[1] Having been at work recently on the book, *The Basic Concepts of Biogeochemistry in Connection with the Scientific Comprehension of Nature*, the author considers it useful—without waiting for its completion, which will necessarily be delayed—to split off and develop separately in *Problems of Biogeochemistry*, certain specific questions, touched upon in the book, to which he finds it necessary to draw attention right away. One such problem, empirically established by the author in this second issue of *Problems of Biogeochemistry*, is the fundamental material-energetic distinction of living matter in the biosphere, from all other of the biosphere's natural objects and occurrences; a distinction that admits of no exception.

The author has approached this question, starting from the study of life as the totality of all living organisms on the planet—that is, the planet's living matter—, taking into account the special structure of the domain, inhabited by living matter—the biosphere, the sole area of the planet, which is lawfully connected with the expanses of cosmic space. It seems to the author, that before now no one has approached the phenomena of life from this side, yet this new approach leads to major consequences, which can be verified by experience and observation. The author considers, that the table published below includes no hypotheses or theories, but rather constitutes an exact presentation of scientific facts and empirical generalizations flowing from those facts. The table does not depart from the framework of science into the domain of philosophical notions, but at the same time it sharply and decisively reveals the significance of life—living matter—in the biosphere, as a planetary phenomenon.

In connection with the general questions raised here, the author, in a third issue now in preparation for publication, poses

---

1. Vernadskii, V. *Problemy biogeokhimii. I. Znachenie biogeokhimii dlia poznaniia biosfery.* [*Problems of Biogeochemistry. I. The importance of biogeochemistry for cognition of the biosphere.*] 2nd ed. (1st ed.—1934). Leningrad, 1935.

the still more general question of "the states of physical space," which concerns not only biogeochemistry, but all investigations of Nature, and which is inseparably connected with the problems of biogeochemistry. The author hopes to publish it in the near future. The topics of these two publications are closely connected.

—*Moscow, September 1938*

I. Basic Concepts

Living matter, the biosphere as an envelope of the planet. Its new geological state—the noösphere. Natural bodies and the natural phenomena of the biosphere—inert, living, and bio-inert. Their system—the scientific apparatus. Left-handedness and right-handedness in living matter as a manifestation of the state of the space it occupies. The free energy of the biosphere as a manifestation of the biogeochemical energy of the living matter in the biosphere.

1.

In my biogeochemical work, which I have pursued systematically and without interruption since the beginning of 1916, I have recently framed conclusions, which point to the deep, unbridgeable distinction—energetic-material in character—between the phenomena of life, and all other processes, occurring in the biosphere; a distinction which, on the one hand, can be expressed with quantitative precision, but which, on the other, calls for new mathematical work in the domain of geometry. Revealed before us, is a new area of the study of life phenomena, which uncovers new facets of the phenomena of life and new possibilities for scientific work. I therefore consider it useful to call attention to these conceptions, rather than waiting for the completion of my reworking of biogeochemistry.

2.

The foundations of biogeochemistry are formed from a few basic conceptions, which *do not contain any hypotheses*, but are

precise and clear scientific concepts—scientific empirical generalizations of the naturalist's experience and observation. Above
all, the very concept *of the living matter of the biosphere* represents such an empirical scientific generalization—one that is as
indisputable as a correctly, scientifically established fact. *The
living matter of the biosphere is the aggregate of all its living organisms.*

In the following I shall use, instead of the concept *"life,"*
the concept *"living matter"* in the indicated sense.

From the standpoint of the biosphere, the individual living
organism is usually lost from view; in first place comes the
aggregate of organisms—living matter. In biogeochemistry, however—in some strictly defined cases—at times it is necessary to
pay attention to the discrete organism, to its individuality. It is
indispensable to do this in those cases, where the activity of Man
appears as a geological factor, as we see happening now, and
the individual personality sometimes becomes vividly apparent
and is reflected in large-scale phenomena of a planetary character. The human personality changes, accelerates, and causes geological processes of enormous significance, through its presence
in the biosphere.

We are living in a brand new, bright geological epoch. Man,
through his labor—and his conscious relationship to life—is
transforming the envelope of the Earth—the geological region
of life, the *biosphere*. Man is shifting it into a new geological
state: Through his labor and his consciousness, the biosphere is
in a process of transition to the *noösphere.*[2] Man is creating
new biogeochemical processes, which never existed before. The
biogeochemical history of the chemical elements—a planetary
phenomenon—is drastically changing. Enormous masses of new,
free metals and their alloys are being created on Earth, for example, ones which never existed here before, such as aluminum,
magnesium, and calcium. Plant and animal life are being changed
and disturbed in the most drastic manner. New species and races
are being created. The face of the Earth is changing profoundly.

---

2. Le Roy, E. *L'exigence idéaliste et le fait d'evolution*, Paris, 1927,
p. 196.

The stage of the noösphere is being created. Within the Earth's biosphere, an intense blossoming is in process, the further history of which will be grandiose, it seems to us.

In this geological process—which is fundamentally biogeochemical—a single individual unit of living matter, out of the totality of humanity—a great personality, whether a scientist, an inventor, or a statesman—can be of fundamental, decisive, directing importance, and can manifest himself as a *geological force*. This sort of manifestation of individuality in processes of enormous biogeochemical importance, is a new planetary phenomenon. It emerged, and began to manifest itself ever more sharply and profoundly in the course of time, *during the most recent tens of thousands of years,* on the background of billions of years of the prior history of the biosphere, when this phenomenon did not exist.

In biogeochemical processes—outside the boundaries of these phenomena—the totality of living beings—living matter, continues to play the basic role. It is characterized as the totality of all organisms, mathematically expressed as the totality of *average* living organisms. Biogeochemistry studies, above all, the manifestation of the totality, not of the average indivisible unit. In the majority of the other biological sciences, we chiefly study the average indivisible unit; and, in the sciences of medicine and animal husbandry, the indivisible unit, individuality, or the single personality has been of outstanding significance during the past millennia.

Morphologically, living matter is manifested in biogeochemistry as a species, genus, race, etc. We distinguish *homogeneous living matter—belonging to a genus, species, etc.—and heterogeneous living matter,* such as the forest, the steppe, or a biotic community in general, consisting of homogeneous forms of living matter, in certain proportions.[3] The convenience of this approach

---

3. Vernadskii, V. *Biosfera.* Leningrad, 1926. Vernadskii, V., *Tr. Biogeokhim. labor. [Works of the Biogeochemical Laboratory].* 1. Leningrad, 1930. Vernadsky, W. *La biosphère.* Paris, 1930. Vernadskii, V. *Biogeokhimicheskie ocherki.* Moscow, 1939 (in the process of publication [Vernadsky's note]).

to the phenomena of life lies in the fact that we do not stray, in our judgments and conceptions, into the shaky domain of hypotheses and philosophical constructs about life, such as dominate the thinking in biology. We do not depart from the domain of scientific facts and scientific empirical generalizations; we stand on their firm ground.

3.

Alongside the concept of living matter, we put forward two other empirical generalizations: the concept of the *medium* of life, as the *biosphere*, and the concept of a *living natural body*. Living matter is found on our planet only in the *biosphere*, which is the domain of life.

This characterization defines the boundaries of the biosphere with absolute precision. According to this definition, the entire *troposphere* of the atmosphere belongs to the biosphere. And now, living organisms—human beings and their inevitable companions: insects, plants, and microorganisms—are penetrating even higher, by themselves or with mechanical assistance, into the *stratosphere*. At the same time, civilized humanity (together with its inevitable living companions) is penetrating several kilometers below the surface of the Earth, deep below the limits of that surface terrain, which is in contact with the troposphere. Today, too, we recognize the planetary significance of the discovery, at the end of last century, that life—chiefly anaerobic, microbial living matter—is to be found in subterranean regions more than three kilometers deep, and probably deeper. The lower boundary of the biosphere thus lies several kilometers below the surface of the geoid.[4] The entire world ocean belongs to the biosphere.

The biosphere constitutes a definite *geological envelope*, sharply differentiated from all other geological envelopes of our

---

4. Vernadskii, V. *O predelakh biosfery. Izvestiia AN SSSR. Seriia geol. [Concerning the boundaries of the biosphere. News of the Academy of Sciences of the U.S.S.R. Geology Series]*, 1937.

planet.[5] This is so, not only because the biosphere is populated by living matter having enormous significance as a geological force, completely reworking the biosphere and transforming its physical, chemical, and mechanical properties. In addition, this is the sole envelope of the planet, penetrated in an appreciable way by cosmic energy, which transforms it even more than living matter does. The main source of this energy is the Sun. The Sun's energy—thermal, light, and chemical [i.e., ultraviolet—trans.] energy—is, together with the energy of the chemical elements, the primary source for the creation of living matter.

Living matter permeates the entire biosphere and to a large extent creates it. Living matter accumulates the energy of the biosphere, mainly the thermal and chemical energy of solar radiation and the chemical energy of the Earth's atoms. It is possible, that radioactive energy plays a certain role in this.[6]

4.

Materially and energetically, the matter constituting the biosphere is acutely heterogeneous. From this standpoint, we must distinguish the main bulk of its matter, which does not belong to living matter, and which I shall call *inert*—nonliving matter. The greater part of this, in terms of weight, consists of solid rocks. But the greatest volume belongs to liquid and gaseous bodies—the ocean and the atmosphere. Here is found—here lives—the totality of the planet's living organisms—its living matter.

Between the living and inert matter of the biosphere, there is a single, continuous material and energetic connection, which is continuously maintained during the processes of respiration, feeding, and reproduction of living matter, and is necessary for

5. Vernadskii, V. *Biosfera*. Leningrad, 1926; *Ocherki geokhimii [Sketches on Geochemistry]*. 2nd ed. Leningrad, 1934 (first published in French in 1924, as *La géochimie*); *Problemy biogeokhimii. I. [Problems of Biogeochemistry. I.]* 2nd ed., Leningrad, 1934.

6. Vernadskii, V. *Ocherki geokhimii [Sketches on Geochemistry]*. Leningrad, 1934; *Biogeokhimicheskie ocherki [Biogeochemical Sketches]*. Moscow, 1939 (in the process of publication [Vernadsky's note]).

its survival: *the biogenic migration of atoms* of the chemical elements, from the inert bodies of the biosphere into the living natural bodies and back again. This appears in the form of *motion*—the departure and arrival of specific chemical compounds and elements to and from living organisms in connection with the processes of feeding, respiration, excretion, and reproduction, characteristic of living matter. These processes define the *biogeochemical energy* of living matter, the chief manifestation of which is the multiplication of living matter.

All of these manifestations of biogenic migration and biogeochemical energy are determined by the dimensions, the chemical composition, and the energy of the biosphere. For this reason, not any arbitrary sorts of organism can exist in the biosphere, but only those organisms strictly determined by the structure of the biosphere. *The living organism and living matter are a lawful function of the biosphere.* People usually forget this. And, in an erroneous manner—especially in philosophical discourse, but also in biology—they counterpose the living organism to its environment, as if these were two independent objects. This sort of counterposition is a logical error. It is especially apparent in philosophy, and *undermines at the core a great number of its conclusions.* I shall not pause here to consider this point more fully.

5.

No less important, is the concept of a *natural body.* Strangely enough, this basic concept, which in essence pervades all natural science, is usually ignored and not subjected to serious logical analysis. And yet, scientists use the concept, almost unconsciously, at every step of their work.

In my youth, I had a clear and conscious experience of its importance. My teacher V.V. Dokuchayev, in his creative work on soil science, put forward the proposition, that soil is a *special natural body,* distinct from other rocks. As is well known, he proved this thesis, and thus made it possible for his contemporaries to grasp, through a striking example of a successful synthesis, the bases of creative work in natural science.[7]

But such events are rare in the history of science and in current scientific life. Normally, debates do not address the fundamental assumptions of scientific knowledge. People do not talk about these assumptions; they forget about them.

Reflecting on this, it is easy to convince oneself, *that all natural science is based upon the concept of a natural body, or a natural phenomenon.* In our further discussion, we shall deal only with the biosphere, and shall consider phenomena involving living matter.

Scientists study in the biosphere only those objects, which are created in the biosphere by forces occurring within the biosphere, or phenomena, produced in the biosphere by those forces. The objects they deal with, may conveniently be termed the *natural bodies* of the biosphere, and the phenomena—*its natural phenomena.* The task of science is to enumerate, describe, and identify all the natural bodies and all the natural phenomena, which exist or have existed in the biosphere. This is the work of generations of scientists, and there are billions of billions of scientific facts and scientific generalizations—i.e., natural bodies and natural phenomena—to be grasped in a scientific manner, counted, and brought into a system. These form the basis of science; from them, empirical generalizations are constructed, which can be brought back once again to the natural bodies and natural phenomena.

This work results in the creation of the basic content of science, for which, strangely, there is not yet any generally accepted expression. I have had to name it, and, perhaps, it is convenient to call it *the scientific apparatus.*[8] This apparatus

---

7. Vernadskii, V. *Ocherki i Rechi [Sketches and Speeches].* Prague, 1922, p. 77. *Problemy biogeokhimii. I. [Problems of Biogeochemistry. I.]* Leningrad, 1934.

8. I have to introduce a *new word* for this old concept, although the enormous significance of the concept it embraces is clear to everyone, as is the exclusive importance of work on the scientific apparatus, in terms of both the time and the labor, spent on it by scientific researchers. This

began to be created in astronomy already thousands of years B.C., and was understood—it came down to us—in the form of numerical data on the positions of the Sun, the stars, and the planets in the Hellenistic compendia (Hipparchus, Ptolemy). This work was revived in the Middle Ages in Central Asia. Everywhere, it was done in the chronicles in the form of precise records of comets, fireballs, meteorites, etc. Starting in the Sixteenth Century, there was a rapid accumulation of data, the evaluation of which was the basis for making the first major generalizations. But even in astronomy, the basic forward motion, which has been continuous and developing rapidly from that time on, began on a large scale only in the Eighteenth Century. In that century— the century of *descriptive natural science*—the effort to precisely enumerate, observe, and describe every natural body and to record every natural phenomenon, became a conscious task of exact natural science.

Linnaeus (1707-1778), basing himself on the work of earlier naturalists, introduced the concept of the *system of Nature* and for the first time calculated the number of species of animals and plants—the species of homogeneous forms of living matter, inhabiting the biosphere. In 1758, he knew a total of 4,162 species of animals (by 1768, the number was 5,936), and in 1768—7,788 species of plants. In all, Linnaeus had distinguished 13,724 species of living organisms by 1768, and even fewer rocks and minerals. Today, the number of species of plants is approaching 200,000, and may possibly exceed 300,000. The number of species of animals is approaching 800,000; in reality, it is probably several million and may reach 10 million. In essence, the *"system of Nature,"* understood in a broad sense, corresponds to what I call the scientific apparatus.

The colossal quantity of numerical data, corresponding to chemical and physical properties of matter—growing like a snowball, always increasing over the course of time, obtained mainly by *scientific experiment,* rather than from observation

---

is a consequence of vestiges of the past, of a time when work in philosophy— rightly so, at that time—was considered more fundamental than scientific work.

of the biosphere, and first created in the biosphere by scientific work, exceeding by many times the quantity of living natural bodies and living matter, and having no limits—in my opinion, makes it logically unclear, inconvenient, and practically useless to term these data a system of Nature. Therefore, the concept of *the scientific apparatus,* which we can appreciate, only because it has been reduced to a scientific system, is simpler. It includes both the system of Nature and the scientific apparatus of the humanities, which is encompassable by a scientific system, albeit thoroughly permeated by individuality.

6.

Every object of natural science is a natural body or natural phenomenon, created by processes of Nature. At the present time many quadrillions, if not more, of natural bodies and phenomena have been scientifically collected, enumerated, and scientifically defined in the system of the scientific apparatus. The number of bodies and phenomena continuously increases, and the system of the scientific apparatus is also continuously being perfected. Thanks to this, we are confronted, ever more acutely, with an infinite quantity of scientific facts to examine. The basic content of science is located in them. Reworked by means of scientific generalization, provisional scientific hypotheses and theories, and embraced by mathematical deduction and analysis, these become *scientific truth,* the precision and profundity of which increases *with each generation.*

This is what distinguishes exact science from philosophy, religion, and art, where *there is no scientific apparatus* and where the scientific truth, sometimes discovered by intuitive creativity, can be recognized as such only when it has been scientifically validated. This creative intuition sometimes comes far in advance of its scientific comprehension, and it is in these domains of human creativity that the scientific truths of the future are hidden, which are unclear to contemporaries. But, we cannot make precise sense of them without science, without grounding them in the scientific apparatus.

7.

It is possible to distinguish three types of natural bodies in the biosphere: *living* bodies (for example, a plant, a beetle, etc.), *inert bodies* (for example, rock, quartz, etc.), and *bio-inert* bodies (such as soil, lake water, etc.).

The biosphere consists of sharply bounded domains, formed by living, inert, and bio-inert bodies—waters, living matter, rocks, air, and so forth. A transition from living bodies to inert bodies takes place when they die; when a living body ceases to exist as such, it is transformed into organogenic rock (for example, bioliths) and inert bodies such as gases.[9] Bioliths are often bio-inert bodies. The direct generation of a living organism from inert bodies is never observed: the principle of F. Redi (all life comes from life) [*omne vivum ex vivo*], is never violated.[10]

The concept of inert (dead) and living natural bodies as sharply distinct natural objects, is a commonplace, ancient notion, inculcated over millennia of history—a concept of "common sense." It cannot provoke any doubts, being clear and intelligible to all.

In scientific work, even over centuries, only a few cases can be found, in which there were doubts about whether a specific natural object should be reckoned a living being or an inert body—whether that given natural phenomenon were a manifestation of the living or the nonliving. One such doubtful case— perhaps the most profound one—is the question of viruses.[11]

Other cases may be the questions J.C. Bose has raised in Calcutta, about whether *life* is not manifest in both living and inert matter, but to different degrees. These are, however, philosophical problems, which Bose tried to solve using the scientific method, as G.T. Fechner had posed the matter less precisely, in

---

9. Samoilov, Ia. *Biolity [Bioliths]*. Moscow, 1929.

10. On Redi's principle, see Vernadskii, V. *Ocherki geokhimii [Sketches on Geochemistry]*, 4th ed., Leningrad, 1934, p. 209.

11. For viruses, it is still unclear whether we are dealing with a new form of organism ("living protein"), or with a protein, which contains the spores of miniscule organisms. It is thought that *the proteins cannot be cleansed of these spores by crystallization.*

philosophical terms, earlier in the Nineteenth Century in Europe. In this case, the question of biogeochemistry's living matter is not involved, since in biogeochemistry, living matter is the totality of living organisms, whereas Fechner and Bose were trying to delve into the material-energetic substance, which is common to the living and the inert body.

8.

The concept of *a bio-inert natural body* is a new concept—defined in exact biogeochemical terms and in distinction from the concepts of inert and living natural bodies. Natural bodies of this sort are clearly expressed in the biosphere and play a big role in how it is organized.[12] *Bio-inert bodies are characteristic of the biosphere*. These are lawful structures, consisting of inert and living bodies simultaneously (for example, soils), all of *the physico-chemical properties* of which have to be adjusted—with sometimes very large corrections—if, in studying them, the activity of the living matter located within them is not taken into account.

The biogenic migration of chemical elements (atoms) plays a big role in their properties—very often the dominant role.

Any soil is a typical bio-inert body. V.V. Dokuchayev had already recognized this clearly.

The overwhelming majority of *terrestrial waters* are bio-inert bodies. There are only isolated instances, in which living matter does not play a fundamental role in them. This is not the case, for example, in hot volcanic waters, which are rich in sulphuric and hydrochloric acid, nor is it the case in strongly saline waters. Nonetheless, even in the Dead Sea there is microbial living matter, although it does not play a decisive role. Rain water is free of living matter in its first moments. All the waters of the oceans and seas, of rivers and lakes, and all of their *bottoms,* are bio-inert bodies. The gas balance, the chemical composition, and the silts of all these waters—their chemistry—are basically determined by living matter.

---

12. Vernadskii, V. *Problemy biogeokhimii [Problems of Biogeochemistry]*. Leningrad, 1935. Vol. 1., 8 f.

The role of bio-inert natural bodies is extraordinary, and has not yet been properly taken into account in how the biosphere is organized.

The process of *the weathering of rocks* is a bio-inert process—a fact that is usually not considered. This circumstance, I think, explains the backwardness of this area of chemical geology (the weathering of the Earth's crust) relative to the contemporary level of knowledge. The biogeochemical approach should contribute much to the solution of this problem.

9.

So far, I have not gone beyond the concepts: living matter, the biosphere, natural bodies, and natural phenomena (inert, living, and bio-inert)—concepts based on the enormous empirical, precise material of experience and observation. These concepts cannot arouse any theoretical doubts whatsoever, nor do they require any new scientific hypotheses or theoretical scientific constructions to be understood. One can calmly proceed with the work, so fruitful for science, of systematizing the accumulated scientific facts and generalizing from them.

But, for an understanding of the matters that now follow, I must necessarily touch upon two new phenomena of great importance, the scientific investigation of which cannot be carried out on the basis of the mere generalization of scientific facts, but requires introducing new concepts and finding a new form of comprehension of the facts. Both of these phenomena are extremely poorly understood from a theoretical standpoint, and their scientific significance has not been appreciated. They are now on the frontier of contemporary scientific knowledge. These are, first, the concept of *right- and left-handedness* and, second, the concept of *biogeochemical energy*.

Right- and left-handedness is an everyday concept, existing since the earliest times, which has hardly been comprehended in a scientific and philosophical way. It was Louis Pasteur, who first drew attention to its paramount importance for understanding the phenomena of life—the living organism, or living matter. Independently of Pasteur, and somewhat earlier, Bechamps had realized this, but Pasteur grasped the question more deeply, and identified within it phenomena, which permit us to penetrate in a precise scientific way into this immense domain of problems, the full significance of which Pasteur himself could not foresee.

The concept of *biogeochemical energy* was introduced by me in 1925, in my report to the Rosenthal Foundation in Paris, which was never published in full. In my book, I deal with this question to the extent possible today. Let us first examine the question of right- and left-handedness in its relation to living matter and to the biosphere.

10.

We do not need, here, to deal with the profound naturalist and experimenter A. Bechamps—an older contemporary of Pasteur, his enemy and rival, who outlived Pasteur by many years, but was unable to obtain the conditions needed for systematic work. He started out from exactly the same fact, as did Pasteur—from the discovery, made at the beginning of the Nineteenth Century, in a small enterprise in Alsace, of the transformation of racemic acid or its salts into left-tartaric acid during the development of wine mold in it. On this basis, a new way of producing left-tartaric acid was established. Pasteur and Bechamps—both profound chemists—saw in this chemical action of the mold as living matter, a remarkable, exclusive property of life—living matter; something not understood, unusual, unknown and, apparently, impossible in ordinary chemical reactions. To reflect upon this and to take note of it—to see the problem involved—was already a big accomplishment, but it was only the first step. It was necessary to investigate the phenomenon, and express it, in specific scientific facts.

Bechamps's circumstances of life did not permit him to do this. But Pasteur connected the new phenomenon with a very special property of enantiomorphous crystals, characterizing—under the influence of living matter—the racemic acids and salts. As a result of that action, an isomer was produced—only the left- or the right-handed one, but not the other, which had perhaps been consumed by the organism. Pasteur correctly saw in this a drastic violation of the law of crystalline symmetry. This violation appeared in the fact, that the right- and left-handed forms manifest completely different degrees of stability in living matter, exhibiting *far from identical chemical behavior*— something never observed with them in inert natural bodies. Evidently, the latter could not occur.

He called this phenomenon *dissymmetry,* but did not draw attention to, and did not connect this with the normal right- and left-handedness of living matter, in its morphological and physiological structures. He studied the phenomenon as a crystallographer and a chemist, but not as a biologist. Pasteur himself did not provide a more precise definition of dissymmetry and did not consider the changes, which had occurred in crystallography, when he returned to these problems again in the last years of his life.

Much more important, was Pasteur's discovery of *molecular dissymmetry,* completely analogous to the dissymmetry of polyhedral crystals. He thereby initiated a whole new science—stereochemistry. Because of it, chemistry was enriched by the concept of *asymmetry* (i.e., the absence of symmetry in the spatial configuration *in the vicinity* of a carbon atom). This term is used simultaneously in chemistry and physics in completely different senses, generating confusion.

11.

The muddle that arose interfered with the work. The molecular dissymmetry, discovered by Pasteur, showed, that the presence of living matter is reflected in the chemical formula, including in solutions, and that *right- and left-handed atomic structures* are found to be non-equivalent in chemical reactions. *They are chemically distinct in living matter, but chemically identical in inert chemical media.* Pasteur did not know, that (as was discovered after his death) this was essentially the same phenomenon he himself had discovered in crystals. For in crystals, he had a spatial distribution of right- and left-handed spiral arrangements of *atoms,* analogous to the atomic structure in molecules. This conclusion emerged in a precise way from the notion of *crystal-*

line space—speaking in contemporary language—geometrically constructed by Ye.S. Fyodorov and A. Schoenflies at the end of the last century. In the coincidence of the 230 groups he identified (there are actually 219), with the arrangements of atoms in crystalline space, Ye.S. Fyodorov saw proof of the atomic construction of chemical compounds. Finally, this was experimentally demonstrated in the Twentieth Century by the x-ray analysis of crystals. The contemporaries of Pasteur—Seeber, Ampère, and Godin—had foreseen this, but Pasteur remained outside the influence of their ideas.

After Pasteur, P. Curie generalized the concept of dissymmetry, considering the phenomenon, discovered by Pasteur in living organisms, as a special case, and applying the concept of dissymmetry to physical phenomena in general—electric and magnetic fields, etc.—as a fundamental postulate of physics. But Curie was not able to complete the development of his ideas; his work was interrupted in full swing, by his sudden death. No coherent presentation of the results he had obtained was left in his papers. It should only be noted, that Curie demonstrated the existence of different forms of "dissymmetry," and logically concluded that a phenomenon, connected with any given form of dissymmetry, must have a cause that possesses the same form of dissymmetry. It is convenient to call this conclusion *P. Curie's principle*.

In view of this state of the matter, I think it will be more correct to leave aside the concept and the word "dissymmetry," and instead employ the older, generally familiar idea of the distinction between right- and left-handedness in organisms, which is so starkly manifested in Man. But since there exists a theory (an erroneous one, it seems to me) that right-handedness in Man emerged only in the Neolithic period, the correct way to proceed will be to substitute for right- and left-handedness, the more general concept, which Curie employed before his death, of *distinct states of space*. He did not manage to prepare a formal presentation of this concept before his death, but it essentially corresponds, of course, to the different forms of dissymmetry, one on which Curie and Pasteur were working.

This concept was widely known among naturalists in the domain of descriptive natural science, and is rooted far back in the Eighteenth Century. Here the subject was often the variable state of space on our planet, connected with its orbital motion around the Sun; that certain motions and phenomena were different, according to whether they took place on a part of the planet moving in the direction of the Sun, or in the opposite direction. Pasteur recognized the possibility of *different states* of cosmic space, by which he explained his discovery that living matter exhibits dissymmetry. Indeed, we should see in the state of space, the basic *geometrical substrate* for all of its material, temporal, and energetic manifestations.

In the present case, there will be a state of space, in which right- and left-handedness, expressed as right- or left-handed spiral structures of atoms, are chemically identical in inert bodies and distinct in living ones. This, one of the most profound geometrical properties of natural bodies, has been given insufficient attention, in philosophy, mathematics, and natural science. But we are all very familiar with it in daily life. We know it from childhood, since a human being is a living body, in which right- and left-handedness are sharply distinguished from one another (including in chemical terms). For example, one person out of 16,000 [sic] is left-handed. In recent times these phenomena have begun to attract greater, but in my opinion still insufficient, attention in biology.

Mathematicians—especially geometers—can no longer ignore this, but need to elaborate this fundamental *geometrical phenomenon.*

I shall return to the question of the state of space, in general, and in connection with its particular manifestation in the non-equivalence of right- and left-handedness, in my next study on the problems of biogeochemistry. Here I cannot go into it further. It seems to me that it is convenient to speak, in this context, about physical space, as Helmholtz proposed.

12.

It is necessary to discuss yet another phenomenon, which has hardly been comprehended by scientific generalizations— *the active energy of living matter in the biosphere.* R. Mayer, almost 100 years ago, took this manifestation of living matter under consideration. He showed that in organogenic minerals— in coal deposits—we have an accumulator of free energy, captured in this form by the living matter of the Carboniferous period, and we use the fossilized solar rays of that time. But the idea in general form—the creation and accumulation of *free energy in the biosphere by living matter* and by the natural processes associated with living matter—arose in the minds of many in the middle of the Nineteenth Century, when the concept of energy itself was developed.

Now I want to address this more concretely: not as the basic question of the energetics of the planet, but as a biogeochemical problem. In 1925, I designated the free energy exhibited by living matter in the biosphere, which essentially amounts to the work, associated with the motion of atoms, and is manifested in the movements of living matter, as *biogeochemical energy* (See Section 15, V). Since biogeochemical energy sharply distinguishes living matter from inert matter, it is indispensable to mention its basic features here.

13.

The biogeochemical energy of living matter is closely linked with three fundamental characteristics of living matter in the biosphere: first, with *the unity of all living matter in the biosphere;* second, with the continuous generation, by living matter in the biosphere, of *free energy, capable of performing work;* and third, with *the colonization of the biosphere by living matter.*

In all three of these cases, the manifestation of biogeochemical energy is different; *taken as a whole, biogeochemical energy is inhomogeneous.* In the final analysis, it is connected with the movement of living matter in the biosphere, with passive or active displacements (relative to living matter), associated with the mobility of masses of living matter in the biosphere, and ultimately reducible to the motion of atoms or chemical elements.

From what I have said, it is clear that biogeochemical energy is not some special form of energy pertaining to life; it is not the *vital energy* that W. Ostwald was looking for—analogous to thermal, chemical, light, electrical energy, etc. It does not affect the law of conservation of energy, but appears in that context as *already known forms of energy*.

We can now trace the real sources of biogeochemical energy with precision. They are, ultimately, the radiant energy of the Sun (light, heat, chemical, and the energy of the chemical elements, from which bodies of living matter are constituted [chemical and thermal energy]). There is probably a contribution from radioactive elements.

An exact quantitative calculation of the caloric effect in life processes, I believe, establishes beyond any doubt that such is its origin. It is, essentially, a result of *the organization of the biosphere and the organization of the living matter* that inhabits the biosphere.

I cannot go into this matter further here. I shall only mention the main forms of manifestation of that organization. The most important is *the biogeochemical energy, connected with the colonization of the planet*. I attempted to calculate it in the form of a definite, for each species of living matter, maximum *velocity of that species' transmission of life*—the perhaps unsuccessful definition I gave it earlier; that is, *the velocity of colonization of the entire planet by a given organism*. This is energy, connected with the *reproduction of living organisms*. Each form of living matter can in this way spread throughout the planet and, within a certain period of time, which is different for each form of living matter, theoretically colonize the entire planet. In the most rapid cases, for bacteria, this process of colonization can occur within one to one-and-a-half days; while for the elephant—one of the slowest-reproducing of all organisms—it would take 1,000 to 1,100 years. At full colonization, the living matter would cover the entire surface of the planet, i.e., it would fill all of its actually existing lines and areas. One of these curved lines, the line of the Earth's equator, i.e. the precisely defined terrestrial line (curve) of maximum length, may be taken as a single parameter for comparison, common to all forms of living matter.

When I speak here about the colonization of the planet, I assume that this process of colonization were to occur under such conditions, as would permit it to proceed normally into the future, if it were not hindered by lack of space—of surface area for colonization. The velocity of colonization, expressed as a magnitude V, may fluctuate within limits ranging from close to the speed of sound in air, more than 33,000 centimeters per second (for some bacteria), to hundredths of a centimeter per second (for the elephant).

In other words, we are talking about the long-term, durable colonization of the planet by an organism under its normal conditions of life, in which it can exist over generations; and not about *explosions* of life, in which the excess of organisms born, dies out due to insufficient food or living space.

These conceptions have not yet entered into the consciousness of science. I am convinced that their employment is a matter for the future. It should be noted, that the velocity of sound corresponds to the real condition, wherein the normal composition of the atmospheric medium, in which the organism lives— even in the case of aquatic organisms (natural waters have their own underwater atmosphere)—, is not destroyed. This shows that biogeochemical energy, so expressed, has nearly reached its physical limits. The velocities obtained in this way may be quantitatively compared with one another; it can be asserted, for example, that the velocity of colonization for the elephant is 10^7 times less than for bacteria.

But the biogeochemical energy of colonization does not subsume all the manifestations of that energy. I shall mention two more of its forms here.

First, the creation of *a mass of a living matter* and *its maintenance,* by the metabolic process, *at a constant value* during the period of the organism's existence.

And, second, the enormous new form of biogeochemical energy, constituted in the biosphere by the technical *work process of the human race,* which is directed in a complex manner by human thought—consciousness. It is remarkable, that the growth of machines within the structure of human society, also proceeds in a geometrical progression over the course of time, just as does the proliferation of any living matter, including human beings.

These manifestations of biogeochemical energy have not been scientifically investigated at all.

It is imperative to direct scientific work into these areas of biogeochemistry, not only because of their great theoretical significance, but also, it seems to me, with a view towards their certain importance for the tasks of the state. In biogeochemistry, it is necessary to make a deliberate approach to the spontaneous process of the biosphere's transformation into the noösphere, which is now taking place.

For this, the paramount task is to assemble facts and study the problems connected with biogeochemical energy. I have no doubt that this will be done sooner or later. I hope to come back to it in my book.

The basic, distinctive feature of biogeochemical energy is clearly and forcefully demonstrated in the increase of *the free energy of the biosphere* over the course of geological time, and is evident in an especially drastic manner in the transition from the biosphere to the noösphere, which is now apparent.

II. Table:
The Fundamental Material-Energetic Distinction of the Living Natural Bodies of the Biosphere from Its Nonliving Bodies

The distinction of the energetic processes of living matter from those of inert matter is located in the context of the same forms of energy, as appear in inert natural bodies. The chemical composition of both types of natural bodies comes down to the same chemical elements—although it is possible that the atomic weights of some or all of the elements are shifted in living matter. This fundamental distinction is observed in the space-time of forms of living matter. It is indispensable also to study, alongside matter and energy, the manifestation of time in living processes. The scientific hypothesis of a special geometrical structure of space for bodies of living matter is admissible, and requires verification—a space not corresponding to Euclidean geometry, but lying at the basis of the material-energetic and temporal properties of living matter, distinguishing it from the inert natural bodies of the biosphere.

14.

On the basis of everything that is currently known about the biosphere, I shall now attempt to express concisely, *without any theories or hypotheses,* that sharp distinction between the living matter of the biosphere, and its inert natural bodies, which is so pronounced and characteristic for the envelope of the Earth, most familiar and closest to us. It seems to me, that this is necessary and important to do right now, before the publication of my book—whenever that might occur. As far as I know, this has never yet been done in such a form and aspect; consequently, it could never before be discussed as a whole—the most important problem lies outside the naturalist's field of vision.

It is extremely important, for naturalists to think about understanding such a fundamental phenomenon in the biosphere.

It is important for them to have at their disposal, not so much the theoretical scientific-philosophical conceptions of life, which today occupy the thought of philosophers, as those exact data, which subsume biology and all of its "definitions of life," grounded in those data.

In the table provided below, I believe I am giving only such empirical generalizations, and that I do not depart from the domain of scientific facts. This is the side of the question, to which attention must now be turned, and these generalizations should be taken as the basis for scientific work.

15.

The acute, unbridgeable distinction between living natural bodies and inert natural bodies of the biosphere can be summarized in condensed form in the following table.

The Fundamental Material-Energetic Distinction of the Living Natural Bodies of the Biosphere from Its Nonliving Bodies

Inert Natural Bodies	Living Natural Bodies

I.

Among the *dispersed* inert natural bodies of the biosphere, there are no bodies analogous to living bodies. Dispersed inert forms are concentrated in the biosphere, just as living forms are, but the former penetrate to greater depths. Still deeper, evidently in the granite layer of the crust, their existence is stifled by the great pressure.

These inert bodies are created in the biosphere by the death of living matter (for example, microscopic organisms), from their secretions and excretions, through the motion of gases or liquid phases, in winds, moving waters, oils, etc. They are also brought into the biosphere from its lower regions by gases or liquids, volcanic explosions and eruptions, and tectonic movements of deeper layers of the Earth's crust. They are created by ordinary physico-chemical processes and can be synthetically reproduced in our laboratories.

Inert dispersed bodies—cosmic dust and meteorites—penetrate the biosphere constantly and continuously from the expanses of cosmic space, partly from the galaxy.

Living natural bodies exist only in the biosphere and *only as dispersed bodies,* in the form of living organisms and their aggregates—living matter. They are observed in both the macroscopic (gravitational field), and in the microscopic cutaway views of reality.

The artificial synthesis of a living natural body has never been accomplished. This indicates that some fundamental condition is required for such a synthesis, which is absent in the laboratory. L. Pasteur identified dissymmetry—a special state of space—as the missing condition (Sections 10-11).

The penetration of living natural bodies into the biosphere from cosmic space is conceivable, but has not been proven so far.

Inert Natural Bodies	Living Natural Bodies

II.

Inert natural bodies are extremely diverse and, taken as a whole, manifest no unifying genetic connection among them.

The inert natural bodies of the biosphere have no common, unifying feature analogous to the cell, protoplasm, and reproduction—features common to all living natural bodies.

Living natural bodies represent a unified *whole—the living matter of the biosphere*—both *morphologically,* having *a single morphological unit—the cell;* as well as *in their material structure,* having the same *protoplasm;* and, finally, *in dynamic terms, as always possessing the ability to reproduce.*

It can hardly be denied, that such a unity of all living natural bodies, is connected with their genetic unity in the course of time.

III.

In inert natural bodies and natural phenomena, there is no distinction in the chemical properties between the left- and right-handed forms of one and the same chemical compound. In inert bodies these are chemically identical. Right- and left-handedness are subject to the strict laws of symmetry for homogeneous solids (monocrystals). In particular, the quantities of right- and left-handed monocrystals of one and the same chemical compound, formed simultaneously in an inert medium—are identical. "Dispersed droplets," i.e., homogeneous crystalline polyhedra—individual specimens of a solid chemical compound—may differ

A chemical distinction between right- and left-handed forms of the same chemical compound, characterizes the state of *the physical space,* occupied by the body of a living organism, and its manifestation in the surrounding medium, in the biosphere. This chemical non-identity is strongly manifested in the solid (crystalline and mesomorphic) and liquid products, formed by biochemical processes. Either right-handed, or left-handed isomers predominate. This phenomenon is acutely and profoundly manifested in the properties of the living matter of the biosphere, right down to the molecules which make up living bodies. The laws of symmetry for

Inert Natural Bodies	Living Natural Bodies

strongly in their internal structure from the usual (isotropic) space of Euclidean geometry, but they do not depart from the framework of that geometry.

Right- and left-handedness are geometrically and chemically identical in inert natural bodies. Both are always present in the same number, and are chemically indistinguishable. One can state, that this chemical identity of the right- and left-handed forms, is a necessary *manifestation* of the *atomic* construction of homogeneous, solid chemical compounds, and of Euclidean physical geometrical space, materially expressed in this way. It is a manifestation of the atomic construction, on the one hand, and of Euclidean geometry, on the other.

the solid crystalline state of matter are violated in a drastic manner.

Such states of space, occupied by bodies of living matter, are created in the biosphere only out of previously existing living natural bodies. They are generated by *birth* (Redi's principle).

One can see here an expression of Curie's principle (Section 11).

It appears that L. Pasteur was right, that *for the primary chemical compounds, essential to life, only the left stero-isomers* exist inside the body of a living organism (in its physical space); the right-handed isomers either do not appear, or are eliminated by the organisms. Unfortunately, until now this enormously important phenomenon, which could easily be established, has still not been verified, and remains only very probable.

IV.

New inert natural bodies are created in the biosphere by physico-chemical and geological processes, irrespective of earlier existing natural bodies, living or inert; they are formed via innumerable pathways from natural bodies, which usually do not resemble the resulting product.

Inert bodies can be formed within living natural bodies. But

A new living natural body, a living organism—is born only from another living organism like it. For each species of living matter there is an alternation of *generations,* coming to be at a certain definite rate over time (Redi's principle).

In geological time, in the course of at least two billion years, living matter has been *plastic*—there is

Inert Natural Bodies	Living Natural Bodies

there is nothing resembling reproduction in the creation of inert natural bodies in the biosphere.

There is no kind of change in inert natural bodies of the biosphere, analogous to the evolutionary process of living matter. Generally speaking, we see in the biosphere today the very same inert natural bodies and the same phenomena of formation of such bodies, as have existed over a period of at least two billion years. In the course of geological time, new inert bodies emerged only under the influence of the evolutionary process of living matter. The creation of such new inert bodies is occurring in a drastic and powerful way—and their significance is growing—in the *noösphere* of the present epoch, as a consequence of human creativity.

a process of *evolution of species*. Evidently, according to laws that have not yet been elucidated (processes of mutation, in part?), a new *species* of living matter is created from time to time; in various living organisms, a new generation appears, which is morphologically and physiologically changed, and clearly different from the preceding generation. *A single, unified evolutionary process,* closely connected with the history of the planet, is observed over the course of not less than two billion years. As shown by Dana (1852), there is a process of formation, within the living matter of the biosphere, of functionally more and more powerful central nervous systems—of the brain. This process moves forward inexorably over the course of time, but with major interruptions on the order of tens, or perhaps hundreds of millions of years.

Thanks to this, from the end of the Pliocene the geological role of living matter in the biosphere abruptly increases—making a jump. Thanks to human creativity, the biosphere is rapidly shifting into to a new state—*the noösphere.*

Inert Natural Bodies	Living Natural Bodies

V.

A dispersed inert natural body—solid or mesomorphic—has no special properties of motion as a single natural body. There are also no such properties in liquid or gaseous inert bodies, which consist of molecules in complex motion and which assume the form of the containers in which they are located. Gaseous bodies exert pressure on the walls of closed containers. Their motion is governed by the laws of temperature and pressure.

There are no liquid or gaseous living natural bodies in the biosphere. The liquids and gases existing in any living body are mixed with colloidal—mesomorphic and solid—structures.

Spontaneous motion, to a large degree self-regulating, is one of the marks of any living natural body in the biosphere.

There are two forms of such motion for living matter. One—*passive*—occurs through reproduction, and is *a common property of all living matter*. The other—*active*—is expressed for the great majority of animals, and for a minority of plants, as the spontaneous movement of individuals and their colonies in *the medium of living matter*.

The first form of motion—spreading in the biosphere, or *colonization of the biosphere*—is analogous, in the nature of its laws, to a gaseous mass, and, like such a gas, it exerts pressure, the magnitude of which depends on the rate of reproduction (the biogeochemical energy of the colonization process). The rate of colonization by living matter within the boundaries of the biosphere approaches a physical maximum—*the speed of sound in the gaseous medium of respiration.*

For microscopic organisms, liv-

Inert Natural Bodies	Living Natural Bodies
	ing in liquids, there is yet another form of motion, which matches the molecular motion of fluids, visible to us in Brownian motion.

VI.

Inert Natural Bodies	Living Natural Bodies
Inert natural bodies are absolutely inert. They change as a result of external causes, being weathered in the biosphere. This bio-inert process proceeds slowly and is manifested in the course of geological time. Inert bodies do not grow and, apparently, do not increase their mass. For inert bodies, we find nothing analogous to the *growth* (and proliferation) of living organisms. To liken the growth of an organism to that of a crystal, is a misunderstanding, as becomes clear upon the first encounter with logical analysis. The atoms of an inert body do not manifest, inside it, any characteristics of motion, analogous to the biogenic migration of atoms.	Living natural bodies live, i.e., *grow and multiply.* Thanks to this, each living organism is the source and center of *a biogenic migration of atoms* from the biosphere into the organism and back again. Thereby each organism is a source of *free energy in the biosphere*—free biogeochemical energy. Biochemically, this biogenic flow of atoms creates an innumerable and continuously changing quantity of chemical molecules in living matter. Most of the chemical compounds generated in living organisms, can be synthesized by different means in the laboratory. But in the biosphere, almost all of those compounds are formed *only* in living matter. Their synthesis occurs within living matter at rates which are unheard of and not yet achievable in our laboratories. Thanks to this, biogeochemical energy appears in the biosphere, in terms of its power, as the fundamental force of change of the biosphere.

Inert Natural Bodies	Living Natural Bodies

VII.

The number of inert natural bodies in the biosphere is determined by the general properties of matter and energy. It does not depend, in any explicit way, on the dimensions of the planet.

The biosphere continuously absorbs and emits matter and energy from and to cosmic space. There exists a continuous matter-energy exchange of inert natural bodies.

Apparently, we see here an established dynamic equilibrium —a manifestation of the same sort of organization (but not mechanism) which is characteristic of the biosphere and living matter.

The number of living natural bodies of the biosphere is quantitatively connected with the dimensions of the biosphere.

The scientific working hypothesis is admissible, but requires verification, that an extraterrestrial exchange of living natural bodies occurs.

VIII.

The size of the area occupied, and the regions in which inert natural bodies appear in the biosphere, are limited by the dimensions of the latter, and can only increase with the expansion of the biosphere.

Evidently, the biosphere expands in the course of geological time, through the motion of living matter. In this process the inert natural bodies of the biosphere play a passive role.

The mass of living matter of the biosphere is close to the limit and, evidently, remains a relatively constant value *on the scale of historical time*. It is determined, above all, by the radiant energy of the Sun, falling on the biosphere, and by the biogeochemical energy of the process of colonization of the planet.

Evidently, the mass of living matter increases in the course of geological time, and the process of the occupation of the Earth's crust by living matter has not yet been completed.

Inert Natural Bodies	Living Natural Bodies

IX.

The minimum dimensions of an inert natural body of the biosphere are determined by the degree of dispersion of matter and energy—the atom, electron, neutron, etc. The maximum dimensions are determined by the dimensions of the biosphere—a bio-inert natural body. The range of sizes is enormous—10^{40} or, probably, even more.

The minimum dimensions of a living natural body are determined by *respiration,* i.e., the gaseous biogenic migration of atoms (and, in the final analysis, by the Loschmidt [Avogadro] number). These dimensions are of the order of 10^{-6} cm. The maximum dimensions have not exceeded a few hundred meters in the course of two billion years. The reasons for this have not been ascertained. The range of sizes is not large: 10^9.

X.

The chemical composition of inert natural bodies of the biosphere is a function of the composition and properties of the surrounding medium *in which they are created.* It is determined in a passive manner by the structure of the biosphere in the course of geological time.

The chemical composition of living natural bodies is created *by those bodies themselves.* Through nutrition and respiration, they select the chemical elements they need for their existence and for the creation of new living natural bodies (the autarchy of living matter). Evidently, in this process they can change the isotopic ratios (change the atomic weights of the chemical elements) in mixtures.

Thus, living organisms create the greater part of their own bodies, as independent and autonomous (within certain defined limits) bodies in the biosphere—the large bio-inert body of the planet.

Inert Natural Bodies	Living Natural Bodies

XI.

The number of different chemical compounds—molecules and crystals—in inert natural bodies of the biosphere (and the Earth's crust) is *limited*. There exist a few thousands of such molecules and crystals. This determines the essentially small number of forms of inert natural bodies of the biosphere.

The number of chemical compounds—molecules and crystals—in living natural bodies is *unlimited*. It is connected with individuality, and is different for each individual unit of living matter. We already know *millions* of species of organisms and *millions of millions* of different molecules and crystal lattices, corresponding to them. Although far from all of them have been described, this character of theirs is beyond any scientific doubt.

XII.

All natural processes in the domain of natural inert bodies—with the exception of radioactivity—reduce the free energy of the biosphere (physico-chemical processes are reversible). In this way, the *free energy* of the biosphere is diminished and its *entropy* is increased.

Natural processes of living matter, as reflected in the biosphere, increase the free energy of the biosphere (i.e., decrease its entropy).

As a result of that process *the free energy of the biosphere increases,* thus showing the fundamental importance of living matter in the structure of the biosphere—and thereby the planet.

Inert Natural Bodies	Living Natural Bodies

XIII.

The chemical composition of inert natural bodies may correspond to an almost theoretically pure chemical compound, with precise stoichiometric proportions among the elements. In minerals, solid solutions predominate (isomorphic mixtures).

Free atoms of chemical elements are dispersed in all inert bodies. These penetrate all terrestrial matter, not entering into the composition of the molecules, and not always entering the nodes of the spatial lattices.

Today we know of two continuously occurring processes, causing the *dispersion of atoms:* the penetration of (cosmic) radiation, and radioactive processes, which cause an uninterrupted dispersion of atoms—always ephemeral—in the terrestrial inert matter of the biosphere. The significance of this phenomenon is just beginning to dawn upon us. It demands theoretical and experimental study.

In the living matter of the biosphere, we always find extraordinarily complex mixtures of chemical molecules. These are always bodies of mesomorphic structure (colloidal, and more rarely crystalline, etc.). *Molecules of water,* chemically and physically bound and retaining their characteristic properties to a great extent, overwhelmingly predominate (outside the stages of the latent states of living matter). They constitute 60 to 99% (or possibly more) of the total weight of living matter. In latent states of living matter, the amount of these molecules ranges between 4% and 15% (possibly less).

There are no stoichiometric proportions in the gross chemical composition of living bodies. But their chemical composition is strictly determined, and more constant than the chemical composition of isomorphic mixtures in natural minerals. This composition is typical for a given *species, race etc., constituting a characteristic signature of each form of living matter.*

In this respect, there are no special biogenic chemical elements for living matter as a whole. All the elements of the biosphere are embraced by living matter. But it is characteristic, that for every chemical element its geochemistry in the biosphere involves the existence of

Inert Natural Bodies	Living Natural Bodies
	living organisms, whose activity concentrates that element, and which are thereby distinguished from other living organisms. *Here the role of living matter is clearly of a planetary character.*

living organisms, whose activity concentrates that element, and which are thereby distinguished from other living organisms. *Here the role of living matter is clearly of a planetary character.*

It is evident, that the elements of water—oxygen and hydrogen—dominate in the overwhelming mass of living matter. Besides them, the dominant elements in protoplasm (C, N, P, S, K, Na, Cl, Ca, Fe, Si, Mg, etc.) must be characteristic of all organisms. The elements in skeletal structures, perhaps, play an even more important role in the biosphere in general: Fe, Ca, Mg, P, S, N, C, H, O, Mn, Si.

The number of chemical elements *necessary* for each species of matter, for its prolonged, normal life, is rapidly increasing as it is studied, and has now reached a total of 60 most studied ones. Without them, normal, prolonged existence is impossible. Dispersed elements (chiefly the so-called trace elements) often play a primary role. It is conceivable, that the number of elements in each living organism exceeds 80.

The phenomena of dispersion of chemical elements appear here, as they do in inert natural bodies. This process evidently is not limited to the planet's matter.

Inert Natural Bodies	Living Natural Bodies

XIV.

With the exception of radioactive decay, isotopic composition (for the terrestrial chemical elements) does not change in inert natural bodies of the *biosphere*.

Evidently, there exist natural processes *outside the limits of the biosphere*—for example, the movement of gases under high pressures and at high temperature in the Earth's crust—which can shift the isotopic ratios.

These shifts do not violate the basic constancy, in first approximation, of atomic weights, since those meteorites (galactic matter) which have been studied give the same atomic weights, with accuracy to the second decimal place.

One of the most important tasks of geochemistry at the moment is to obtain a more precise definition of the atomic weight of chemical elements in inert bodies, than is possible through chemistry.

Evidently, a shift (within certain ranges) in the isotopic composition (atomic weights) inside living organisms is *a characteristic property of living matter*. This has been proven for hydrogen, carbon, and potassium, and is probable for oxygen and nitrogen. This phenomenon calls for precise investigation.

It is becoming more than probable, that a chemical element, upon entering a living organism, changes its isotopic composition.

Since this process must be connected with an expenditure of energy, we should expect to observe, in the biogenic migration of chemical elements, which links together the living and inert matter in the biosphere, a considerable delay in the exit of these elements from the cycles of biogenic migration.

This phenomenon was noted by K.M. von Baer for nitrogen a long time ago. It is possible, that it is a general phenomenon.

Inert Natural Bodies	Living Natural Bodies

XV.

The overwhelming majority of solid and mesomorphic natural bodies of the biosphere are characterized by their stability in the course of geological time—more than two billion years. This explains the small number of types of such bodies. W. Bragg correctly pointed out, that among crystalline structures (and, obviously, molecules) of the Cosmos, only the most stable and firm have persisted over the course of time. It seems to me, that we can see in this fact the result of an extremely long-term state of the Cosmos, which we are studying.

The study of the radioactivity of crust rocks shows, that the atoms of the basic material of the lithosphere *have not moved from their relative positions in the course of hundreds of millions, up to two billion years,* while remaining the whole time in motion.

The picture changes totally when we look at the living bodies of the biosphere.

A huge majority of these change in form through the process of evolution, and transform into other species or races of living matter. *This is a manifestation of time, in the living matter of the biosphere.*

This phenomenon is rather more complex than we imagine it to be in our understanding of evolution, since the evolutionary process has not yet been expressed in quantitative terms and its rate of change has not been quantitatively estimated (which is now possible). Despite the plasticity of living matter, there are cases of some organisms that are completely fixed. The organism does not change its morphological-physiological structure, remaining in the contemporary biosphere a living witness of the biosphere's past. Here we are talking about hundreds of millions of years (for Radiolaria from the Algonkian era and Lingulae from the Cambrian period—more than two billion years). Unfortunately, this *phenomenon of morphological constancy*—these persistent life forms—has not yet been studied by biologists.

Evidently, a continuous migra-

Inert Natural Bodies	Living Natural Bodies
	tion of atoms occurs inside living bodies, sharply contrasting with their immobility inside inert atomic structures over the course of time. The method of [radioactively] tagged atoms is beginning to reveal to us a new process of continuous biogenic substitution within the molecules, in which atoms of one and the same kind are exchanged—*an uninterrupted intramolecular biogenic flow of atoms.*

XVI.

All physico-chemical processes in inert natural bodies are reversible in time. The space, in which they occur—the space of Euclidean geometry—is in an isotropic or anisotropic crystalline state.	The physico-chemical processes, which create living natural bodies in the biosphere, are irreversible in time. It is possible, that this will turn out to be a consequence of a special state of space-time, having a substrate that corresponds to a non-Euclidean geometry. At the moment, this may be put forward as a scientific working hypothesis, to be verified. From this hypothesis the possibility follows logically, that there exist, *in our reality, phenomena of the transition of geometrically different states of space, one into another. The existence of the living matter of the Earth's biosphere is one such manifestation.*

III. Supplementary Explanations

The admissibility of the conception of different states of space-time existing simultaneously in the biosphere. **Its geometrical heterogeneity.** *In the biosphere, time should be studied in the same way as matter and energy. The working hypothesis of a special geometrical state of the living matter of the biosphere, corresponding to one of the Riemannian geometries.*

16.

Analyzing the above Table (Section 15), we see that the distinctions between living and inert bodies in the biosphere can be reduced to three basic parameters: (1) differences in energetic characteristics, (2) differences in chemical characteristics, and (3) differences in space-time characteristics.

It seems to me, that the first parameters do not require any special interpretation from the standpoint of scientific work. When the point of departure for the explanation of Nature was Man, it was inevitable that Man be taken as the standard of comparison, leading to acceptance of the primacy of philosophy over science. In this connection, people thought they saw in living natural bodies the manifestation of a special *vital force* (this came from pondering mental processes), which sharply and definitively distinguished living from dead. I leave aside the even earlier, animistic views. All of these conceptions, both new and old, have departed, or are departing, from the domain of modern science into the past.

The latest vitalist conceptions are based not on scientific data—which serve, rather, to illustrate them—but on philosophical notions (Driesch's entelechy, for example, and so forth). The notion of a special vital energy (W. Ostwald) is likewise more connected with philosophical, than with scientific data. Facts have failed to confirm its actual existence.

The provenance of the energy of living matter (Section 7) is beyond any doubt. It is completely confirmed by quantitative, experimental calculations.

17.

Likewise, there is no need to discuss chemical composition. There are no special, life-bearing, biogenic chemical elements, as was still thought quite recently (Section 15, XIV).

The possibility is not excluded, incidentally, that chemical elements may have a different atomic weight, but then analogous changes should occur also in inert natural bodies outside the biosphere (and, perhaps, sometimes within it?). All of these phenomena require systematic scientific study.

Beyond a doubt, the overwhelming majority of biochemically formed molecules sharply differ, from the chemical compounds of inert natural bodies. In the latter, such molecules do not form. Thanks to biogenic migration, however, they do form in the geochemical cycles of the biosphere, where atoms freely move from living bodies to inert ones, and back again. The reaction takes place by utilization of the same energy.

The possibility must be considered, of delays in the biogenic migration of chemical elements, in the event their atomic weight changes (Section 15, XIV). This will be decided by experiment and observation in the near future.

18.

But, for space-time, matters are more complex. On the one hand, we enter here into a domain that has not yet been investigated scientifically; and, on the other, we address that substrate of all natural processes (their geometry), which the naturalist is accustomed to leaving aside, unexamined, in his scientific work.

This substrate—the geometrical state of physical space—lies deeper than all physico-chemical processes. But, I think, it is even more real than they are.

At present, the reigning notion—sometimes wrongly posited as an axiom—is that one and the same geometry is manifested in all terrestrial phenomena. But the naturalist cannot construct his conceptions on the basis of axioms, not even logical axioms, because their axiomatic character cannot be demon-

strated except by scientific experiment, experience, and observation. Logic is always less comprehensive than Nature (the biosphere, in this case), since logic corresponds to an abstraction,
i.e., a simplified picture of Nature.

In considering the *possibility* of the simultaneous occurrence
of different geometries on our planet, we must verify their existence experimentally. If the naturalist comes upon phenomena,
which permit him to check this by experiment and observation,
he is obliged to do so.

Before our present century, only three-dimensional Euclidean geometry was considered in scientifically studied phenomena. In the new scientific-philosophical conceptions, connected
with Einstein's constructions, four-dimensional space is considered; this space corresponds, in the opinion of some, to a Riemannian, rather than a Euclidean space. Theoretical physics is rightly
searching for new pathways here, but it has not carried its analysis through to the end, as logic demands.

19.

Before going further, it is indispensable to clarify, to what
extent it is possible, in our scientific reality, to admit the simultaneous manifestation of *spaces, characterized by different geometries,* in different domains.

It seems to me, that people today assume that such a thing
is impossible, without submitting the question to analysis. We
can see this from the history of geometry. In his time, Lobachevsky allowed the possibility, that the structure of the space
of scientific reality was defined by a new geometry, which he
had discovered, rather than by Euclidean geometry. He tried to
arrive at an experimental test of this conclusion, by taking a real
measurement of the largest star triangles in the heavens. At the
present time, Eddington is trying to detect a true four-dimensional space—one of the Riemannian spaces—corresponding to
Einstein's conception of the Cosmos.

But all of this is only the simplest, most abstract conception
of the Cosmos, which might satisfy the geometer and the theoretical physicist, but which contradicts the entire empirical knowledge of the naturalist.

Another conception is logically possible—the conception of *the geometrical inhomogeneity of reality*. It is closer to precise empirical knowledge, without contradicting what we know scientifically: *It is the supposition, that, in different cases and different manifestations of the Cosmos, different geometries may be manifested in phenomena under scientific study.*

The hypothesis of a single unified geometry for the Cosmos as a whole, for the entirety of reality, is inseparably connected with the hypothesis, that the propositions of geometry originate as special properties of our reason. The history of geometry refutes this.

20.

This leads me to the following considerations. We know now, that there can be a whole array of geometries, and that they may be divided into three types—Euclidean, Lobachevskian, and Riemannian—,and that all of them are irreproachable and equally true. At present, the work of generalization is proceeding successfully, to bring them all into *a single generalized geometry*.

But at the present moment, the history of science clearly demonstrates that geometry and its laws, with respect to their fundamental basis, are adduced in empirical fashion, like all other scientific generalizations of the properties of matter and energy. The foundation, from which these laws are derived in deductive fashion, is the precise scientific observation and experience of the thinker. In science today, one can hardly proceed from other philosophical and unscientific notions about the genesis of the laws of geometry, as a starting point, and then see in them a logical manifestation of human reason. I always prefer, wherever it is scientifically permissible, not to depart from an empirical scientific basis.

Starting from such a basis, one can, if necessary, allow that reality is geometrically inhomogeneous, that different geometries may be manifested in different phenomena, and that we must take this into account in our scientific work. *In the biosphere we confront this sort of geometrical heterogeneity.*

21.

For us, space is inseparable from time. This conception is not a consequence of the theoretical propositions of Einstein, but was obtained independently of them and much earlier. I have tried to show this in another location.

We are presently living through an extremely important epoch in the development of science. For the first time, the object of scientific investigation is *time,* which for centuries remained outside its scope. This circumstance characterizes the science of our time and distinguishes it from the science of the Nineteenth Century. It is now becoming clear, that time is an extremely complex manifestation of reality, and that the content of this concept is extremely rich.

Speaking about space-time, we merely indicate the inseparability of one from the other. *For science there is no space without energy and matter, nor, in exactly the same sense, without time.* The conception of Minkowski and his predecessors, about time as a fourth dimension of space, is a mathematical abstraction having no logical grounding in scientific reality; it is a fiction, which does not correspond to the real content of science, nor to a true scientific conception of time. Time is not a dimension of metric geometry. Of course, time can be expressed in geometry by a vector, but it is obvious that such a representation of time does not subsume all of its properties in the natural phenomena studied by the naturalist; it provides him nothing real by way of knowledge. He has no use for it.

Twentieth-Century science is now at a stage, when *the moment has arrived to study time, in the same way as we study the energy and matter filling space.* Minkowski's time, considered as the fourth dimension of Euclidean space, does not correspond to the time, which is actually observed in physical space. We should not forget, that in concrete scientific work, we, generally speaking, are not dealing with the abstract absolute space of geometry. At every step, we are dealing with the much more complex *real space of Nature.*

In a vacuum and very often in gaseous media we can extremely often, without need of corrections, use all the conclusions that follow from the properties of the abstract space of

Euclidean geometry. But, not always. Already in most of the problems we face, involving fluids and solid bodies, we cannot do this. In connection with this, it is convenient, as we shall see, to distinguish the real space of Nature—in this case the biosphere—as *a physical space,* from geometrical space; in the manner, that Helmholtz apparently, first proposed to do.

In exactly the same way, the naturalist's *time* is not the geometrical time of Minkowski, is not the time of mechanics and theoretical physics, or chemistry, and is not the time of Galileo or Newton.

In Section 15, I indicated the sharp empirical distinction of time for living and inert natural bodies of the biosphere. In living natural bodies it is manifested in the *succession of generations*— a phenomenon which is absolutely absent in inert bodies.

The succession of generations is the characteristic biological manifestation of time, sharply distinguishing one form of living matter from another, with different scales of comparison for each. It is also possible to find a common scale for all of these.

22.

Proceeding from everything said above, it is convenient for purposes of organizing scientific work, to take as a scientific working hypothesis, that the space inside a living organism is different from the space inside inert natural bodies of the biosphere; that this space does not correspond to a special state of living matter within the bounds of Euclidean geometry, and that time is expressed in this space by a polar vector. The existence of right- and left-handedness, and their physico-chemical non-equivalence, point to a different geometry than Euclidean—the geometry of space inside living matter.

From my discussions with geometers, it has become clear to me that the geometry, corresponding to the required conditions, has not yet been elaborated. According to indications by Academician N.N. Luzin and Professor S. P. Finikov, it is possible, that it is one of the geometries of the Riemannian type; perhaps one of those pointed to, but not elaborated, by Cartan. This geometry reduces all space to a point, endowed with the germ of a vector.

It were desirable, that these questions attract the attention of geometers. The investigative work of naturalists, in reality, always employs the mathematical constructions of geometers. Without them, it cannot develop correctly. On the other hand, mathematical thinking grows and discovers its new domains, when scientific thought or the life around us confronts it with new problems. *The geometrical character of the space, occupied by the living matter of the biosphere,* is such a new problem. Characteristic for that space are polar vectors (i.e., the absence both of a center of symmetry and of complex symmetry); the non-equivalence of right- and left-handedness (their failure to appear in combination or appearance in only partial combination); the marked chemical non-identity of right- and left-handed phenomena and compounds, and atomic structures (molecules and monocrystals). Characteristic is the conspicuous absence, in living organisms, of plane surfaces and straight lines; the symmetry of living organisms is distinguished by the curved lines and curved surfaces, characteristic of Riemannian geometries. One more identifying mark, which is usual for Riemannian geometries, is a finite and closed space, sharply distinguished from its surroundings, and autonomous. This is completely coherent with the character of aloofness of living organisms in the biosphere, their autarchy.

Which of the array of Riemannian geometries is appropriate here? What are its geometrical characteristics? It seems to me, that this task cannot be ignored by our geometers. It deserves their attention in and of itself as a geometrical problem.

All the more so, because it is connected with a still more general physical problem: with the question of the geometrical states of *physical space,* which have been very little touched upon by philosophical and physical thought.

In the next article I shall try to present a concept of this problem.

I consider it a pleasant duty to express my gratitude to N.N. Luzin and S.P. Finikov, who helped me with valuable suggestions in the course of our conversations.

—*Uzkoye, June 1938*

About the Author

LYNDON H. LAROUCHE, JR. emerged, over the course of the 1970s and 1980s, to rank among the most controversial international political figures of his time. This controversy, which also features such related issues as his efforts to destroy the international drug traffic and his initiating role in formulating what President Ronald Reagan announced on March 23, 1983 as the "Strategic Defense Initiative (SDI)," is principally rooted not just in domestic U.S. issues, but also in global political-economic considerations.

The recent, fresh demonstration of his exceptional qualifications as a long-range economic forecaster, has placed LaRouche at the center of the presently erupting global systemic crisis of the world's economy. Thus, the relevant resumé is that which helps to situate his career in terms of his actual and prospective role in dealing with that present global crisis.

LaRouche as an Economist

Both Lyndon LaRouche's standing as an internationally known economist, and his exceptional successes as a long-range forecaster, are the outgrowths of his original discoveries of physical principle, dating from a project conducted during the 1948-1952 interval. These discoveries arose out of his opposition to Bertrand Russell devotee Professor Norbert Wiener's efforts, as in the latter's 1948 *Cybernetics,* to apply so-called "information theory" to communication of ideas. As part of that same project, he also opposed Russell devotee John von Neumann's efforts to degrade real economic processes to solutions for systems of simultaneous linear inequalities.

The outcome of this project was LaRouche's introduction of axiomatically non-linear notions of individual human cognition, explicitly, to that science of physical economy which had been first established by the relevant 1671-1716 work of Gottfried Leibniz. His own work located the determining, nonlinear factor in increase of society's potential relative population-density in the relations exemplified by the role of the machine-tool principle in linking proof-of-principle experiments to the development of advanced designs of both products and productive processes.

In his subsequent search for a metrical standard for this treatment of the functional role of cognition, he adopted the Leibniz-Gauss-Riemann standpoint, as represented by Bernhard Riemann's 1854 habilitation dissertation. Hence, the employment of Riemannian conceptions to LaRouche's own discoveries became known as the LaRouche-Riemann Method.

His work is best known through his success in two long-range forecasts. The first of these was developed during 1959-1960, forecasting, that, if the axiomatic policy-shaping assumptions of the Truman and Eisenhower Presidencies persisted, the second half of the 1960s would experience a series of international financial-monetary crises, leading toward a breakdown in the existing Bretton Woods agreements: This occurred during the interval from the British sterling devaluation of November 1967 through the breakdown of the Bretton Woods agreements, on Aug. 15-16, 1971.

The second was premised upon the implications of the 1971 breakdown. He forecast, that, if the dominant powers resorted to a combination of increasingly rapacious, monetarist forms of austerity measures, the result would be, not a new cyclical crisis, but, rather, a systemic crisis, a "general breakdown crisis" of the global system. Since the October 1987 U.S. stock market crisis, and the strategic, economic, financial, and monetary decisions of the 1989-1992 interval, the existing global financial-monetary system has become locked into the presently erupting series of seismic-like shocks expressing such a global systemic, or "general breakdown crisis.

A Figure of Political Controversy

His work and activities as an economist have always intersected a continuing commitment, since military-service experience in postwar India, to what has been often termed "a just new world economic order": the urgency of affording what have been sometimes termed "Third World nations," their full rights to perfect national sovereignty, and to access to the improvement of their educational systems and economies through employment of the most advanced science and technology. On this account, he has continued the same quarrel with the policies of the British Empire and Commonwealth which U.S. President Franklin Roosevelt had, on these same issues, with Britain's wartime Prime Minister, Winston Churchill.

To similar effect, he opposed the economic and related policy-matrices of the administrations of Presidents Truman and Eisenhower, and Nixon, Carter, Reagan, and Bush (most notably). Today, inside U.S. domestic and foreign-economic policy, his commitment is typified by intractable opposition to the relevant policies of Henry A. Kissinger, of Robert Bartley's *Wall Street Journal,* and also the neo-malthusian doctrinaires generally. On these issues of both U.S. domestic and foreign policies, he is aligned with the tradition of what used to be known as the "American System of political-economy," as that patriotic, anti-British tradition is typified by the policies of Benjamin Franklin, and such adversaries of the dogmas of British East India Company apologist Adam Smith as U.S. Treasury Secretary Alexander Hamilton, Philadelphia's Mathew and Henry Carey, Friedrich List, and President Abraham Lincoln. He has always supported the kinds of "dirigist" policies associated with that American System tradition, and that tradition's emphasis upon fostering investment in scientific and technological progress, and development of basic economic infrastructure, against the "free trade" and related dogmas of the Haileybury and positivist schools.

Since his studies of the 1948-1952 interval, he has always situated the deep political basis for the opposition between the two modern camps in economic policy in the struggle of those forces which find their self-interest in national economy, such as farmers, industrial entrepreneurs, and operatives, against those oligarchical financier interests which loot the national economy through mechanisms of financial and analogous forms of usury.

In a related matter, he has located the historically exceptional importance of the American Revolution and Federal Constitution in the fact, that although the ideas of the American Revolution were products of the European tradition of the Fifteenth-Century Renaissance, North America provided the relevant strategic distance from a Europe still dominated by those combinations of feudal landed aristocracy and feudal financier oligarchy which were typified by the Castlereagh-Metternich alliance at the Vienna Congress. Thus, the nation-states of Europe emerged chiefly as quasi-republican, parliamentary reforms within nations still ruled from the top by feudal oligarchies, such as the United Kingdom, rather than true republics, such as the 1789 U.S. Federal Republic.

On this account, as soon as LaRouche began to achieve some degree of political influence, first inside the U.S.A., and then abroad, he came into increasingly embittered political conflict with the financier-oligarchical strata and their lackeys, both inside the U.S.A. and internationally. In the U.S.A., these are the combination of oligarchical families formerly associated with the New England opium-traders, Manhattan bankers in the tradition of Aaron Burr, Martin van Buren, August Belmont, and J.P. Morgan, and those who cling to the tradition of Southern slave-holding.

Additionally, since 1964-1972, he has been a leading organizer of the opposition to the 1964-1972 cultural paradigm shift. On this account, he has become a leading target of bitter enmity from ideologues of such sundry New Age cults as the "rock-drug-sex counterculture, post-industrial utopianisms" generally, and "neo-malthusian" forms of anti-scientific, "environmentalist" fads.

As a result of that, he has been the target of sundry known efforts to eliminate him, even physically, by sundry official and private agencies inside the U.S.A. and abroad. This pattern is typified by a 1973 plot directed by the U.S. Federal Bureau of Investigation, as admitted in official documents subsequently released, and by a 1983-1988 U.S. official operation run under the cover of Executive Order 12333.

Campaigns for Public Office

He has campaigned repeatedly for the office of U.S. President, beginning 1976: six times for the Democratic Party's Presidential nomination. In each of the 1976, 1980, and 1984 campaigns, the leading motive was the same: the virtual inevitability of a long-term, downward slide into a global, systemic financial and monetary crisis, unless certain specific types of changes in economic, financial, monetary, and social policies were introduced. In 1988, the theme of the campaign was the imminent collapse of the Soviet system, and prospective early reunification of Germany, beginning in Eastern Europe as early as 1989. In 1992, the theme was the fact that a financial-monetary "mudslide" was already in progress, leading toward a threatened general financial-monetary collapse sometime during the course of the decade. In 1996, that the outbreak of a general, global financial-monetary systemic crisis was imminent. The premises offered for this perspective were always the same, the long-term prospect for a breakdown crisis, already forecast in the setting of the 1971 breakdown of the Bretton Woods agreements. In the 2000 campaign, the theme was the immediate need for a bankruptcy reorganization along the principles of his plan for a New Bretton Woods.

As of Dec. 27, 2000 LaRouche declared his candidacy for the 2004 Democratic Presidential nomination, and is presently campaigning actively to build political support nationally and internationally, for the New Bretton Woods-Landbridge alternative to the onrushing global depression and war.

During each of those campaigns, the proposed remedy was always the same: a fundamental reform of the planet's economic, financial, and monetary systems, emphasizing: a) a return to the best features of the 1950s Bretton Woods system; b) the general replacement of central banking by the kind of national banking which U.S. Treasury Secretary Hamilton attributed to the U.S. Federal Constitution's implications; c) a just new world economic order as a new quality of partnership among sovereign nation-states; d) emphasis on both large-scale development of basic economic infrastructure, adequate food supplies, and fostering of growth of per-capita productivity through investment in scientific and technological progress.

During the 1976-1984 campaigns, a leading included feature, were proposals for measures of scientific and technological cooperation between the U.S.A. and U.S.S.R., to realize what Dr. Edward Teller described, in late 1982, as "the common aims of mankind." Exemplary of such proposals was the original, 1979 version of the "SDI," featured as a leading plank of the 1980 campaign for the Democratic nomination. In 1988, SDI was superseded by a program of "food for peace," premised upon the cascading economic crisis expected for Eastern Europe and the Soviet Union, beginning 1989. For 2000, the campaign just ended was intended chiefly to foster the early establishment of a "New Bretton Woods" agreement, centered around cooperation between the Presidents of the U.S.A. and China. The campaign was geared to foster the realization of that objective by the incumbent U.S. President, William Clinton. The aim was to establish a new form of global financial and monetary stability, one consistent with the principles of a just new world economic order, one established in time to prevent the presently ongoing process of financial, monetary, and economic collapse from plunging the planet, very soon, into a planetary New Dark Age.

Science and Classical Art

The central feature of all his activities, is emphasis upon those sovereign cognitive powers of the individual human mind whose functions are merely typified by validated discoveries of physical principle. Since his original discoveries of the 1948-1952 interval, he has always emphasized that the processes responsible for discovery of physical principles are identical in nature with those responsible for the composition of metaphor in great compositions in Classical forms of poetry, music, tragedy, and plastic arts. This view he acquired in rejecting Immanuel Kant's Romantic dogma for aesthetics. Accordingly, he rejects the empiricist, Cartesian, and positivist notions of both "objective science," and the separation of science from art. He treats science and art as intrinsically subjective, rather than objective, as the subjective generation of objectively validatable new principles of science, new ideas spawned as resolutions of metaphor.

These were leading considerations in his co-founding of the scientific association, the Fusion Energy Foundation, during the mid-1970s, and his support for his wife Helga Zepp LaRouche's founding of the international Club of Life and international Schiller Institute, during the 1980s. During the 1980s, he launched a project for clarifying certain crucial principles of Classical musical composition and performance, out of which one important book has been produced. He is currently working with some among his collaborators in developing improved approaches to education, based, inclusively, upon pedagogical models adduced variously from the scientific work of Classical Greek culture, Leonardo da Vinci, Johannes Kepler, Gottfried Leibniz, Carl Gauss, and Bernhard Riemann. The principle underlying this effort, is that the student must know, rather than merely learn the subject-matter, this by reenacting the original act of discovery of a principle in such a fashion that the student reexperiences the mental processes employed by the original discoverer of that principle. This is his definition of the Classical Humanist method in education.

Born: 8 September 1922, Rochester, New Hampshire, U.S.A.

Parents: Lyndon Hermyle LaRouche, Sr., native-born citizen, internationally known technological consultant to Footwear Manufacturers; Jessie Weir LaRouche, native-born citizen.

Married: December 1977, Helga Zepp LaRouche, native and citizen of Germany, specialist in Nicholas of Cusa, Friedrich Schiller; founder and director of the Schiller Institute; political figure of Germany.

Son: Daniel Vincent LaRouche, born August 1956; data-processing specialist.

Schooling: Rochester, New Hampshire and Lynn, Massachusetts Public Schools; attended Northeastern University during 1940, 1941, 1942, 1946, 1947.

Military: AUS, 1944-1946. Overseas service in India, Burma.

Professional: Management Consultant, Economist 1947-1948, 1952-1972. Founder: (1974) *Executive Intelligence Review* weekly; Co-Founder: (1975) Fusion Energy Foundation; Member: Schiller Institute.

Books: *So, You Wish To Learn All About Economics?* (1984, 1995) *The Science of Christian Economy* (1991) and many others.

Political: Candidate for U.S. Presidential nomination of Democratic Party: 1980, 1984, 1988, 1992, 1996, 2000, 2004. U.S. Presidential Candidate, U.S. Labor Party, 1976. Candidate, U.S. Representative, Virginia, 1990.

Conviction: Convicted and sentenced on conspiracy charges, December 1988 (imprisoned 1989-1994), in a political show-trial which was described (1989) by Germany law specialist Professor Friedrich A. Freiherr von der Heydte as comparable to the scandal of the case of France's Captain Alfred Dreyfus: "Everything we have been able to find out about the trial against Lyndon H. LaRouche, has been yet another painful reminder that the exploitation of the judicial system for the achievement of political ends, is unfortunately a method used repeatedly today in the West as well as the East." Testifying Sept. 2, 1994 before a Commission investigating the same case, former U.S. Attorney General Ramsey Clark described the case as representing "a broader range of deliberate cunning and systematic misconduct over a longer period of time utilizing the power of the Federal government than any other prosecution by the U.S. Government in my time or to my knowledge."

Sponsors

The publisher would like to thank the following people, whose generosity in contributing to the broad circulation of these works by Lyndon H. LaRouche, Jr., has made publication of this book possible.

Elizabeth C. Acheson
Anna Ahlers
John Ajemian
Lewis J. Alary
Dorothy R. Alder
Carmen Alexander
Ashmead & Janice Ali
Luqman Ali
Jerry A. Anderson
Mark Carlton Anderson
Paul C. Anderson
Phillip Armstrong
Ray L. Arnold
Paul Bader
John Bailey
Normand Belanger
Glenn A. Berney
John E. Bigelow
Elvera Bluemlein
H. Dickson S. Boenning
Mrs. Lynn L. Bollinger
John Borrelli, Jr.
Ronald A. Bowden
Ruth E. Brown
Reginald C. Buchanan
Richard W. Burden

Martha L. Cheers
David and Lydia Cherry
Mr. Dennis Chinn
Charles Chresfield
Vincent Civale
Virginia Cobb
Richard Stevens Condon
Douglas T. Crawford
Walter Dallas
Alvin L. Davis
Sharon L. Del Principe
Gerald DeMarinis
Ms. Julie Devlieg
Juan A. Diaz
Barrera Dan Dickson
Helen H. Dilmore
Michael F. DiMarco
Michael Dobson
David J. Dodge
Lillian Dudek
Arthur V. Dunn
June M. Eby
Katherine Edwards
Alfred A. Eichner
Cherrie Elder
Donald C. Errickson

Pearl K. Fine
Ronald C. Force
Dewitt H. Fox
William L. Franchuk
Paul D. Frelich
Mary Frueholz
Phillip Funk
Hugh Gallagher
Wilbur D. Garrels
William Gasper
John Lee Gastley
Jean Gates
Julia Gerland
Jeffrey L. Gernon
Paul Gerrish
Todd A. Gilchrist
Mike Glynn
David Goulart
Joan Greenberg
Molly Grose
Elizabeth Gulick
Valere Hache
Mr. Doug Haley
Geneva C. Hall
Jeremiah Hallaren
Howland B. Hanson
John Hamilton
Donald Hammond
Ann C. Hanse
Clara A. Harter
James E. Harwood
Mary T. Hazelbaker
Lillian Heard
Robert J. Heartland
Floyd Hemmer
Yvonne Henk
Mr. Apolinar Herrera
Verna S. Hess

Janet Hetzel
Charles J. Hill
Louise Hines
Clovis Hinton
William H. Horning
Celia Thaxter Hubbard
Winifred W. Ingram
Evangelyn Johnson
Rev. A. James Johnson
Tom and Laura Jones
Edward Joshie
Ella Mae Joy
J. William Kaeser
Ted Kennedy
Eugene Klymyshyn
Raymond Knepp
Harry Knights
Margaret Kopi
Martin W. Kron
Wesley Kujawski
Thomas R. Lacey
Rodney Leeb
Robert Lincoln
Barrie Luttge
Beverly MacNeil
Henry Macon
Luigi Marietti, Sr.
Nicholas A. Maris
Jean Maurice Masse
Mrs. Vada McClendon
Richard McMeekin
Augusta J. McWethy
Dale Merrick
Edith Messina
James T. Michaelson
Matt Miovac
Michael Mirand
Dr. Roberto Moran

Cornelius U. Morgan
Laura Morland
Erna B. Morris
Anthony Morss
D.S. Moyer
Ray Lynn Mull
Alexander K. Murphy
Helen C. Murray
Sable Nelson and Dolores
 Johnson
Barbara A. Novak
Ned Nurge
Lillian O'Daniel
Thomas P. O'Leary
Mr. & Mrs. E. Orem
Adeline G. Perdew
Keith Perez
H.J. and Lucille G. Perry
A. Viola Peterson
Thomas F. Peterson, Jr.
Harry Pierce
Paul H. Pina
Marjorie Pipitt
Paul M. Portanova
Bonita Potts
Elizabeth K. Putnam
James M. Ryan
Susie E. Salayko
Steve Salem
William A. Samber
Thomas Santry, Jr.
Ralph Saul, Jr.
Mr. Baldwin Sawyer
Joseph J. Scavullo
Lawrence J. Schaeffer
Anton P. Schaffner, Sr.
Albert H. Schneider
Rita M. Schneider

Ekkehart Schwarz
Donald F. Schwarzkopf
Eugene & Lee Shannon
Steven R. Shaw
Audrey Sheehan
Roy Sheumaker
John K. Shrader, D.V.M.
John and Renee Sigerson
Mary Ann Simons
Carol A. Smith
Michael W. Sperry
Claudine Steiner
Rosemarie Stendahl
Jack Stockwell
James R. Straub
Maryann Sullivan
Bill Swift
Olive Thornton
Lillie Trent
Peter Umana
Paul Valentino
Richard Van Bergen
Robert H. Van Hee
Rao Veeramachaneni
John Veldman
Jean Vigneault and Brigitte
 Bergeron
Mrs. Frances Viviani
William A. Watson
Ty Weiler
John R. Wheeler, Jr.
Arthur Whitaker
Alice Wickey
Gerald Wilkin
Lorraine Wilson
Bishop L.C. Young
Ella Zimmerman